SCIENTIFIC PRACTICES IN EUROPEAN HISTORY, 1200–1800

Scientific Practices in European History, 1200–1800 presents and situates a collection of extracts from both widely known texts, by such figures as Copernicus, Newton, and Lavoisier, and lesser known but significant items, all chosen to provide a perspective on topics in social, cultural, and intellectual history and to illuminate the concerns of the early modern period.

The selection of extracts highlights the emerging technical preoccupations of this period, while the accompanying introductions and annotations make these occasionally complex works accessible to students and non-specialists. The book follows a largely chronological sequence and helps to locate scientific ideas and practices within broader European history.

The primary source materials in this collection stand alone as texts in themselves, but in illustrating the scientific components of early modern societies they also make this book ideal for teachers and students of European history.

Peter Dear is Professor of the History of Science at Cornell University, USA. His previous publications include *Revolutionizing the Sciences: European Knowledge and Its Ambitions, 1500–1700* (Princeton, NJ: Princeton University Press, 2009), *The Intelligibility of Nature: How Science Makes Sense of the World* (Chicago: University of Chicago Press, 2006), and *Discipline and Experience: The Mathematical Way in the Scientific Revolution* (Chicago: University of Chicago Press, 1995).

SCIENTIFIC PRACTICES IN EUROPEAN HISTORY, 1200–1800

A Book of Texts

Peter Dear

Routledge
Taylor & Francis Group

LONDON AND NEW YORK

First published 2018
by Routledge
2 Park Square, Milton Park, Abingdon, Oxon OX14 4RN

and by Routledge
711 Third Avenue, New York, NY 10017

Routledge is an imprint of the Taylor & Francis Group, an informa business

British Library Cataloguing in Publication Data
A catalogue record for this book is available from the British Library

Library of Congress Cataloging in Publication Data
Names: Dear, Peter, 1958-
Title: Scientific practices in European history, 1200–1800:
a book of texts/Peter Dear.
Description: Abingdon, Oxon: Routledge, 2017. | Includes bibliographical references and index.
Identifiers: LCCN 2017007956 | ISBN 9781138656406 (hardback: alk. paper) | ISBN 9781138656413 (pbk.: alk. paper) | ISBN 9781315114453 (ebook: alk. paper)
Subjects: LCSH: Science–Europe–Early works to 1800. | Science–Early works to 1800. | Science–Europe–History.
Classification: LCC Q124.97 .D43 2017 | DDC 500–dc23
LC record available at https://lccn.loc.gov/2017007956

ISBN: 978-1-138-65640-6 (hbk)
ISBN: 978-1-138-65641-3 (pbk)
ISBN: 978-1-315-11445-3 (ebk)

Typeset in Garamond Three and Helvetica
by Deanta Global Publishing Services, Chennai, India

CONTENTS

CONTENTS

CONTENTS

FIGURES

TABLES

ACKNOWLEDGEMENTS

I would like to thank Carin Berkowitz for encouraging me to take the approach adopted by this book, and three anonymous referees for useful advice.

INTRODUCTION

This is a book for those who teach courses on European and world history at the university and college level. Although its author is an historian of science, it is not meant to be a history of science or to cover the standard topical register of the history of science; it is for historians who teach the social, political, cultural, and intellectual history of Europe, and aims to provide them with materials that can broaden their approach to include activities often set aside in survey courses as technical, specialist, and arcane.

Although there is general agreement that science has become a major force in world history, it has tended to resist incorporation into overarching historical narratives. To be sure, there are some excellent textbook aids to understanding the history of science and technology on the large scale,[1] but these accounts conform to stories forged within the disciplinary confines of their own specialties. If the teacher of historical survey courses wishes to make use of them, it will be possible only by virtue of buying into those stories themselves, which tend to displace the other stories that a general historical survey course may well prefer to privilege. This book, by contrast, endeavours to provide materials that can be used for a wide range of approaches, leaving to the course's instructor decisions about what place the chosen extracts should play in his or her particular course. In some cases that place may seem fairly obvious (as with the pieces by Petty and Malthus), whereas in others the relevance of the passages to some extra-scientific theme will remain for the instructor's own determination. The introductory remarks accompanying each extract will point out possible directions, as will, less directively, the

---

1   Good examples include Lesley B. Cormack and Andrew Ede, *A History of Science in Society: From Philosophy to Utility*, 3nd ed. (Toronto: University of Toronto Press, 2016); Peter J. Bowler and Iwan Morus, *Making Modern Science: A Historical Survey* (Chicago: University of Chicago Press, 2005).

annotations, but the hope is that historians, whatever their specialty, will find material of interest here that can sometimes provide new angles of approach to otherwise familiar terrain. Links between different passages are noted where appropriate (between Acosta and Halley, for example), but such links are not intended to exhaust the possibilities of the material. The book aims at stimulating the perception of connections and of distant contexts rather than mandating them.

The historian looking for primary-source material in English to assign to students is nowadays faced with an embarrassment of riches: so much is available online, in facsimile as well as in transcribed form, that merely offering to present selections from the history of science might seem otiose. However, the purpose of this volume is to make available selections that represent in some fashion a characteristic, if sometimes also extraordinary, practice or activity to be found in the world in which it took place, and thereby to augment the student's perception of the interconnections between things in the past, in which technical knowledge enterprises (if that expression can stand as a capacious term for scientific work) formed part of the fabric of human life. In a sense, such materials could be assembled almost at random, since all would in some way or another embody this general property. But from a pedagogical perspective the items assembled here are, while various, all notable for their revelation of practices, tendencies or directions that were commonly understood at the time, or that would be brought fully to life at later times, or even would be unknowingly replicated in future endeavours of which their authors knew nothing. In this latter sense, the history of science is always teleological, the interest or significance of an episode deriving from what it reveals about processes and tendencies that are largely latent in that episode's present, but fully realised in later periods. At the same time, the commonplace can also reveal much: whether Lilly's astrological assumptions, widely shared among his contemporaries, or the technical conventions of Sacrobosco's *De Sphaera*—then generally known among the literate, even if less familiar to the light-drenched urban dwellers of today.[2]

Technical content has been kept to a reasonable minimum in the materials presented here, but it has not been eliminated. To have done so would have betrayed one of the central purposes of the book, which is to allow the integration of procedures that were routine or else emergent, and that were in some way consequential for the societies in which they were embedded, into the narratives that historians weave. No one will be overcome by the technical demands of the following extracts, although some of the extracts may require close attention. Understanding them helps in training the historian's (and the

---

2   The early stages of that modern light-drenching are represented in the piece by Murdoch on coal gas.

student's) mind to enter into ways of being that structured worlds of the past, whether these involved astrological prognostication or trade winds.

The texts and authors included here could be expanded indefinitely, of course, by the very nature of the enterprise. The fact that these texts are principally western European, and written by (usually) well-to-do men, reflects certain cultural dominances and hegemonies that are part and parcel of the history of scientific cultures, and may help to explain some related dominances and hegemonies in European history more generally. The presentation of the materials follows a broad chronological sequence, but is deliberately non-systematic: my intention is to avoid the imposition of an overarching narrative, however much readers may choose to infer one.

1

NAVIGATING

One of the more notable aspects of intellectual endeavour in the High Middle Ages is the disjunction between theoretical knowledge (the preserve of the literate) and practical knowledge. This is especially well known in the case of cathedral building, where the highly skilled builders seem to have eschewed formal, written architectural plans and calculations derived from theory-based mechanical engineering in favour of informal artisanal judgments and assessments as the work proceeded. A curious example of this uneasy relationship is provided by an unusual text from the thirteenth century, Petrus Peregrinus's letter "On the Magnet" (dated 1269), in which Petrus discusses, in Latin, the learned language, practical instruments of the sort recently adopted into European navigational practice (the magnetic compass), together with a strikingly systematic experimental, or deliberately experiential, investigation of the properties of magnetic stones, as well as a consideration of possible theoretical explanations of this remarkable behaviour. Petrus describes his concern accordingly as being with "philosophical instruments," a notable combination of purposes.

Source: Petrus Peregrinus, *On the Magnet*, trans. Brother Arnold (New York: McGraw, 1904). Public domain. Part I, chaps. 1–10; Part II, chap. 3.

Part I

Chapter I

Purpose of this work

Dearest of Friends:

At your earnest request, I will now make known to you, in an unpolished narrative, the undoubted though hidden virtue of the lodestone,[1] concerning which philosophers up to the present time give us no information, because it is characteristic of good things to be hidden in darkness until they are brought to light by application to public utility. Out of affection for you, I will write in a simple style about things entirely unknown to the ordinary individual. Nevertheless I will speak only of the manifest properties of the lodestone, because this tract will form part of a work on the construction of philosophical instruments.[2] The disclosing of the hidden properties of this stone is like the art of the sculptor by which he brings figures and seals into existence. Although I may call the matters about which you inquire evident and of inestimable value, they are considered by common folk to be illusions and mere creations of the imagination. But the things that are hidden from the multitude will become clear to astrologers and students of nature, and will constitute their delight, as they will also be of great help to those that are old and more learned.

Chapter II

Qualifications of the experimenter

You must know, my dear friend, that whoever wishes to experiment, should be acquainted with the nature of things, and should not be ignorant of the motion of the celestial bodies. He must also be skillful in manipulation in order that, by means of this stone, he may produce these marvelous effects. Through his own industry he can, to some extent, indeed, correct the errors

---

1 Lodestone (sometimes "loadstone") is naturally occurring magnetic rock (largely magnetite) that has a high iron content, rendering it magnetically polarizable by terrestrial magnetism.

2 The idea of a "philosophical instrument" implied that the work of the instrument supplied knowledge concerning the nature of natural phenomena rather than simply being useful for practical purposes. Nonetheless, in this text Petrus focuses on precisely the use of magnetic instruments rather than on their natural–philosophical meanings.

that a mathematician would inevitably make if he were lacking in dexterity.[3] Besides, in such occult[4] experimentation, great skill is required, for very frequently without it the desired result cannot be obtained, because there are many things in the domain of reason which demand this manual dexterity.

Chapter III

Characteristics of a good lodestone

The lodestone selected must be distinguished by four marks—its color, homogeneity, weight and strength. Its color should be iron-like, pale, slightly bluish or indigo, just as polished iron becomes when exposed to the corroding atmosphere. I have never yet seen a stone of such description which did not produce wonderful effects. Such stones are found most frequently in northern countries, as is attested by sailors who frequent places on the northern seas, notably in Normandy, Flanders and Picardy. This stone should also be of homogeneous material; one having reddish spots and small holes in it should not be chosen; yet a lodestone is hardly ever found entirely free from such blemishes. On account of uniformity in its composition and the compactness of its innermost parts, such a stone is heavy and therefore more valuable. Its strength is known by its vigorous attraction for a large mass of iron; further on I will explain the nature of this attraction. If you chance to see a stone with all these characteristics, secure it if you can.

Chapter IV

How to distinguish the poles of a lodestone

I wish to inform you that this stone bears in itself the likeness of the heavens, as I will now clearly demonstrate. There are in the heavens two points more important than all others, because on them, as on pivots, the celestial sphere revolves: these points are called, one the Arctic or north pole, the other the Antarctic or south pole. Similarly you must fully realize that in this stone there are two points styled respectively the north pole and the south pole.[5] If you are very careful, you can discover these two points in a general way.

---

3 Petrus stresses here the artisanal dimension of working with the lodestone rather than the theoretical dimension represented by "mathematicians."

4 "Occult" meaning, literally, "hidden." This work on the lodestone counts as occult because the causes of magnetic behavior were not manifest.

5 Compare this discussion of the poles in the heavens and on a lodestone with the approach taken by Gilbert (Chapter 6). For Gilbert, the poles on a lodestone reflect the poles of a revolving earth, not the poles of a revolving celestial sphere carrying the entire heavens around with it.

One method for doing so is the following: with an instrument with which crystals and other stones are rounded let a lodestone be made into a globe and then polished. A needle or an elongated piece of iron is then placed on top of the lodestone and a line is drawn in the direction of the needle or iron, thus dividing the stone into two equal parts. The needle is next placed on another part of the stone and a second median line drawn. If desired, this operation may be performed on many different parts, and undoubtedly all these lines will meet in two points just as all meridian or azimuth circles meet in the two opposite poles of the globe. One of these is the north pole, the other the south pole. Proof of this will be found in a subsequent chapter of this tract. A second method for determining these important points is this: note the place on the above-mentioned spherical lodestone where the point of the needle clings most frequently and most strongly; for this will be one of the poles as discovered by the previous method. In order to determine this point exactly, break off a small piece of the needle or iron so as to obtain a fragment about the length of two fingernails; then put it on the spot which was found to be the pole by the former operation. If the fragment stands perpendicular to the stone, then that is, unquestionably, the pole sought; if not, then move the iron fragment about until it becomes so; mark this point carefully; on the opposite end another point may be found in a similar manner. If all this has been done rightly, and if the stone is homogeneous throughout and a choice specimen, these two points will be diametrically opposite, like the poles of a sphere.

Chapter V

How to discover the poles of a lodestone and how to tell which is north and which south

The poles of a lodestone having been located in a general way, you will determine which is north and which south in the following manner: take a wooden vessel rounded like a platter or dish, and in it place the stone in such a way that the two poles will be equidistant from the edge of the vessel; then place the dish in another and larger vessel full of water, so that the stone in the first-mentioned dish may be like a sailor in a boat. The second vessel should be of considerable size so that the first may resemble a ship floating in a river or on the sea. I insist upon the larger size of the second vessel in order that the natural tendency of the lodestone may not be impeded by contact of one vessel against the sides of the other. When the stone has been thus placed, it will turn the dish round until the north pole lies in the direction of the north pole of the heavens, and the south pole of the stone points to the south pole of the heavens. Even if the stone be moved a thousand times away from its position, it will return thereto a thousand times, as by natural instinct.

Since the north and south parts of the heavens are known, these same points will then be easily recognized in the stone because each part of the lodestone will turn to the corresponding one of the heavens.

Chapter VI

How one lodestone attracts another

When you have discovered the north and the south pole in your lodestone, mark them both carefully, so that by means of these indentations they may be distinguished whenever necessary. Should you wish to see how one lodestone attracts another, then, with two lodestones selected and prepared as mentioned in the preceding chapter, proceed as follows: Place one in its dish that it may float about as a sailor in a skiff, and let its poles which have already been determined be equidistant from the horizon, i.e., from the edge of the vessel. Taking the other stone in your hand, approach its north pole to the south pole of the lodestone floating in the vessel; the latter will follow the stone in your hand as if longing to cling to it. If, conversely, you bring the south end of the lodestone in your hand toward the north end of the floating lodestone, the same phenomenon will occur; namely, the floating lodestone will follow the one in your hand. Know then that this is the law: the north pole of one lodestone attracts the south pole of another, while the south pole attracts the north. Should you proceed otherwise and bring the north pole of one near the north pole of another, the one you hold in your hand will seem to put the floating one to flight. If the south pole of one is brought near the south pole of another, the same will happen. This is because the north pole of one seeks the south pole of the other, and therefore repels the north pole. A proof of this is that finally the north pole becomes united with the south pole. Likewise if the south pole is stretched out towards the south pole of the floating lodestone, you will observe the latter to be repelled, which does not occur, as said before, when the north pole is extended towards the south. Hence the silliness of certain persons is manifest, who claim that just as scammony[6] attracts jaundice on account of a similarity between them, so one lodestone attracts another even more strongly than it does iron, a fact which they [conjecture falsely but which is] really true as shown by experiment.

Chapter VII

How iron touched by a lodestone turns towards the poles of the world

It is well known to all who have made the experiment, that when an elongated piece of iron has touched a lodestone and is then fastened to a light block of

---

6   A purgative resin extracted from Convolvulus (bindweed).

wood or to a straw and made float on water, one end will turn to the star which has been called the Sailor's star[7] because it is near the pole; the truth is, however, that it does not point to the star but to the pole itself. A proof of this will be furnished in a following chapter. The other end of the iron will point in an opposite direction. But as to which end of the iron will turn towards the north and which to the south, you will observe that that part of the iron which has touched the south pole of the lodestone will point to the north and conversely, that part which had been in contact with the north pole will turn to the south. Though this appears marvelous to the uninitiated, yet it is known with certainty to those who have tried the experiment.[8]

Chapter VIII

How a lodestone attracts iron

If you wish the stone, according to its natural desire, to attract iron, proceed as follows: mark the north end of the iron and towards this end approach the south pole of the stone, when it will be found to follow the latter. Or, on the contrary, to the south part of the iron present the north pole of the stone and the latter will attract it without any difficulty. Should you, however, do the opposite, namely, if you bring the north end of the stone towards the north pole of the iron, you will notice the iron turn round until its south pole unites with the north end of the lodestone. The same thing will occur when the south end of the lodestone is brought near the south pole of the iron. Should force be exerted at either pole, so that when the south pole of the iron is made touch the south end of the stone, then the virtue in the iron will be easily altered in such a manner that what was before the south end will now become the north and conversely. The cause is that the last impression acts, confounds, or counteracts and alters the force of the original movement.

Chapter IX

Why the north pole of one lodestone attracts the south pole of another and vice versa

As already stated, the north pole of one lodestone attracts the south pole of another and conversely; in this case the virtue of the stronger becomes active, whilst that of the weaker becomes obedient or passive. I consider the

---

7   That is, Polaris, the pole star, which was sometimes also called, significantly, the "lode star," or guiding star.

8   An implication of experientially verifiable marvels, a notion reminiscent of Francis Bacon's philosophy.

following to be the cause of this phenomenon: the active agent requires a passive subject, not merely to be joined to it, but also to be united with it, so that the two make but one by nature. In the case of this wonderful lodestone this may be shown in the following manner: Take a lodestone which you may call A DA D, in which A is the north pole and D the south; cut this stone into two parts, so that you may have two distinct stones; place the stone having the pole A so that it may float on water and you will observe that A turns towards the north as before; the breaking did not destroy the properties of the parts of the stone, since it is homogeneous; hence it follows that the part of the stone at the point of fracture, which may be marked B, must be a south pole; this broken part of which we are now speaking may be called A BA B. The other, which contains D, should then be placed so as to float on water, when you will see D point towards the south because it is a south pole; but the other end at the point of fracture, lettered C, will be a north pole; this stone may now be named C D. If we consider the first stone as the active agent, then the second, or C D, will be the passive subject. You will also notice that the ends of the two stones which before their separation were together, after breaking will become one a north pole and the other a south pole. If now these same broken portions are brought near each other, one will attract the other, so that they will again be joined at the points B and C, where the fracture occurred. Thus, by natural instinct, one single stone will be formed as before. This may be demonstrated fully by cementing the parts together, when the same effects will be produced as before the stone was broken. As you will perceive from this experiment, the active agent desires to become one with the passive subject because of the similarity that exists between them. Hence C, being a north pole, must be brought close to B, so that the agent and its subject may form one and the same straight line in the order A B, C D and B and C being at the same point. In this union the identity of the extreme parts is retained and preserved just as they were at first; for A is the north pole in the entire line as it was in the divided one; so also D is the south pole as it was in the divided passive subject, but B and C have been made effectually into one. In the same way it happens that if A be joined to D so as to make the two lines one, in virtue of this union due to attraction in the order C D A B, then A and D will constitute but one point, the identity of the extreme parts will remain unchanged just as they were before being brought together, for C is a north pole and B a south, as during their separation. If you proceed in a different fashion, this identity or similarity of parts will not be preserved; for you will perceive that if C, a north pole, be joined to A, a north pole, contrary to the demonstrated truth, and from these two lines a single one, B A C D, is formed, as D was a south pole before the parts were united, it is then necessary that the other extremity should be a north pole, and as B is a south pole, the identity of the parts of the former similarity is destroyed. If you make B the south pole as it was before they united, then D must become north, though it was south in the original stone; in this way neither the identity nor similarity of parts is preserved. It is becoming that when the two are united into one, they should bear the same likeness as the agent, otherwise nature would be called upon to do what is impossible. The same incongruity would occur if you were to join *B* with *D* so as to make the line *A B D C*, as is plain to any person who reflects a moment. Nature, therefore, aims at being and also at acting in the best manner possible; it selects the former motion and order rather than the second because the identity is better preserved. From all this it is evident why the north pole attracts the south and conversely, and also why the south pole does not attract the south pole and the north pole does not attract the north.

Chapter X

An inquiry into the cause of the natural virtue of the lodestone[9]

Certain persons who were but poor investigators of nature held the opinion that the force with which a lodestone draws iron, is found in the mineral veins themselves from which the stone is obtained; whence they claim that the iron turns towards the poles of the earth, only because of the numerous iron mines found there. But such persons are ignorant of the fact that in many different parts of the globe the lodestone is found; from which it would follow that the iron needle should turn in different directions according to the locality; but this is contrary to experience. Secondly, these individuals do not seem to know that the places under the poles are uninhabitable because there one-half the year is day and the other half night. Hence it is most silly to imagine that the lodestone should come to us from such places. Since the lodestone points to the south as well as to the north, it is evident from the foregoing chapters that we must conclude that not only from the north pole but also from the south pole rather than from the veins of the mines virtue flows into the poles of the lodestone. This follows from the consideration that wherever a man may be, he finds the stone pointing to the heavens in accordance with the position of the meridian; but all meridians meet in the poles of the world; hence it is manifest that from the poles of the world, the poles of the lodestone receive their virtue.[10] Another necessary consequence of this is that the needle does not point to the pole star, since the meridians

---

9   This chapter is strikingly "natural philosophical" in tone, concerned with philosophical causal explanation rather than with instrumental use of the lodestone.

10   Note again that by "poles of the world" Petrus refers to the poles of the celestial sphere, not to the poles of the earth; the poles, like latitudes, were prototypically celestial points and lines, only secondarily reflected by the surface of the central spherical earth. Only when the earth was displaced and put in motion by Copernicus did this sense of priority begin to change.

do not intersect in that star but in the poles of the world. In every region, the pole star is always found outside the meridian except twice in each complete revolution of the heavens. From all these considerations, it is clear that the poles of the lodestone derive their virtue from the poles of the heavens. As regards the other parts of the stone, the right conclusion is, that they obtain their virtue from the other parts of the heavens, so that we may infer that not only the poles of the stone receive their virtue and influence from the poles of the world, but likewise also the other parts, or the entire stone from the entire heavens. You may test this in the following manner: A round lodestone on which the poles are marked is placed on two sharp styles as pivots having one pivot under each pole so that the lodestone may easily revolve on these pivots. Having done this, make sure that it is equally balanced and that it turns smoothly on the pivots. Repeat this several times at different hours of the day and always with the utmost care. Then place the stone with its axis in the meridian, the poles resting on the pivots. Let it be moved after the manner of bracelets so that the elevation and depression of the poles may equal the elevation and depressions of the poles of the heavens of the place in which you are experimenting. If now the stone be moved according to the motion of the heavens, you will be delighted in having discovered such a wonderful secret; but if not, ascribe the failure to your own lack of skill rather than to a defect in nature.[11] Moreover, in this position I consider the strength of the lodestone to be best preserved. When it is placed differently, i.e., not in the meridian, I think its virtue is weakened or obscured rather than maintained. With such an instrument you will need no timepiece, for by it you can know the ascendant at any hour you please, as well as all other dispositions of the heavens which are sought for by astrologers.

Part II

. . .

Chapter III

The art of making a wheel of perpetual motion[12]

In this chapter I will make known to you the construction of a wheel which in a remarkable manner moves continuously. I have seen many persons vainly

---

11 To be clear: Petrus is asserting here that the spherical lodestone, properly mounted and oriented, will replicate the motions of the heavens by itself revolving on its axis. If this experiment were to fail, the failure would merely demonstrate the incompetence of the experimenter.

12 Like the preceding material, this chapter shows that Petrus's apparently forward-looking, "scientific" treatise nonetheless incorporates ideas and experimental findings that would not now be accepted.

busy themselves and even becoming exhausted with much labor in their endeavors to invent such a wheel. But these invariably failed to notice that by means of the virtue or power of the lodestone all difficulty can be overcome. For the construction of such a wheel, take a silver capsule like that of a concave mirror, and worked on the outside with fine carving and perforations, not only for the sake of beauty, but also for the purpose of diminishing its weight. You should manage also that the eye of the unskilled may not perceive what is cunningly placed inside. Within let there be iron nails or teeth of equal weight fastened to the periphery of the wheel in a slanting direction, close to one another so that their distance apart may not be more than the thickness of a bean or a pea; the wheel itself must be of uniform weight throughout. Fasten the middle of the axis about which the wheel revolves so that the said axis may always remain immovable. Add thereto a silver bar, and at its extremity affix a lodestone placed between two capsules and prepared in the following way: When it has been rounded and its poles marked as said before, let it be shaped like an egg; leaving the poles untouched, file down the intervening parts so that thus flattened and occupying less space, it may not touch the sides of the capsules when the wheel revolves. Thus prepared, let it be attached to the silver rod just as a precious stone is placed in a ring; let the north pole be then turned towards the teeth or cogs of the wheel somewhat slantingly so that the virtue of the stone may not flow diametrically into the iron teeth, but at a certain angle; consequently when one of the teeth comes

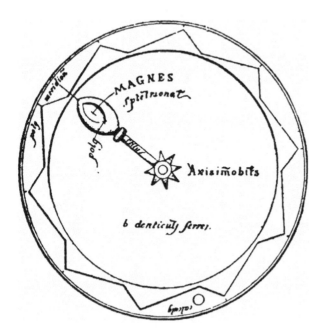

Figure 1.1 Perpetual motion wheel.

near the north pole and owing to the impetus of the wheel passes it, it then approaches the south pole from which it is rather driven away than attracted, as is evident from the law given in a preceding chapter. Therefore such a tooth would be constantly attracted and constantly repelled. In order that the wheel may do its work more speedily, place within the box a small rounded weight made of brass or silver of such a size that it may be caught between each pair of teeth; consequently as the movement of the wheel is continuous in one direction, so the fall of the weight will be continuous in the other. Being caught between the teeth of a wheel which is continuously revolving, it seeks the centre of the earth in virtue of its own weight, thereby aiding the motion of the teeth and preventing them from coming to rest in a direct line with the lodestone. Let the places between the teeth be suitably hollowed out so that they may easily catch the body in its fall, as shown in the diagram above [Figure 1.1].

Farewell: finished in camp at the siege of Lucera on the eighth day of August, Anno Domini MCCLXIX.

2

MODELLING A DISPUTATION (*QUAESTIO* FROM AQUINAS)

The most characteristic academic exercise in the medieval university was the disputation. A student needed to display skill at formal disputation in order to graduate at any level, or degree, whether the bachelor's, master's, or doctor's; consequently, developing such skill by participating in disputations was a regular part of university life. The standard form was that of oppositional contestation: there were only two sides to the argument, each directly opposed to the other. A proposition was introduced, and one participant charged to uphold it; his opponent's task was to deny it. The arguments were judged by masters as to their logical validity and dexterity (according to the precise taught forms of the syllogism), as well as on their content, which would typically draw on a knowledge of relevant authoritative texts, such as those of Aristotle. The literary version of a disputation was the genre known as *Quaestiones*, and the following extracts are from the work of a master of the form, the great thirteenth-century theologian Thomas Aquinas. Among the many things to be learned from Aquinas's discussion is what it might be like to inhabit a world that contains angels and miracles.

Source: Thomas Aquinas, *Disputed Questions concerning the Power of God*, trans. the English Dominican Fathers (Westminster, MD: The Newman Press, 1952, reprint of 1932 edition). Public Domain. Q. VI: Article I (selections).

Q. VI: Article I

Can God Do Anything in Creatures That is Beyond Nature, Against Nature, Or Contrary to the Course of Nature?

{Con. Gen. iii, 98, 99, 100}

THE first point of inquiry is whether God can do anything in creatures that is beyond or against nature, or contrary to the course of nature: and seemingly he cannot.

1. The (ordinary) gloss[1] on Romans xi, 24, *Contrary to nature thou wert grafted*, says: "God the author of all natures does nothing against nature."
2. Another gloss on the same passage observes: "God can no more act against the law of nature than he can act against himself." Now he can nowise act against himself because *he cannot deny himself* (2 Tim. ii, 13). Therefore he cannot act against the order of nature.
3. Just as the order of human justice derives from divine justice, so does the order of nature derive from divine wisdom since it is this that *orders all things sweetly* (Wis. viii, x). Now God cannot act against the order of human justice: further, he would be the cause of sin which alone is contrary to the order of justice. Since then God's wisdom is no less than his justice, it would seem that neither can he act against the order of nature.
4. Whenever God works in creatures through the innate laws of nature, he does not act against the course of nature. Now God cannot fittingly work in a creature independently of the innate laws of nature. Therefore he cannot fittingly work against the course of nature. The minor proposition is proved as follows. Augustine says (*De Trin.* iii, 11, 12) that visible apparitions were shown to the patriarchs by means of the angelic ministrations, inasmuch as God governs bodies through spirits. In like manner he governs the lower bodies through the higher (*ibid.* 4): and it may also be said that he directs all effects through their causes. Since then the laws of nature are implanted in natural causes, it would seem that God cannot fittingly work in natural effects, except by means of the natural laws: and thus he will do nothing contrary to the course of nature.
5. God cannot make *yes* and *no* to be true at the same time: because since this is incompatible with the very nature of being as such, it is also incompatible with a creature: and the first of things created was being (*De Causis*, p. 54). Now the aforesaid principle, being the first principle of all, to which all others are reduced (*Metaph.* iv), must be implied in every necessary proposition, and its opposite in every impossible proposition. Since then things that are contrary to the course of nature are impossible in nature, for instance that a blind man be made to see, or a dead man to live, they imply the opposite of the aforesaid proposition. Therefore God cannot do what is contrary to the course of nature.
6. A gloss on Ephesians iii says that God does not change his will so as to act against the causes which he had established by his will. Now God established natural causes by his will. Therefore he neither does nor can do anything contrary to them, inasmuch as he cannot change: for to do

---

1   The "ordinary gloss" refers to the textual commentaries by Church Fathers that commonly accompanied the Vulgate translation of the Bible.

anything contrary to that which one has deliberately decided would seem to point to a change in one's will.

7. The good of the universe is a good of order, and to this the course of nature belongs. But God cannot act against the good of the universe, since it is due to his sovereign goodness that all things are good in relation to the order of the universe. Therefore God cannot do anything contrary to the order of nature.

8. God cannot be the cause of evil. Now according to Augustine (*De Nat. Boni iv*) evil is the privation of measure, form and order. Therefore God cannot do anything contrary to the course of nature which belongs to the order of the universe.

9. It is written (Gen. ii, 2) that *on the seventh day God rested from all the work which he had done*, and this because as the (ordinary) gloss observes, he ceased to produce new works. Now in the works of the six days he did nothing contrary to the course of nature: wherefore Augustine (*Gen. ad. lit.* ii) says that in discussing the works of the six days we do not ask what God might have done miraculously, but what was compatible with nature which he established then. Therefore neither did God afterwards do anything contrary to the course of nature.

10. According to the Philosopher[2] (*Metaph.* vii) nature causes order in all things. Now God cannot do anything that is not in order, since according to Romans xiii, i: *Those that are of God are well ordered.* Therefore he cannot do anything contrary to nature.

11. Nature no less than human reason is from God. But God cannot act against the principles of reason, for instance that the genus be not predicated of its species, or that the side of a square be not proportionate to the diameter. Neither therefore can he act against the principles of nature.

12. The entire course of nature derives from divine wisdom even as the products of art proceed from art, according to Augustine in his commentary on Jo. i, 3, 4: *That which was made, was life in him.* Now a craftsman does nothing against the principles of his art except by mistake: and this cannot happen to God. Therefore God does nothing contrary to the course of nature.

...

These three points being established, namely that God is the author of being in all things of nature; that he has proper knowledge and providence in respect of each individual; and that he does not act of natural necessity, it follows that he can act independently of the course of nature in the production of particular effects—either as regards being by producing in natural things a

---

2 A usual way in medieval scholasticism of referring to Aristotle.

new form which nature is unable to produce, for instance, the form of glory; or by producing a form in a particular matter, as sight in a blind man: or as regards operation, by restraining the action of nature from doing what it would naturally do, for instance, by hindering fire from burning (Dan. iii, 49, 50), or water from flowing, as happened in the Jordan (Jos. iii, 13).

Reply to the First Objection. Both God and nature act against individual nature: for instance, it is against the nature of this or that particular fire that it be extinguished: wherefore the Philosopher says (*De Coelo et Mundo*, ii[3]) that corruption, decrepitude, and in general all defects are contrary to nature: whereas nothing in nature acts against universal nature. For particular nature denotes the relation of a particular cause to a particular effect, while universal nature denotes the relation of the first agent in nature, which is the heavens, to all agents in the lower world. And seeing that none of the lower bodies acts save by virtue of the heavenly body, it is impossible for any natural body to act against universal nature: while the very fact that anything acts against a particular nature, is in accord with universal nature. Now just as the heaven is the universal cause in respect of lower bodies, so God is the universal cause in respect of all beings, and in comparison with him even the heaven is a particular cause. For nothing prevents one and the same cause from being universal in relation to things below it, and particular in relation to those above it: thus if we take the predicables, animal is universal in relation to man, and particular in relation to substance. Accordingly just as by the power of the heavens something can happen that is contrary to this or that particular nature, and yet not contrary to nature simply, since it is in accord with universal nature: even so by the power of God something can occur that is contrary to universal nature which is dependent on the power of the heavens; without being contrary to nature simply, since it will be in accord with the supremely universal nature, dependent on God in relation to all creatures. It is in this sense that Augustine in the gloss quoted says that God does nothing contrary to nature: wherefore he goes on to say, because "the nature of each thing is what God does in it."

The *Reply to the Second Objection* is evident from what has just been said: because in that gloss Augustine refers to the supreme law of nature which is God's ordinance with regard to all creatures.

Reply to the Third Objection. As we have already explained, although God can do something contrary to the relation between one creature and another, he cannot do anything contrary to a creature's relation to himself. Now the justice of a man consists chiefly in his being duly referred to God: so that

---

3   Evidently here referring to Aristotle's *De caelo*.

God cannot do anything contrary to the order of justice. On the other hand the course of nature is dependent on the relation of one creature to another, wherefore God can act against the course of nature.

Reply to the Fourth Objection. Just as God can produce effects in nature without employing natural causes, so also can he without the ministry of the angels: but the reason for his doing so is not the same in both cases. He acts independently of natural causes in order that being unable to ascribe the effect to visible causes we may be compelled to attribute it to some higher cause, and that thus a visible miracle may be a manifestation of the divine power. But the activities of the angels are not visible; wherefore their ministrations do not hinder us from ascribing something to the divine power. For this reason Augustine does not say that God is unable to work without the ministry of the angels, but that he does not do so.

Reply to the Fifth Objection. Just as God cannot make *yes* and *no* to be true at the same time, so neither can he do what is impossible in nature in so far as it includes the former impossibility. Thus for a dead man to return to life clearly involves a contradiction if we suppose that his return to life is the natural effect of an intrinsic principle, since a dead man is essentially one who lacks the principle of life. Wherefore God does not do this but he makes a dead man to regain life from an extrinsic principle: and this involves no contradiction. The same applies to other things that are impossible to nature, and which God is able to do.

Reply to the Sixth Objection. God does not change his will when he does anything contrary to natural causes: because from eternity he foresaw and decreed that he would do what he does in time. Wherefore he so ordered the course of nature, that by his eternal decree he preordained whatsoever he would at some time do independently of that course.

Reply to the Seventh Objection. When God does anything outside the course of nature he does not put aside the entire order of the universe wherein its good consists, but the order of some particular cause to its effect.

Reply to the Eighth Objection. Penal evil[4] is contrary to the order between one part of the universe and another part; and in like manner every evil that is a defect of nature. But sinful evil is contrary to the order between the whole universe and its last end, inasmuch as the will in which sinful evil resides is deprived by sin of its order in relation to the last end of the universe.

---

4   This is an evil that God imposes on Man as punishment for his misdeeds.

Wherefore God cannot be the cause of this evil: since he cannot act against the latter order, although he can act against the former.

Reply to the Ninth Objection. God does not work miracles except in creatures that already exist, and in some way existed already in the works of the six days. Hence miraculous works, in a manner of speaking, existed already materially in the works of the six days, although it was not befitting that anything should be done miraculously contrary to the course of nature, when nature itself was being established.

Reply to the Tenth Objection. Nature is the cause of order in all natural things, but not in all things absolutely speaking.

Reply to the Eleventh Objection. The logician and the mathematician consider things in their abstract principles, so that in logic and mathematics nothing is impossible except what is contrary to the abstract notion of a thing. These things involve a contradiction and consequently are of themselves impossible. Such impossibilities God cannot do.[5] On the other hand the physicist studies individual matter, wherefore he reckons as an impossibility, even that which is impossible to an individual. But nothing prevents God from being able to do what is impossible to lower agents.

Reply to the Twelfth Objection. The divine art is not fully extended in producing creatures: so that God can by his art do something otherwise than the course of nature requires. Hence although he can do something contrary to the course of nature it does not follow that he can act against his art: since even a human craftsman can by his art produce another work in a different way to that in which he produced a previous work.

---

5   Such metaphysical restriction on God's freedom of action was a Thomist position particularly odious to the Bishop of Paris, Étienne Tempier, who issued a list of 219 condemned propositions of various kinds in 1277, a list soon endorsed by the pope (see "Condemnation of 1277" in *Stanford Encyclopedia of Philosophy*). Shortly after Thomas was canonized, in 1323, the erring propositions that he had upheld were removed from the ruling.

3

MAKING SENSE OF THE COSMOS

Learned people in the Middle Ages (largely churchmen, who made up the only demographic group likely to be literate), if they had any interest in the natural clock that was the sky and its celestial bodies, might have had recourse to a widely known Latin text that taught them how to compute the motions of the heavens. The most common such text from the thirteenth century onwards had been written by a (perhaps British) scholar who taught at the University of Paris. He was known as John of Holywood, or Sacrobosco, and his book was *On the Sphere*, or *De sphaera*. *De sphaera* served in medieval universities up into the sixteenth century as the standard beginners' book on astronomy. It was first printed in 1472.

The focus of the work, the celestial sphere, indicates the basic function of this kind of astronomy. The celestial sphere was the fundamental referent of mathematical astronomy, and we do well to remember that the fictitious circles of the equator and the lines of latitude, as well as the north and south poles, like the ecliptic (the circle traversed by the sun against the backdrop of the stars in the course of a year), were in origin lines inscribed in the sky, on the inner surface of the imaginary sphere surrounding the spherical, central earth. Only by projection onto the earth's surface were these features secondarily identifiable with the terrestrial globe (remember that the poles served no kinematic function for the immobile earth of the Middle Ages; they were the points around which the spherical heavens rotated).

Source: Sacrobosco, *De sphaera*, English trans. Lynn Thorndike (Chicago: University of Chicago Press, 1949). Open access. Chapters 1–4, pp. 118–123.

Proemium

Contents of the Four Chapters.—The treatise on the sphere we divide into four chapters, telling, first, what a sphere is, what its center is, what the axis of a sphere is, what the pole of the world is, how many spheres there are, and what the shape of the world is. In the second we give information concerning the circles of which this material sphere is composed and that supercelestial one, of which this is the image, is understood to be composed. In the third we talk about the rising and setting of the signs, and the diversity of days and nights which happens to those inhabiting diverse localities, and the division into climes. In the fourth the matter concerns the circles and motions of the planets, and the causes of eclipses.

Chapter One

Sphere defined.—A sphere is thus described by Euclid: A sphere is the transit of the circumference of a half-circle upon a fixed diameter until it revolves back to its original position. That is, a sphere is such a round and solid body as is described by the revolution of a semicircular arc.

By Theodosius a sphere is described thus: A sphere is a solid body contained within a single surface, in the middle of which there is a point from which all straight lines drawn to the circumference are equal, and that point is called the "center of the sphere." Moreover, a straight line passing through the center of the sphere, with its ends touching the circumference in opposite directions, is called the "axis of the sphere." And the two ends of the axis are called the "poles of the world."

Sphere divided.—The sphere is divided in two ways, by substance and by accident. By substance it is divided into the ninth sphere, which is called the "first moved" or the *primum mobile*; and the seven spheres of the seven planets, of which some are larger, some smaller, according as they the more approach, or recede from, the firmament. Wherefore, among them the sphere of Saturn is the largest, the sphere of the moon the smallest....

By accident the sphere is divided into the sphere right and the sphere oblique. For those are said to have the sphere right who dwell at the equator, if anyone can live there. And it is called "right" because neither pole is elevated more for them than the other, or because their horizon intersects the equinoctial circle and is intersected by it at spherical right angles. Those are said to have the sphere oblique who live this side of the equator or beyond it. For to them one pole is always raised above the horizon, and the other is always depressed below it. Or it is because their artificial horizon intersects the equinoctial at oblique and unequal angles.

The Four Elements.—The machine of the universe is divided into two, the ethereal and the elementary region. The elementary region, existing subject to continual alteration, is divided into four. For there is earth, laced, as it were, as the center in the middle of all, about which is water, about water air, about air fire, which is pure and not turbid there and reaches to the sphere of the moon, as Aristotle says in his book of *Meteorology*. For so God, the glorious and sublime, disposed. And these are called the "four elements" which are in turn by themselves altered, corrupted and regenerated.[1] The elements are also simple bodies which cannot be subdivided into parts of diverse forms and from whose commixture are produced various species of generated things. Three of them, in turn, surround the earth on all sides spherically, except in so far as the dry land stays the sea's tide to protect the life of animate beings. All, too, are mobile except earth, which, as the center of the world, by its weight in every direction equally avoiding the great motion of the extremes, as a round body occupies the middle of the sphere.[2]

The Heavens.—Around the elementary region revolves with continuous circular motion the ethereal, which is lucid and immune from all variation in its immutable essence. And it is called "Fifth Essence"[3] by the philosophers. Of which there are nine spheres, as we have just said: namely, of the moon, Mercury, Venus, the sun, Mars, Jupiter, Saturn, the fixed stars, and the last heaven.[4] Each of these spheres incloses its inferior spherically.

Their Movements.—And of these there are two movements. One is of the last heaven on the two extremities of its axis, The Arctic and Antarctic poles, from east through west to east again, which the equinoctial circle divides through the middle. Then there is another movement, oblique to this and in the opposite direction, of the inferior spheres on their axes, distant from the former by 23 degrees. But the first movement carries all the others with it in its rush about the earth once within a day and night, although they strive against it, as in the case of the eighth sphere one degree in a hundred years.[5] This second movement is divided through the middle by the zodiac, under which each of the seven planets has its own sphere, in which it is borne by its own motion, contrary to the movement of the sky, and completes it in varying

1 The four Aristotelian elements were mutually interchangeable, as befitted their explanatory function; these were not immutable elements.
2 This and the following section on the matter of the heavens integrate the astronomical account with natural–philosophical, or "physical," content, in what is otherwise a largely mathematical treatment.
3 *Quintessentia*, or "quintessence"; hence "quintessential."
4 This last sphere served to provide the very slow motion corresponding to the precession of the equinoxes.
5 Actually a degree every 72 years or so.

spaces of time—in the case of Saturn in thirty years, Jupiter in twelve years, Mars in two, the sun in three hundred and sixty-five days and six hours, Venus and Mercury about the same, the moon in twenty-seven days and eight hours.

Revolution of the Heavens from East to West.—That the sky revolves from east to west is signified by the fact that the stars, which rise in the east, mount gradually and successively until they reach mid-sky and are always at the same distance apart, and, thus maintaining their relative positions, they move toward their setting continuously and uniformly. Another indication is that the stars near the North Pole, which never set for us, move continuously and uniformly, describing their circles about the pole, and are always equally near or far from one another. Wherefore, from those two continuous movements of the stars, both those that set and those which do not, it is clear that the firmament is moved from east to west.

...

The Earth a Sphere.—That the earth, too, is round is shown thus. The signs and stars do not rise and set the same for all men everywhere but rise and set sooner for those in the east than for those in the west; and of this there is no other cause than the bulge of the earth. Moreover, celestial phenomena evidence that they orientals than for westerners. For one and the same eclipse of the moon which appears to us in the first hour of the night appears to orientals about the third hour of the night, which proves that they had night and sunset before we did, of which setting the bulge of the earth is the cause.

Further Proofs of This.—That the earth also has a bulge from north to south and vice versa is shown thus: To those living toward the north, certain stars are always visible, namely, those near the North Pole, while others which are near the South Pole are always concealed from them. If, then, anyone should proceed from the north southward, he might go so far that the stars which formerly were always visible to him now would tend toward their setting. And the farther south he went, the more they would be moved toward their setting.[6] Again, that same man now could see stars which formerly had always been hidden from him. And the reverse would happen to anyone going from the south northward. The cause of this is simply the bulge of the earth. Again, if the earth were flat from east to west, the stars would rise as soon for westerners as for orientals, which is false. Also, if the earth were flat from north to south and vice versa, the stars which were always visible to anyone would continue to be so wherever he went, which is false. But it seems flat to human sight because it is so extensive.

6   That is, closer towards the northern horizon.

Surface of the Sea Spherical.—That the water has a bulge and is approximately round is shown thus: Let a signal be set up on the seacoast and a ship leave port and sail away so far that the eye of a person standing at the foot of the mast can no longer discern the signal. Yet if the ship is stopped, the eye of the same person, if he has climbed to the top of the mast, will see the signal clearly. Yet the eye of a person at the bottom of the mast ought to see the signal better than he who is at the top, as is shown by drawing straight lines from both to the signal. And there is no other explanation of this thing than the bulge of the water. For all other impediments are excluded, such as clouds and rising vapors.

Also, since water is a homogeneous body, the whole will act the same as its parts. But parts of water, as happens in the case of little drops and dew on herbs, naturally seek a round shape. Therefore, the whole, of which they are parts, will do so.

The Earth Central.—That the earth is in the middle of the firmament is shown thus. To persons on the earth's surface the stars appear of the same size whether they are in mid-sky or just rising or about to set, and this is because the earth is equally distant from them. For if the earth were nearer to the firmament in one direction than in another, a person at that point of the earth's surface which was nearer to the firmament would not see half of the heavens. But this is contrary to Ptolemy and all the philosophers, who say that, wherever man lives, six signs rise and six signs set, and half of the heavens is always visible and half hid from him.

And a Mere Point in the Universe.—That same consideration is a sign that the earth is as a center and point with respect to the firmament, since, if the earth were of any size compared with the firmament, it would not be possible to see half the heavens. Also, suppose a plane passed through the center of the earth, dividing it and the firmament into equal halves. An eye at the earth's center would see half the sky, and one on the earth's surface would see the same half. From which it is inferred that the magnitude of the earth from surface to center is inappreciable and, consequently, that the magnitude of the entire earth is inappreciable compared to the firmament.[7]

---

7   This idea that the size of the earth is negligible in relation to the size of the entire universe was later echoed in much expanded form in Copernicus's assertion that the earth's orbit around the sun in his heliocentric scheme of the universe must also be negligible in relation to the size of the entire universe. In each case, the assumption of negligibility was necessary in order to account for the inability to detect any measurable parallax of the fixed stars: in the first case, diurnal parallax, as the heavens rotated overhead during the course of a night and hence any particular star would vary slightly in its distance from an observer on the earth's surface (that is, an observer offset from the universe's exact centre, which coincided with the centre of the earth), and in the second case, annual parallax, as the sun moved around its orbit with consequent varying distance from any particular part of the stellar sphere.

Also Alfraganus[8] says that the least of the fixed stars which we can see is larger than the whole earth. But that star, compared with the firmament, is a mere point. Much more so is the earth, which is smaller than it.

The Earth Immobile.—That the earth is held immobile in the midst of all, although it is the heaviest, seems explicable thus. Every heavy thing tends toward the center. Now the center is a point in the middle of the firmament. Therefore, the earth, since it is heaviest, naturally tends towards that point. Also, whatever is moved from the middle toward the circumference ascends. Therefore, if the earth were moved from the middle toward the circumference, it would be ascending, which is impossible.

Measuring the Earth's Circumference.—The total girth of the earth by the authority of the philosophers Ambrose, Theodosius, and Eratosthenes is defined as comprising 252,000 stades,[9] which is allowing 700 stades for each of the 360 parts of the zodiac. For let one take an astrolabe on a clear starry night and, sighting the pole through both apertures in the indicator, note the number of degrees where it is. Then let our measurer of the cosmos proceed directly north until on another clear night, observing the pole as before, the indicator stands a degree higher. After this let the extent of his travel be measured, and it will be found to be 700 stades. Then, allowing this many stades for each of the 360 degrees, the girth of the earth is found.

8   Al-Farghani was a ninth-century Arabic astronomer, known in the Latin West as Alfraganus, who, *inter alia*, estimated the dimensions of the geocentric universe described by Ptolemy.
9   A stade is a furlong, i.e. one-eighth of a mile, where the mile in question here is presumably a Roman mile.

4

REORDERING THE COSMOS

Nicolaus Copernicus proposed a new arrangement of the universe in a short work, which long remained in manuscript, that came to be known as the *Commentariolus* ("Little Commentary"). Dating from around 1512 (experts differ), the work proposed that the system of the universe inherited from the writings of the ancient Greeks Aristotle and Ptolemy, in which the heavens revolve around a stationary, central earth, be replaced by one in which the spheres of the heavens revolve around the Sun, itself now stationary at the centre and with the earth and the five planets, Mercury, Venus, Mars, Jupiter, and Saturn, rotating about it.[1] Copernicus developed the idea into its full mathematical form in his *De revolutionibus orbium coelestium* ("On the Revolutions of the Celestial Spheres"), published in 1543. The new system was not in itself productive of better predictions of celestial motions (the old earth-centred approach was capable of doing just as well when handled with Copernicus's mathematical skill), but the new, restructured universe was to cause much controversy due to its overturning of established authority and apparent violation of literal readings of Scripture. Copernicus, a canon in the Catholic Church in his native Poland, dedicated the work to the Pope.

Source: Nicolaus Copernicus, *De revolutionibus orbium coelestium* ("On the Revolutions of the Celestial Spheres"), Preface, slightly modified translation from Charles W. White (ed.), *Prefaces and Prologues to Famous Books*, Harvard Classics vol. 39 (New York: P.F. Collier, 1910), pp. 52–57.

---

1   This made the earth itself into a planet instead of the unique object that it had been hitherto. Only the Moon continued to orbit the earth.

Dedication of the revolutions of the heavenly bodies

By Nicolaus Copernicus (1543)

To Pope Paul III

I can easily conceive, most Holy Father, that as soon as some people learn that in this book which I have written concerning the revolutions of the heavenly bodies, I ascribe certain motions to the Earth, they will cry out at once that I and my theory should be rejected. For I am not so much in love with my conclusions as not to weigh what others will think about them, and although I know that the meditations of a philosopher are far removed from the judgment of the laity, because his endeavor is to seek out the truth in all things (so far as this is permitted by God to the human reason), I still believe that one must avoid theories altogether foreign to orthodoxy. Accordingly, when I considered in my own mind how absurd a performance it must seem, to those who know that the judgment of many centuries has approved the view that the Earth remains fixed as center in the midst of the heavens, if I should on the contrary assert that the Earth moves, I was for a long time at a loss to know whether I should publish the commentaries which I have written in proof of its motion, or whether it were not better to follow the example of the Pythagoreans and of some others, who were accustomed to transmit the secrets of Philosophy not in writing but orally, and only to their relatives and friends, as the letter from Lysis to Hipparchus bears witness. They did this, it seems to me, not as some think, because of a certain selfish reluctance to give their views to the world, but in order that the noblest truths, worked out by the careful study of great men, should not be despised by those who are vexed at the idea of taking great pains with any forms of literature except such as would be profitable, or by those who, if they are driven to the study of Philosophy for its own sake by the admonitions and the example of others, nevertheless, on account of their stupidity, hold a place among philosophers similar to that of drones among bees. Therefore, when I considered this carefully, the contempt which I had to fear because of the novelty and apparent absurdity of my view nearly induced me to abandon utterly the work I had begun.

My friends, however, in spite of long delay and even resistance on my part, withheld me from this decision. First among these was Nicolaus Schonberg, Cardinal of Capua, distinguished in all branches of learning. Next to him comes my very dear friend, Tidemann Giese, Bishop of Culm, a most earnest student, as he is, of sacred and, indeed, of all good learning. The latter has often urged me, at times even spurring me on with reproaches, to publish and at last bring to the light the book which had lain in my study not nine years merely, but already going on four times nine.[2] Not a few other very eminent and scholarly men made the same request, urging that I should no

---

2   A reference to a remark by the Roman poet Horace; see also the same reference in Wright's introduction to Gilbert's *De magnete*, below.

longer through fear refuse to give out my work for the common benefit of students of Mathematics. They said I should find that the more absurd most men would think this theory of mine concerning the motion of the Earth, the more admiration and gratitude it would command after they saw in the publication of my commentaries the mist of absurdity cleared away by most transparent proofs. So, influenced by these advisors and this hope, I have at length allowed my friends to publish the work, as they had long besought me to do.

But perhaps Your Holiness will not so much wonder that I have ventured to publish these studies of mine, after having taken such pains in elaborating them that I have not hesitated to commit to writing my views of the motion of the Earth, as you will be curious to hear how it occurred to me to venture, contrary to the accepted view of mathematicians, and well-nigh contrary to common sense, to form a conception of any terrestrial motion whatsoever. Therefore I would not have it unknown to Your Holiness, that the only thing which induced me to look for another way of reckoning the movements of the heavenly bodies was that I knew that mathematicians by no means agree in their investigations thereof. For, in the first place, they are so much in doubt concerning the motion of the sun and the moon that they cannot even demonstrate and prove by observation the constant length of a complete year; and in the second place, in determining the motions both of these and of the five other planets,[3] they fail to employ consistently one set of first principles and hypotheses, but use methods of proof based only upon the apparent revolutions and motions. For some employ concentric circles only; others, eccentric circles and epicycles; and even by these means they do not completely attain the desired end. For, although those who have depended upon concentric circles have shown that certain diverse motions can be deduced from these,[4] yet they have not succeeded thereby in laying down any sure principle corresponding indisputably to the phenomena. These, on the other hand, who have devised systems of eccentric circles, although they seem in great part to have solved the apparent movements by calculations by these eccentrics, have nevertheless introduced many things which seem to contradict the first principles of the uniformity of motion.[5] Nor have they been able to discover or calculate from these the main point, which is the

3   The sun and moon were often counted as "planets" to mark their movements against the backdrop of the so-called "fixed" stars, which they exhibited much like the five naked-eye planets Mercury, Venus, Mars, Jupiter, and Saturn.

4   Evidently referring to the nested-sphere approach introduced by Eudoxus in the fourth century BC, in which planets, sun, and moon are each attached to spheres centred on the earth that rotate uniformly around it. This approach found new champions, such as Fracastoro, in the early sixteenth century.

5   Copernicus here alludes to the basic principle of ancient Greek astronomy, claimed by Simplicius in the sixth century AD to have been first stated by Plato, that celestial motions should be nothing but circular and uniform.

shape of the world and the fixed symmetry of its parts; but their procedure has been as if someone were to collect hands, feet, a head, and other members from various places, all very fine in themselves, but not proportionate to one body, and no single one corresponding in its turn to the others, so that a monster rather than a man would be formed from them.[6] Thus in their process of demonstration, which they term a "method," they are found to have omitted something essential, or to have included something foreign and not pertaining to the matter in hand. This certainly would never have happened to them if they had followed fixed principles; for if the hypotheses they assumed were not false, all that resulted therefrom would be verified indubitably. Those things which I am saying now may be obscure, yet they will be made clearer in their proper place.

Therefore, having turned over in my mind for a long time this uncertainty of the traditional mathematical methods of calculating the motions of the celestial bodies, I began to grow disgusted that no more consistent scheme of the movements of the system of the universe, set up for our benefit by that best and most law abiding Architect of all things, was agreed upon by philosophers who otherwise investigate so carefully the most minute details of this world. Wherefore I undertook the task of rereading the books of all the philosophers I could get access to, to see whether anyone ever was of the opinion that the motions of the celestial bodies were other than those postulated by the men who taught mathematics in the schools. And I found first, indeed, in Cicero, that Niceta perceived that the Earth moved; and afterward in Plutarch I found that some others were of this opinion, whose words I have seen fit to quote here, that they may be accessible to all:

> Some maintain that the Earth is stationary, but Philolaus the Pythagorean says that it revolves in a circle about the fire of the ecliptic, like the sun and moon. Heraklides of Pontus and Ekphantus the Pythagorean make the Earth move, not changing its position, however, confined in its falling and rising around its own center in the manner of a wheel.

Taking this as a starting point, I began to consider the mobility of the Earth; and although the idea seemed absurd, yet because I knew that the liberty had been granted to others before me to postulate all sorts of little circles for explaining the phenomena of the stars, I thought I also might easily be

---

6   The criticism concerns the fact that in an earth-centred system, the relative sizes of the orbits of each of the planets cannot be determined, since only the *direction* of planets in the sky, seen from the earth's central position, can be measured, and not their *distances* from it. Thus, as far as direct measurement is concerned, Mercury could be farther away from the centre than Saturn rather than (as was usually assumed without geometrical demonstration) Saturn being at the greater distance.

permitted to try whether by postulating some motion of the Earth, more reliable conclusions could be reached regarding the revolution of the heavenly bodies than those of my predecessors.[7]

And so, after postulating movements that in this work I ascribe to the Earth, I have found by much long study that if the movements of the stars [i.e. planets][8] are attributed to the circular motion of the Earth and are calculated for the revolution of each one, not only do their phenomena follow logically therefrom, but the relative positions and magnitudes both of the planets and all their orbits, and of the heavens themselves, become so closely related that in none of its parts can anything be changed without causing confusion in the other parts and in the whole universe.[9] Therefore, in the course of the work I have followed this plan: I describe in the first book all the positions of the spheres together with the movements which I ascribe to the Earth, in order that this book might contain, as it were, the general scheme of the universe. Thereafter in the remaining books, I set forth the motions of the other stars and of all their orbits together with the movement of the Earth, in order that one may see from this to what extent the movements and appearances of the other stars and their orbits can be saved, if they are transferred to the movement of the Earth. Nor do I doubt that ingenious and learned mathematicians will sustain me, if they are willing to recognize and weigh, not superficially, but with that thoroughness which Philosophy demands above all things, those matters which have been adduced by me in this work to demonstrate these theories. In order, however, that both the learned and the unlearned equally may see that I do not avoid anyone's judgment, I have preferred to dedicate these lucubrations of mine to Your Holiness rather than to any other, because, even in this remote corner of the world where I live, you are considered to be the most eminent man in dignity of rank and in love of all learning and even of mathematics, so that by your authority and judgment you can easily suppress the bites of slanderers, albeit the proverb hath it that there is no remedy for the bite of a sycophant.

If perchance there shall be idle talkers, who, though they are ignorant of all mathematical sciences, nevertheless assume the right to pass judgment on these things, and if they should dare to criticize and attack this work of mine because of some passage of scripture which they have falsely distorted for their own purpose, I care not at all; I will even despise their judgment as foolish. For it is not unknown that Lactantius,[10] otherwise a famous writer but a poor mathematician, speaks most childishly of the shape of the Earth when he makes fun of those who said that the Earth has the form of a sphere. It should

---

7 In other words, Copernicus justifies his innovation by claiming that it had legitimate classical roots.

8 Here called "stars" as a generic use of the term for the specific case of the planets.

9 Thereby solving the difficulty mentioned in n.6, above.

10 A late-antique Church Father, c.AD 300.

not seem strange then to zealous students, if some such people shall ridicule us also. Mathematics is written for mathematicians, to whom, if my opinion does not deceive me, our labors will seem to contribute something to the ecclesiastical state whose chief office Your Holiness now occupies; for when not so very long ago, under Leo X, in the Lateran Council the question of revising the ecclesiastical calendar was discussed, it then remained unsettled, simply because the length of the years and months, and the motions of the sun and moon were held to have been not yet sufficiently determined. Since that time, I have given my attention to observing these more accurately, urged on by a very distinguished man, Paul, Bishop of Sempronia, who at that time had charge of the matter. But what I may have accomplished herein I leave to the judgment of Your Holiness in particular, and to that of all other learned mathematicians; and lest I seem to Your Holiness to promise more regarding the usefulness of the work than I can perform, I now pass to the work itself.

5

SEEING NEW THINGS: THE NEW WORLD

European cultural centres opened up to new experiences with reports from what they soon called "the New World," following Columbus's first voyage of 1492. In the course of the sixteenth century, Iberian reports of what was to be found in the Americas were published to reveal novelties unimagined in the classical texts that had long informed the worldview of learned Europeans. Natural history and forms of comparative anthropology expanded the conceivable in previously unexampled ways. Acosta's *Natural and Moral History of the Indies* (1555) is one of the most celebrated such works, and was translated into English (as well as other vernaculars) during the period precisely because of the immense interest that it generated. Acosta is especially concerned, in the passages reproduced here, in assessing these recent novelties in the light of accepted scriptural and historical authorities, so as to integrate existing established knowledge with the novelties that are its chief subject.

Source: Jose de Acosta, *Natural and Moral History of the Indies* [*De Orbe Novo*], trans. 1604 (Biodiversity Library, an 1880 edition). Some additional paragraphing added.

pp. 15–19:

Chapter VI.—That there is Land and Sea Under the two Poles

It is no small labour to have unfolded this doubt with this knowledge and resolution, that there is a Heaven in these parts of the Indies, which doth cover them as in Europe, Asia, and Affricke. And this point serveth often against many Spaniards, who being here, sigh for Spaine, having no discourse but of their countrie. They wonder, yea, they grow discontented with us, imagining that we have forgotten and make small accompt of our native soyle. To whom we answer, that the desire to returne into Spaine doth nothing trouble us, being as neere unto Heaven at Peru, as in Spaine: as saint Ierome saith well, writing unto Paulinus; That the gates of Heaven are as neere unto Brittanie, as to Ierusalem. But although the Heaven doth compasse in the world of all parts, yet must we not imagine that there is land necessarily on all parts of the world. For being so, that the two elements of earth and water make one globe or bowle,[1] according to the opinion of the most renowned ancient authors, (as Plutarch testifieth) and as it is prooved by most certaine demonstrations, wee may coniecture, that the sea doth occupie all this part, which is under the Antartike or southerne Pole, so as there should not remaine any place in these partes for the earth, the which saint Augustine doth very learnedly hold against them that maintaine the Antipodes, saying, that although it bee prooved, and wee believe that the worlde is round like to a bowle, wee may not therefore inferred, that in this other part of the worlde, the earth is uncovered, and without water. Without doubt, saint Augustine speakes well upon this point; and as the contrary is not proved, so doth it not follow, that there is any land discovered at the Antarticke Pole.[2]

The which experience hath now plainely taught us, for although the greatest part of the world under the Pole Antarticke be sea, yet is it not altogether, but there is likewise land, so as in all parts of the world, the earth and water imbrace one another, which truly is a thing to make us admire and glorifie the Arte of the soveraigne Creator. We knowe then by the holy Scripture, that in the beginning of the worlde, the waters were gathered together in one place, so as the earth remained uncovered. Moreover, the same holy Writte doth teach us, that these gatherings together of the water were called Sea; and as there be many, so of necessitie there must be many Seas. And this diversitie of seas is not onely in the Mediterranean Sea, whereas one is called Euxine, another the Caspian, an other the Erythrean or redde Sea, another the Persian, an other of Italie, and so many others. But also in the great Ocean, which the holy Scripture doth usually call a gulph: although really and in trueth it be but a Sea, yet in many and divers manners: as in respect of Peru and all America, the one is called the North Sea, the other the South; and at the East Indies, the one is called the Indian Sea, the other that of China. And I have observed, as well by my owne navigation, as by the relation of others, that the Sea is never divided from the Lande above a thousand Leagues. And althoughe the great Ocean stretcheth farre, yet doth it never passe this measure.

1   The so-called "terraqueous globe."
2   These sorts of discussions about the habitability of other parts of the globe understood in relation to the lines (such as the Tropics) on the celestial sphere were important to Columbus's plans to seek new lands to the south and west. See discussion on the sphere in the extract from Sacrobosco (Chapter 3), and on Columbus and ideas about the Tropics in Nicolás Wey Gómez, *The Tropics of Empire: Why Columbus Sailed South to the Indies* (Cambridge, MA: MIT Press, 2008).

I will not for all this affirme that wee sayle not above a thousand leagues in the Ocean, which were repugnant to trueth, being well knowne that the shippes of Portugal have sailed foure times as much and more, and that the whole world may bee compassed about by sea, as wee have seene in these dayes, without any further doubt. But I say and affirme, that of that which is at this day discovered, there is no land distant from any other firme land, by direct line, or from some Islands neere unto it above a thousand leagues; and so betwixt two firme lands there is no greater distance of sea, accompting from the nearest parts of both the lands: for, from the ends of Europe or Affricke and their coasts, to the Canaries, the Isles of Açores, Cape Verd and others in the like degree, are not above three hundred leagues, or five hundred from the Mayne land. From the saide Ilands running along to the West Indies, there are scant nine hundred leagues, to the Ilands of saint Dominick, the Virgins, the Happy Ilands and the rest; and the same Ilands runne along in order to the Ilands of Barlovent which are Cuba, Hispaniola, and Boriquen; from the same Ilands unto the Mayne land are scarce two or three hundred leagues, and in the nearest part farre lesse.

The firme land runnes an infinite space; from Terra Florida to the land of Patagones, and on the other side of the South, from the Straight [sic] of Magellan, to the Cape of Mendoce, there runnes a long Continent but not very large; for the largest is here in Peru, which is distant from Brazil about a thousand leagues. In this South Sea, although they have not yet discovered the ende towards the West, yet of late they have found out the Ilands which they call Salomon, the which are many and great, distant from Peru about eyght hundred leagues. And for that wee finde by observation, that whereas there bee many and great Ilandes, so there is some firme Land not farre off, I my selfe with many others doe believe that there is some firme land neere unto the Ilands of Salomon, the which doth answere unto our America on the West part, and possibly might runne by the height of the South, to the Straightes of Magellan.

Some hold that Nova Guinea is firme Land, and some learned men describe it neere to the Ilands of Salomon; so as it is likely, a good parte of the world is not yet discovered, seeing at this day our men sayle in the South Sea unto China and the Philipines; and wee say, that to go from Peru to those parts, they passe a greater Sea, then in going from Spaine to Peru. Moreover, wee know, that by that famous Straight of Magellan these two Seas doe ioyne and continue one with an other (I say the South sea with that of the North) by that part of the Antarticke Pole, which is in fiftie one degrees of altitude. But it is a great question, wherein many have busied themselves, whether these two Seas ioyne together in the North part; but I have not heard that any unto this day could attayne unto this point: but by certaine likelihoods and coniectures, some affirme there is an other Straight under the North, opposite to that of Magellan. But it sufficeth for our subiect, to knowe that there is a firme Land on this Southerne part, as bigge as all Europe, Asia, and

Affricke; that under both the Poles we finde both land and sea, one imbracing an other. Whereof the Ancients might stand in doubt, and contradict it for want of experience.[3]

. . .

pp. 53–57:

Chapter XVIII.—Wherein an answere is made to them that say that in times passed they have sayled through the Ocean as at this day

That which is alleaged to the contrary of that which hath beene spoken, that Saloman's Fleet sayled in three yeeres, is no sufficient proofe, seeing the holy Scripture doth not directly affirme, that this voyage continued three yeeres, but that it was made once in three yeeres. And although wee graunt that the voyage lasted three yeeres, it might bee, as it is likely, that this Fleet sayling towards the East Indies was stayed in their course by the diversity of Ports and Regions, which they discovered; as at this day, in all the South Sea, they sayle from Chile to newe Spaine, the which voyage, although it bee more certaine, yet is it longer by reason of the turnings they are forced to make upon the Coast, and they stay in divers Portes. And in trueth I doe not find in ancient books that they have lanched farre into the Ocean, neyther can I beleeve that this their sayling was otherwise then they use at this day in the Mediterranean Sea; which makes learned men to coniecture that in old time they did not sayle without owers [oars], for that they went alwayes coasting along the shoare; and it seems the holy Scripture doth testifie as much, speaking of that famous voyage of the Prophet Ionas, where it sayes, that the Marriners being forced by the weather, rowed to land.

Chapter XIX.—That we may coniecture how the first inhabitants of the Indies came thither by force of weather, and not willingly

Having shewed that there is no reason to beleeve that the first Inhabitants of the Indies came thither purposely, it followeth then, that if they came by Sea, it was by chance or by force of weather, the which is not incredible, notwithstanding the vastnesse of the Ocean, seeing the like hath happened

---

3 An interestingly explicit expression of doubt in the reliability of the Ancients, prompted by the new geographical discoveries. See on this theme Joyce Appleby, *Shores of Knowledge: New World Discoveries and the Scientific Imagination* (New York: Norton, 2013).

in our time, when as that Marriner, whose name we are yet ignorant of, to the end so great a worke, and of such importance, should not be attributed to any other Author then to God, having, through tempest, discovered this new world, left for payment of his lodging, where he had received it, to Christopher Columbus, the knowledge of so great a secret. Even so it might chance that some of Europe or Affricke in times past, have bin driven by foule weather, and cast upon unknowne lands beyond the Ocean. Who knoweth not that most, or the greatest part of the Regions in this newe world, were discovered by this means, the which we must rather attribute to the violence of the weather then to the spirit and industrie of those which have discovered. And to the end we may know that it is not in our time onely that they have undertaken such voiages, through the greatnesse of our shippes, and the valour and courage of our men, we may reade in Plinie that many of the Ancients have made the like voyages, he writes in this manner: "It is reported that Caius Caesar, sonne to Augustus Caesar, having charge upon the Arabian Sea, did there see and finde certaine pieces and remainders of Spanish shippes that had perished." And after he saith: "Nepos reportes of the Northern circuite, that they brought to Quintus Metellus Cæler, companion in the Consulship to Caius Affranius (the same Metellus being then Proconsul in Gaule) certaine Indians which had beene presented by the King of Suevia; the which Indians, sailing from India, for their trafficke, were cast upon Germanie by force of tempest."

Doubtles, if Plinie speaketh truth, the Portugales in these daies, saile no further then they did in those two shipwrackes, the one from Spaine to the Red Sea, the other from the East Indies to Germanie. The same Author writes in another place that a servant of Annius Plocanius, who farmed the customes of the Red Sea, sailing the course of Arabia, there came so furious a Northerne wind, that in fifteene daies he passed Caramania and discovereed Hippuros, a port in Taprobane, which at this day we call Sumatra. And they report of a shippe of Carthage, which was driven out of the Mediterranean Sea by a Northerne wind, to the view of this new world. The which is no strange thing to such as have any knowledge of the sea, to know that sometimes a storme continues long and furious, without any intermission. I my selfe going to the Indies, parting from the Canaries, have in fifteene daies discovered the first land peopled by the Spaniards. And without doubt this voiage had beene shorter, if the Mariners had set up all their sailes to the Northerne winds that blew. It seemes therefore likely to me that, in times past, men came to the Indies against their wills, driven by the furie of the winds. In Peru, they make great mention of certaine Giants, which have been in those parts, whose bones are yet seene at Manta and Puerto Viejo, of a huge greatnes, and by their proportion they should be thrice as big as the Indians. At this day they report that the Giants came by sea, to make warre with those of the Countrie, and that they made goodly buildings, whereof at this day they shew a well, built with stones of great price. They say moreover, that these men committing abominable sinnes, especially against nature, were consumed by fire from heaven. In like sort, the Indians of Yea and Arica report, that in old time they were wont to saile farre to the Ilandes of the West, and made their voiages in Seales skinnes blowne up. So as there wants no witnesses to prove that they sailed in the South sea before the Spaniards came thither.

Thus we may well conjecture that the new world began to be inhabited by men that have been cast upon that coast by the violence of the Northerne winds, as wee have seen in our age. So it is, being a matter verie considerable, that the workes of nature of greatest importance for the most part have been found out accidentally, and not by the industrie and diligence of man. The greatest part of phisicall hearbes, of Stones, Plants, Mettals, Perle, gold, Adamant, Amber, Diamont, and the most part of such like things, with their properties and vertues, have rather come to the knowledge of men by chance then by art or industrie, to the end wee may know that the glorie and praise of such wonders should be attributed to the providence of the Creator, and not to mans understanding; for that which we thinke to happen accidentally proceedes alwaies from the ordinance and disposition of God, who does all things with reason.

6

PRACTICAL KNOWLEDGE, EXPERIMENTAL MANIPULATION, AND NATURAL PHILOSOPHY

<hr>

William Gilbert's Latin work of 1600, *De magnete* ("On the magnet") was a remarkable and widely read work of natural philosophy that the likes of Kepler and Galileo read and took very seriously. Gilbert held that the earth revolves on its axis, thereby shifting the poles from their natural home in the heavens to the surface of the earth, where they defined that terrestrial axis. It is a matter of conjecture as to whether Gilbert also subscribed to the Copernican view that this revolving earth also orbited the sun, stationary at the centre (see on this Stephen Pumfrey, *Latitude and the Magnetic Earth: The True Story of Queen Elizabeth's Most Distinguished Man of Science* [Cambridge: Icon Books, 2002]). The association between magnetism and navigation, represented by the magnetic compass, was an important part of Gilbert's book, which drew on much practical lore from seamen. Wright's preface, below, elaborates on these matters.

Source: William Gilbert, *De magnete*, trans. Sylvanus P. Thompson (London: Chiswick Press, 1900): most of Edward Wright's preface, and Bk. 6, chap. 1.

TO THE MOST EMINENT AND LEARNED MAN DR. WILLIAM GILBERT, a distinguished Doctor of Medicine amongst the Londoners, and Father of Magnetick Philosophy, an Encomiastic Preface of Edward Wright on the subject of these books Magnetical.

Should there by chance be any one, most eminent Sir, who reckons as of small account these magnetical books and labours of yours, and thinks these studies of yours of too little moment, and by no means worthy enough of the attention of an eminent man devoted to the weightier study of Medicine: truly he must deservedly be judged to be in no common degree void of understanding. For that the use of the magnet is very important and wholly admirable is better known for the most part to men of even the lowest class than to need from me at this time any long address or commendation. Nor truly in my judgment could you have chosen any topick either more noble or more useful to the human race, upon which to exercise the strength of your philosophic intellect; since indeed it has been brought about by the divine agency of this stone, that continents of such vast circuit, such an infinite number of lands, islands, peoples, and tribes, which have remained unknown for so many ages, have now only a short time ago, almost within our own memory, been quite easily discovered and quite frequently explored, and that the circuit of the whole terrestrial globe also has been more than once circumnavigated by our own countrymen, Drake and Cavendish; a fact which I wish to mention to the lasting memory of these men.

For by the pointing of the iron touched by a loadstone, the points of South, North, East, and West, and the other quarters of the world are made known to navigators even under an overcast sky and in the darkest night; so that thus they always very easily understand to which point of the world they ought to direct their ship's course; which before the discovery of this wonderful virtue of the [magnetick][1] was clearly impossible. Hence in old times (as is established in histories), an incredible anxiety and immense danger was continually threatening sailors; for at the coming on of a tempest and the obscuring of the view of sun and stars, they were left entirely in ignorance whither they were making; nor could they find out this by any reasoning or skill. With what joy then may we suppose them to have been filled, to what feelings of delight must all shipmasters have given utterance, when that index magnetical first offered itself to them as a most sure guide, and as it were a Mercury, for their journey? But neither was this sufficient for this magnetical Mercury; to indicate, namely, the right way, and to point, as it were, a finger in the direction toward which the course must be directed; it began also long ago to show distinctly the distance of the place toward which it points. For since the index magnetical does not always in every place look toward the same point of the North, but deviates from it often, either toward the East or toward the West, yet always has the same deviation in the same place, whatever the place is, and steadily preserves it; it has come about that from that deviation, which they call variation, carefully noticed and observed in any maritime places, the same places could afterwards also be found by navigators from the drawing near and approach to the same variation as that of these same places, taken in conjunction with the observation of the latitude.

Thus the Portuguese in their voyages to the East Indies had the most certain indications of their approach to the Cape of Good Hope; as appears from the narrations of Hugo van Lynschoten and of the very learned Richard Hakluyt, our countryman. Hence also the experienced skippers of our own country, not a few of them, in making the voyage from the Gulf of Mexico to

---

1 As in the Thompson translation; Greek: *boreodeixis* or "north-showing."

the islands of the Azores, recognized that they had come as near as possible to these same islands; although from their sea-charts they seemed to be about six hundred British miles from them. And so, by the help of this magnetick index, it would seem as though that geographical problem of finding the longitude, which for so many centuries has exercised the intellects of the most learned Mathematicians, were going to be in some way satisfied; because if the variation for any maritime place whatever were known, the same place could very readily be found afterward, as often as was required, from the same variation, the latitude of the same place being not unknown.

It seems, however, that there has been some inconvenience and hindrance connected with the observation of this variation; because it cannot be observed excepting when the sun or the stars are shining. Accordingly, this magnetick Mercury of the sea goes on still further to bless all shipmasters, being much to be preferred to Neptune himself, and to all the sea-gods and goddesses; not only does it show the direction in a dark night and in thick weather, but it also seems to exhibit the most certain indications of the latitude. For an iron index, suspended on its axis (like a pair of scales), with the most delicate workmanship so as to balance in æquilibrio, and then touched and excited by a loadstone, dips to some fixed and definite point beneath the horizon (in our latitude in London, for example, to about the seventy-second degree), at which it at length comes to rest. But under the æquator itself, from that admirable agreement and congruency which, in almost all and singular magnetical experiments, exists between the earth itself and a terrella (that is, a globular loadstone)[2], it seems exceedingly likely (to say the very least), and indeed more than probable, that the same index (again stroked with a loadstone) will remain in æquilibrio in an horizontal position. Whence it is evident that this also is very probable, that in an exceedingly small progress from the South toward the North (or contrariwise) there will be at least a sufficiently perceptible change in that declination; so that from that declination in any place being once carefully observed along with the latitude, the same place and the same latitude may be very easily recognized afterward, even in the darkest night and in the thickest mist by a declination instrument.

Wherefore to bring our oration at length back to you, most eminent and learned Dr. Gilbert (whom I gladly recognize as my teacher in this magnetick philosophy), if these books of yours on the Magnet had contained nothing else, excepting only this finding of latitude from magnetick declination, by you now first brought to light, our shipmasters, Britains, French, Belgians, and Danes, trying to enter the British Channel or the Straits of Gibraltar from

2   This is Gilbert's name for a "little earth," a small sphere of magnetic material (lodestone) that acted as a model of the magnetic earth itself. He then argued for the direct relevance of his experiments with a terrella to the properties of the earth itself, in a remarkable display of metaphorical inference.

the Atlantick Ocean in dark weather, would still most deservedly judge them to be valued at no small sum of gold. But that discovery of yours about the whole globe of the earth being magnetical, although perchance it will seem to many "most paradoxical," producing even a feeling of astonishment, has yet been so firmly defended by you at all points and confirmed by so many experiments so apposite and appropriate to the matter in hand, in Bk. 2, chap. 34; Bk. 3, chap. 4 and 12; and in almost the whole of the fifth book, that no room is left for doubt or contradiction. I come therefore to the cause of the magnetick variation, which hitherto has distracted the minds of all the learned; for which no mortal has ever adduced a more probable reason than that which has now been set forth by you for the first time in these books of yours on the Magnet.

The [northerly pointing][3] of the index magnetical in the middle of the ocean, and in the middle of continents (or at least in the middle of their stronger and more lofty parts), its inclining near the shore toward those same parts, even by sea and by land, agreeing with the experiments Bk. 4, chap. 2, on an actual terrella (made after the likeness of the terrestrial globe, uneven, and rising up in certain parts, either weak or wanting in firmness, or imperfect in some other way),—this inclination having been proved, very certainly demonstrates the probability that that variation is nought else than a certain deviation of the magnetick needle toward those parts of the earth that are more vigorous and more prominent. Whence the reason is readily established of that irregularity which is often perceived in the magnetick variations, arising from the inæquality and irregularity of those eminences and of the terrestrial forces. Nor of a surety have I any doubt, that all those even who have either imagined or admitted points attractive or points respective in the sky or the earth, and those who have imagined magnetick mountains, or rocks, or poles, will immediately begin to waver as soon as they have perused these books of yours on the Magnet, and willingly will march with your opinion.

Finally, as to the views which you discuss in regard to the circular motion of the earth and of the terrestrial poles, although to some perhaps they will seem most supposititious, yet I do not see why they should not gain some favour, even among the very men who do not recognize a sphærical motion of the earth; since not even they can easily clear themselves from many difficulties, which necessarily follow from the daily motion of the whole sky. For in the first place it is against reason that that should be effected by many causes, which can be effected by fewer; and it is against reason that the whole sky and all the sphæres (if there be any) of the stars, both of the planets and the fixed stars, should be turned round for the sake of a daily motion which can be explained by the mere daily rotation of the earth. Then whether will

3   Greek: *orthoboreodeixis*.

it seem more probable, that the æquator of the terrestrial globe in a single second (that is, in about the time in which any one walking quickly will be able to advance only a single pace) can accomplish a quarter of a British mile (of which sixty equal one degree of a great circle on the earth), or that the æquator of the primum mobile in the same time should traverse five thousand miles with celerity ineffable; and in the twinkling of an eye should fly through about five hundred British miles, swifter than the wings of lightning, if indeed they maintain the truth who especially assail the motion of the earth). Finally, will it be more likely to allow some motion to this very tiny terrestrial globe; or to build up with mad endeavour above the eighth of the fixed sphæres those three huge sphæres, the ninth (I mean), the tenth, and the eleventh, marked by not a single star, especially since it is plain from these books on the magnet, from a comparison of the earth and the terrella, that a circular motion is not so alien to the nature of the earth as is commonly supposed.

Nor do those things which are adduced from the sacred Scriptures seem to be specially adverse to the doctrine of the mobility of the earth; nor does it seem to have been the intention of Moses or of the Prophets to promulgate any mathematical or physical niceties, but to adapt themselves to the understanding of the common people and their manner of speech, just as nurses are accustomed to adapt themselves to infants, and not to go into every unnecessary detail.[4] Thus in Gen. i. v. 16, and Psal. 136, the moon is called a great light, because it appears so to us, though it is agreed nevertheless by those skilled in astronomy that many of the stars, both of the fixed and wandering stars, are much greater. Therefore neither do I think that any solid conclusion can be drawn against the earth's mobility from Psal. 104, v. 5; although God is said to have laid the foundations of the earth that it should not be removed for ever; for the earth will be able to remain evermore in its own and self-same place, so as not to be moved by any wandering motion, nor carried away from its seat (wherein it was first placed by the Divine artificer). We, therefore, with devout mind acknowledging and adoring the inscrutable wisdom of the triune Divinity (having more diligently investigated and observed his admirable work in the magnetical motions), induced by philosophical experiments and reasonings not a few, do deem it to be probable enough that the earth, though resting on its centre as on an immovable base and foundation, nevertheless is borne around circularly.

But passing over these matters (concerning which I believe no one has ever demonstrated anything with greater certainty), without any doubt those matters which you have discussed concerning the causes of the variation and

---

4   This was a point central to Galileo's famous defence of the motion of the earth against allegations that the doctrine violated the plain words of scripture, given in his "Letter to the Grand Duchess Christina" of 1615.

of the magnetick dip below the horizon, not to mention many other matters, which it would take too long to speak of here, will gain very great favour amongst all intelligent men, and especially (to speak after the manner of the Chemists) amongst the sons of the magnetick doctrine.[5] Nor indeed do I doubt that when you have published these books of yours on the Magnet, you will excite all the diligent and industrious shipmasters to take no less care in observing the magnetick declination beneath the horizon than the variation. Since (if not certain) it is at least probable, that the latitude itself, or rather the effect of the latitude, can be found (even in very dark weather) much more accurately from that declination alone, than can either the longitude or the effect of the longitude from the variation, though the sun itself is shining brightly or all the stars are visible, with the most skilful employment likewise of all the most exact instruments.

Nor is there any doubt but that those most learned men, Peter Plancius (not more deeply versed in Geography than in observations magnetical), and Simon Stevinus, the most distinguished mathematician, will rejoice in no moderate degree, when they first see these magnetical books of yours, and observe their "port-finder" [Greek: *limeneuretikê*, or *Haven-finding Art*], enlarged and enriched by so great and unexpected an addition; and without doubt they will urge all their own shipmasters (as far as they can) to observe also everywhere the magnetick declination below the horizon no less than the variation. May your Magnetical Philosophy, therefore, most learned Dr. Gilbert, come forth into the light under the best auspices, after being kept back not till the ninth year only (as Horace prescribes), but already unto almost a second nine,[6] a philosophy rescued at last by so many toils, studyings, watchings, with so much ingenuity and at no moderate expense maintained continuously through so many years, out of darkness and dense mist of the idle and feeble philosophizers, by means of endless experiments skilfully applied to it; yet without neglecting anything which has been handed down in the writings of any of the ancients or of the moderns, all which you did diligently peruse and perpend. Do not fear the boldness or the prejudice of any supercilious and base philosophaster, who by either enviously calumniating or stealthily arrogating to himself the investigations of others seeks to snatch a most empty glory. Verily *Envy detracts from great Homer's genius; but Whoever thou art, Zoilus, thou hast thy name from him.*[7] May

---

5   An allusion to the secretive brotherhood of alchemists, a (somewhat fictitious) fra-
    ternity often referred to in mystical writings, and an ideology of knowledge quite
    opposed to the ideal of open and public sharing of scientific discoveries that Wright
    seems to endorse.
6   A standard classical reference to Horace also to be found in Copernicus's preface to *De
    revolutionibus* (Chapter 4), where he writes regarding his delay in publication that it
    was "not nine years merely, but already going on four times nine."
7   Zoilus was an ancient critic of Homer.

your new physiology of the Magnet, I say (kept back for so many years), come forth now at length into the view of all, and your Philosophy, never to be enough admired, concerning the great Magnet (that is, the earth); for, believe me (*If there is any truth in the forebodings of seers*), these books of yours on the Magnet will avail more for perpetuating the memory of your name than the monument of any great Magnate placed upon your tomb.

. . .

BOOK SIXTH. *CHAP. I.* ON THE GLOBE OF THE EARTH, THE *great magnet*. Hitherto our subject hath been the loadstone and things magnetical: how they conspire together, and are acted upon, how they conform themselves to the terrella and to the earth. Now must we consider separately the globe itself of the earth. Those experiments which have been proved by means of the terrella, how magnetick things conform themselves to the terrella, are all or at least the principal and most important of them, displayed by means of the earth's Body: And to the earth things magnetical are in all respects associate. First, as in the terrella the æquator, meridians, parallels, axis, poles are natural boundaries, as numerous experiments make plain: So also in the earth these boundaries are natural, not mathematical only (as all before us used to suppose). These boundaries the same experiments display and establish in both cases alike, in the earth no less than in the terrella. Just as on the periphery of a terrella a loadstone or a magnetick piece of iron is directed to its proper pole: so on the earth's surface are there turnings-about, peculiar, manifest, and constant on either side of the æquator. Iron is indued [*sic*] with verticity by being extended toward a pole of the earth, just as toward a pole of the terrella: By its being placed down also, and cooling toward the earth's pole after the pristine verticity has been annulled by fire, it acquires new verticity, conformable to its position earthward. Iron rods also, when placed some considerable time toward the poles, acquire verticity merely by regarding the earth; just as the same rods, if placed toward the pole of a loadstone, even without touching it, receive polar virtue. There is no magnetick body that in any way runs to the terrella which does not also wait upon the earth. As a loadstone is stronger at one end on one side or other of its æquator: so is the same property displayed by a small terrella upon the surface of a larger terrella. According to the variety and artistick skill in the rubbing of the magnetick iron upon the terrella, so do the magnetick things perform their function more efficiently or more feebly. In motions toward the earth's body, as toward the terrella a variation is displayed due to the unlikeness, inequality, and imperfection of its eminences: So every variation of the versorium or mariners' compass, everywhere by land or by sea, which thing has so sorely disturbed men's minds, is discerned and recognized as due to the same causes. The magnetick dip (which is the wonderful turning of magnetick things to the body of the terrella) in systematick course, is seen in clearer light to be the same thing upon the earth. And that single experiment, by a wonderful indication, as with a finger, proclaims the grand magnetick nature of the earth to be innate and diffused through all her inward parts. A magnetick vigour exists then in the earth just as in the terrella, which is a part of the earth, homogenic in nature with it, but rounded by Art, so as to correspond with the earth's globous shape and in order that in the chief experiments it might accord with the globe of the earth.

7

SEEING NEW THINGS: THE HEAVENS

———◆◆◆◆◆———

Novelties also began to be noticed in the heavens. According to the received view drawn from Aristotle, the heavens were cyclical in their motions and essentially unchanging; perhaps even more fundamentally, all objects in the heavens were already known, at least in principle. The human senses were accommodated to their objects, argued Aristotle and the philosophers of the universities, so that the unaided senses were capable of perceiving anything perceptible that exists. But in 1610 the Italian mathematician Galileo Galilei announced that he had found things in the heavens that were entirely novel and unsuspected. Furthermore, he had done so with the aid of an artificial optical instrument that he called a *perspicillo* (sometimes translated as "spyglass" and soon to be known as a "telescope"). Most striking among these novelties were four satellites apparently revolving around the planet Jupiter; Galileo subsequently suggested that an appropriate set of tables for the motions of these Jovian moons could be used to enable them as a kind of cosmic clock to be used in determining terrestrial longitude. This technique was used in the seventeenth century, although it was not found practicable for use at sea.

Source: Galileo Galilei, *Sidereus nuncius* (1610), trans. Edward Stafford Carlos (1880), rev. Peter Barker (Oklahoma: Byzantium Press, 2004). Extracts reproduced by permission of copyright holder. Preface, and pp. 5r–6v, 11r–13r, 28r–28v.

The Herald of the Stars

To the Most Serene Cosimo de' Medici the Second, Fourth Grand Duke of Tuscany.

There is certainly something very noble and large minded in the intention of those who have endeavored to protect from envy the noble achievements of distinguished men, and to rescue their names, worthy of immortality, from oblivion and decay. This desire has given us the lineaments of famous men, sculptured in marble, or fashioned in bronze, as a memorial of them to future ages; to the same feeling we owe the erection of statues, both ordinary and equestrian; hence, as the poet says, has originated expenditure, mounting to the stars, upon columns and pyramids; with this desire, lastly, cities have been built, and distinguished by the names of those men, whom the gratitude of posterity thought worthy of being handed down to all ages. For the state of the human mind is such that, unless it be continually stirred by the counterparts of matters obtruding themselves upon it from without, all recollection of the matters easily passes away from it.

But others, having regards for more stable and more lasting monuments, secured the eternity of the fame of great men by placing it under the protection, not of marble or bronze, but of the Muses' guardianship and the imperishable monuments of literature. But why do I mention these things, as if human wit, content with these regions, did not dare to advance further; whereas, since she well understood that all human monuments do perish at last by violence, by weather, or by age, she took a wider view, and invented more imperishable signs, over which destroying Time and envious Age could claim no rights; so, betaking herself to the sky, she inscribed on the well-known orbs of the brightest stars—those everlasting orbs—the names of those who, for eminent and god-like deeds, were accounted worthy to enjoy an eternity in company with the stars. Wherefore the fame of Jupiter, Mars, Mercury, Hercules, and the rest of the heroes by whose names the stars are called, will not fade until the extinction of the splendor of the constellations themselves. But this invention of human shrewdness, so particularly noble and admirable, has gone out of date ages ago, inasmuch as primeval heroes are in possession of those bright abodes, and keep them by a sort of right; into whose company the affection of Augustus in vain attempted to introduce Julius Caesar; for when he wished that the name of the Julian constellation should be given to a star, which appeared in his time, one of those which the Greeks and the Latins alike name, from their hair-like tails, comets,[1] it vanished in a short time and mocked his too eager hope. But we are able to read the heavens for your highness, most Serene Prince, far more truly and more happily, for scarcely have the immortal graces of your mind begun to shine on earth, when bright stars present themselves in the heavens, like tongues to tell and celebrate your most surpassing virtues to all time. Behold therefore, four stars reserved for your famous name, and those not belonging to the common and less conspicuous multitude of fixed stars, but in the bright ranks of the planets, four stars which, with different motions among themselves, together hold their paths and orbs with marvelous speed around the planet Jupiter, the most glorious of all the planets, as if they were his own children, while all the while with one accord they complete all together mighty revolutions every twelve years round the center of the universe, that

---

1   From the Latin *coma*, the hair.

is, round the Sun. But the Maker of the Stars himself seemed to direct me by clear reasons to assign these new planets to the famous name of your Highness in preference to all others. For just as these stars, like children worthy of their sire, never leave the side of Jupiter by any appreciable distance, so who does not know that clemency, kindness of heart, gentleness of manners, splendor of royal blood, nobleness in public functions, wide extent of influence and power over others, all of which have fixed their common abode and seat in your Highness, who, I say, does not know that all these qualities, according to the providence of God, from whom all good things do come, emanate from the benign star of Jupiter? Jupiter, Jupiter, I maintain, at the instant of the birth of your Highness having at length emerged from the turbid mists of the horizon, and being in possession of the middle quarter of the heavens, and illuminating the eastern angle, from his own royal house, from that exalted throne, looked out upon your most happy birth, and poured forth into a most pure atmosphere all the brightness of his majesty, in order that your tender body and your mind, though that was already adorned by God with still more splendid graces, might imbibe with your first breath the whole of that influence and power.[2] But why should I use only plausible arguments when I can almost absolutely demonstrate my conclusion? It was the will of Almighty God that I should be judged by your most serene parents not unworthy to be employed in teaching your highness mathematics, which duty I discharged, during the four years just passed, at that time of the year when it is customary to take a relaxation from severer studies. Wherefore, since it evidently fell to my lot by God's will, to serve your highness, and so to receive the rays of your surpassing clemency and beneficence in a position near your person, what wonder is it if you have so warmed my heart that it thinks about scarcely anything else day and night, but how I, who am indeed your subject not only by inclination, but also by my very birth and lineage, may be known to be most anxious for your glory, and most grateful to you? And so, inasmuch as under your patronage, most serene COSIMO, I have discovered these stars, which were unknown to all astronomers before me, I have, with very good right, determined to designate them with the most august name of your family. And as I was the first to investigate them, who can rightly blame me if I give them a name, and call them the MEDICEAN STARS, hoping that as much consideration may accrue to these stars from this title, as other stars have brought to other heroes? For not to speak of your most serene ancestors, to whose everlasting glory the monuments of all history bear witness, your virtue alone, most Mighty Sire, can confer on those stars an immortal name. For who can doubt that you will not only maintain

---

2   These attributions to Jupiter of a role related to Cosimo's birth are of course astrological in nature. Galileo, like all other astronomers of the period, was competent as a
deviser of horoscopes; astronomy and astrology were not yet sharply separated.

and preserve the expectations about yourself which you have aroused by the very happy beginning of your government, high though they be, but also that you will far surpass them, so that when you have conquered others like yourself, you may still vie with yourself, and become day by day greater than yourself and your greatness?

Accept, then, most clement Prince, this addition to the glory of your family, reserved by the stars for you, and may you enjoy for many years those good blessings, which are sent to you not so much from the stars as from God, the Maker and Governor of the stars.

Padua, March 12, 1610

Your Highness' Most Devoted Servant,

Galileo Galilei

...

pp. 5r–6v:

In the present small treatise I set forth some matters of great interest for all observers of natural phenomena to look at and consider. They are of great interest, I think, both from their intrinsic excellence, and from their absolute novelty, and also on account of the instrument by the aid of which they have been presented to my apprehension.

The number of the Fixed Stars which observers have been able to see without artificial powers of sight up to this day can be counted. It is therefore decidedly a great feat to add to their number, and to set distinctly before the eyes other stars in myriads, which have never been seen before, and which surpass the old, previously known, stars in number more than ten times.

Again, it is a most beautiful and delightful sight to behold the body of the Moon, which is distant from us nearly sixty [semi-]diameters[3] of the Earth, as near as if it was at a distance of only two of the same measures; so that the diameter of this same Moon appears about thirty times larger, its surface about nine hundred times, and its solid mass nearly 27,000 times larger than when it is viewed only with the naked eye; and consequently any one may know, with the certainty that is due to the use of our senses, that the Moon certainly does not possess a smooth and polished surface, but one rough and uneven, and, just like the face of the Earth itself, is everywhere full of vast protuberances, deep chasms, and sinuosities.

Then to have got rid of disputes about the Galaxy or Milky Way, and to have made its nature clear to the very senses, not to say to the understanding, seems by no means a matter which ought to be considered of slight importance. In addition to this, to point out, as with one's finger, the nature of those stars

3　The brackets correct a slip in Galileo's original.

which every one of the astronomers up to this time has called cloudlike, and to demonstrate that it is very different from what has hitherto been believed, will be pleasant, and very fine.

But that which will excite the greatest astonishment by far, and which indeed especially moved me to call the attention of all astronomers and philosophers, is this, namely, that I have discovered Four Erratic Stars, neither known nor observed by any one of the astronomers before my time, which have their revolutions round a certain bright star, one of those previously known, like Venus and Mercury round the Sun, and are sometimes in front of it, sometimes behind it, though they never depart from it beyond certain limits. All which facts were discovered and observed a few days ago by the help of a telescope devised by me, through God's grace first enlightening my mind.

Perchance other discoveries still more excellent will be made from time to time by me or by other observers, with the assistance of a similar instrument, so I will first briefly record its shape and preparation, as well as the occasion of its being devised, and then I will give an account of the observations made by me.

About ten months ago a report reached my ears that a Dutchman had constructed a telescope, by the aid of which visible objects, although at a great distance from the eye of the observer, were seen distinctly as if near; and some proofs of its most wonderful performances were reported, which some gave credence to, but others contradicted. A few days after, I received confirmation of the report in a letter written from Paris by a noble Frenchman, Jacques Badovere, which finally determined me to give myself up first to inquire into the principle of the telescope, and then to consider the means by which I might compass the invention of a similar instrument, which a little while after I succeeded in doing, through deep study of the theory of Refraction; and I prepared a tube, at first of lead, in the ends of which I fitted two glass lenses, both plane on one side but on the other side one spherically convex, and other concave. Then bringing my eye to the concave lens I saw objects satisfactorily large and near, for they appeared one-third of the distance off and nine times larger than when they are seen with the natural eye alone. I shortly afterwards constructed another telescope with more nicety, which magnified objects more than sixty times. At length, by sparing neither labor nor expense, I succeeded in constructing for myself an instrument so superior that objects seen through it appear magnified nearly a thousand times, and more than thirty times nearer than if viewed by the natural powers of sight alone. It would be altogether a waste of time to enumerate the number and importance of the benefits which this instrument may be expected to confer, when used by land or sea. But without paying attention to its use for terrestrial objects,[4] I betook myself to observations of the heavenly bodies; and first of all, I viewed the Moon as near as if it was scarcely two [semi-]diameters of the

---

4   In fact, Galileo did not turn his telescope to the heavens until December of 1609.

Earth distant. After the Moon, I frequently observed other heavenly bodies, both fixed stars and planets, with incredible delight; and, when I saw their very great number, I began to consider about a method by which I might be able to measure their distances apart, and at length I found one. And here it is fitting that all who intend to turn their attention to observations of this kind should receive certain cautions. For, in the first place, it is absolutely necessary for them to prepare a most perfect telescope, one which will show very bright objects distinct and free from any mistiness, and will magnify them at least 400 times, for then it will show them as if only one-twentieth of their distance off. For unless the instrument be of such power, it will be in vain to attempt to view all the things which have been seen by me in the heavens, or which will be enumerated hereafter.

...

pp. 11r–13r:

These phenomena which we have reviewed are observed in the bright tracts of the Moon. In the great spots we do not see such differences of depressions and prominences as we are compelled to recognize in the brighter parts, owing to the change of their shapes under different degrees of illumination by the Sun's rays according to the manifold variety of the Sun's position with regard to the Moon. Still, in the great spots there do exist some spaces rather less dark than the rest, as I have noted in the illustrations,[5] but these spaces always have the same appearance, and the depth of their shadow is neither intensified nor diminished; they do appear indeed sometimes a little more shaded, sometimes a little less, but the change of colour is very slight, according as the Sun's rays fall upon them more or less obliquely; and besides, they are joined to the adjacent parts of the spots with a very gradual connection, so that their boundaries mingle and melt into the surrounding region. But it is quite different with the spots which occupy the brighter parts of the Moon's surface, for, just as if they were precipitous crags with numerous rugged and jagged peaks, they have well-defined boundaries through the sharp contrast of light and shade. Moreover, inside those great spots certain other tracts are seen brighter than the surrounding region, and some of them very bright indeed, but the appearance of these, as well as of the darker parts, is always the same; there is no change of shape or brightness or depth of shadow, so that it becomes a matter of certainty and beyond doubt that their appearance is owing to real dissimilarity of parts, and not to unevennesses only in their configuration, changing in different ways the shadows of the same parts according to the variations of their illumination by the Moon, which really happens in the case of the other smaller spots occupying the brighter portion

5   Omitted.

of the Moon, for day by day they change, increase, decrease, or disappear, inasmuch as they derive their origin from the shadows of prominences.

But here I feel that some people may be troubled with grave doubt, and perhaps seized with a difficulty so serious as to compel them to feel uncertain about the conclusion just explained and supported by so many phenomena. For if that part of the Moon's surface which reflects the Sun's rays most brightly is full of sinuosities, protuberances, and cavities innumerable, why, when the Moon is increasing, does the outer edge which looks toward the west, or when the Moon is waning, the other half-circumference towards the east, and at full-moon the whole circle, appear not uneven, rugged and irregular, but perfectly round and circular, as sharply defined as if marked out with a pair of compasses, and without the indentations of any protuberances or cavities? And most remarkably so, because the whole unbroken edge belongs to that part of the Moon's surface which possesses the property of appearing brighter than the rest, which I have said to be throughout full of protuberances and cavities. For not one of the great spots extends quite to the circumference, but all of them are seen to be together away from the edge. Of this phenomenon, which affords a handle for such serious doubt, I produce two causes, and so two solutions of the difficulty. The first solution which I offer is this: if the protuberances and cavities in the body of the Moon existed only on the edge of the circle that bounds the hemisphere which we see, then the Moon might, or rather must, show itself to us with the appearance of a toothed wheel, being bounded with an irregular and uneven circumference; but if, instead of a single set of prominences arranged along the actual circumference only, very many ranges of mountains with their cavities and ruggednesses are set one behind the other along the extreme edge of the Moon, and that too not only in the hemisphere which we see, but also in that which is turned away from us, but still near the boundary of the hemisphere, then the eye, viewing them afar off, will not at all be able to detect the differences of prominences and cavities, for the intervals between the mountains situated in the same circle, or in the same chain, are hidden by the jutting forward of other prominences situated in other ranges, and especially if the eye of the observer is placed in the same line with the tops of the prominences mentioned. So on the Earth, the summits of a number of mountains close together appear situated in one plane, if the spectator is a long way off and standing at the same elevation. So when the sea is rough, the tops of the waves seem to form one plane, although between the billows there is many a gulf and chasm, so deep that not only the hulls, but even the bulwarks, masts, and sails of stately ships are hidden amongst them. Therefore, as within the Moon, as well as round her circumference, there is a manifold arrangement of prominences and cavities, and the eye, regarding them from a great distance, is placed in nearly the same plane with their summits, no one need think it strange that they present themselves to the visual ray which just grazes them as an unbroken line quite free from unevennesses. To this explanation may be added another, namely, that there is round the body of the Moon, just as round the Earth, an envelope of some substance denser than the rest of the ether, which is sufficient to receive and reflect the Sun's rays, although it does not possess so much opaqueness as to be able to prevent our seeing through it—especially when it is not illuminated. That envelope, when illuminated by the Sun's rays, renders the body of the Moon apparently larger than it really is, and would be able to stop our sight from penetrating to the solid body of the Moon, if its thickness were greater; now, it is of greater thickness about the circumference of the Moon, greater, I mean, not in actual thickness, but with reference to our sight-rays, which cut it obliquely; and so it may stop our vision, especially when it is in a state of brightness, and may conceal the true circumference of the Moon on the side towards the Sun. This may be understood more clearly from the adjoining figure, in which the body of the Moon, ABC, is surrounded by an enveloping atmosphere, DEG. An eye at F penetrates to the middle parts of the Moon, as at A, through a thickness, DA, of the atmosphere; but towards the extreme parts a mass of atmosphere of greater depth, EB, shuts out its boundary from our sight. An argument in favor of this is that the illuminated portion of the Moon appears of larger circumference than the rest of the orb which is in shadow. Perhaps also some will think that this same cause affords a very reasonable explanation why the greater spots on the Moon are not seen to reach to the edge of the circumference on any side, although it might be expected that some would be found about the edge as well as elsewhere; and it seems credible that there are spots there, but that they cannot be seen because they are hidden by a mass of atmosphere too thick and bright for the sight to penetrate.[6]

...

pp. 28r–28v:

These are my observations upon the four Medicean planets, recently discovered for the first time by me; and although it is not yet permitted to me to deduce by calculation from these observations the periods of these bodies, yet I may be allowed to make some statements, based upon them, well worthy of attention. In the first place, since they are sometimes behind, sometimes before Jupiter, at like distances, and withdraw from this planet

---

6 All of these arguments, about mountains, roughnesses, and even an atmosphere on the moon, were designed to reduce the differences between the earth and the moon, and hence between the terrestrial and the celestial realms. For Aristotle, whose natural philosophy dominated European learned thought in this period, the terrestrial and celestial were physically distinct realms. Galileo, with ambitions to vindicate the moving earth proposed by Copernicus, wished to break down the distinction so that the (terrestrial) earth could be regarded, without paradox, as part of the heavens, just like the (celestial) moon.

towards the east and towards the west only within very narrow limits of divergence, and since they accompany this planet alike when its motion is retrograde and direct, it can be a matter of doubt to no one that they perform their revolutions about this planet, while at the same time they all move as one around the center of the world in twelve years. They revolve in unequal circles, which is evidently the conclusion to be drawn from the fact that I have never been permitted to see two planets in conjunction when their distance from Jupiter was great, whereas near Jupiter two, three, and sometimes all, have been found closely packed together. It follows from what is said above that the revolutions of the planets which describe the smallest circles round Jupiter are the most rapid, for the stars nearest to Jupiter are often to be seen in the east, when the day before they have appeared in the west, and contrariwise. Also the planet traversing the greatest orb seems to me, after carefully weighing the occasions of its returning to positions previously noticed, to have a periodic time of half a month. Besides, we have a notable and splendid argument to remove the scruples of those who can tolerate the revolution of the planets round the Sun in the Copernican system, yet are so disturbed by the motion of one Moon about the Earth, while both travel around the Sun in an orb over the course of a year, that they consider that this theory of the constitution of the universe must be upset as impossible; for now we have not one planet only revolving about another, while both traverse a vast orb about the Sun, but our sense of sight presents to us four stars circling about Jupiter, like the Moon about the Earth, while all of them together with Jupiter traverse a great orb moving around the Sun in the space of twelve years. Lastly, I must not pass over the consideration of the reason why it happens that the Medicean stars, in performing very small revolutions about Jupiter, seem sometimes more than twice as large as at other times. We can by no means look for the explanation in the mists of the Earth's atmosphere, for they appear increased or diminished, while the discs of Jupiter and neighboring fixed stars are seen quite unaltered. That they approach and recede from the Earth at the points of their revolutions nearest to and furthest from the Earth to such an extent as to account for so great changes seems altogether untenable, for a strict circular motion can by no means show those phenomena; and an elliptical motion (which in this case would be nearly rectilinear) seems to be both untenable and by no means in harmony with the phenomena observed. But I gladly publish the explanation which has occurred to me upon this subject, and submit it to the judgment and criticism of all true philosophers. It is certain that when atmospheric mists intervene the Sun and Moon appear larger, but the fixed stars and planets less than they really are; hence the former luminaries, when near the horizon, are larger than at other times, but stars appear smaller, and are frequently scarcely visible; also they are still more diminished if those mists are bathed in light; so stars appear very small by day and in the twilight, but the Moon does not appear so, as I have previously remarked. Moreover,

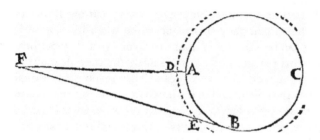

Figure 7.1 An atmosphere for the moon. From Galileo, *Sidereus nuncius.*

it is certain that not only the Earth, but also the Moon, has its own vaporous sphere enveloping it, for the reasons which I have previously mentioned, and especially for those which shall be stated more fully in my System, and we may consistently decide that the same is true with regard to the rest of the planets. So that it seems to be by no means an untenable opinion to place round Jupiter also an orb denser than the rest of the ether, about which the MEDICEAN planets revolve, like the Moon about the sphere of the elements. And that by the interposition of this orb they appear smaller when they are in apogee. But when in perigee, through the absence or attenuation of that orb, they appear larger. Lack of time prevents my going further into these matters; kind Reader, expect more on these subjects shortly.[7]

FINIS

7 In the event, not to appear until Galileo's *Dialogue Concerning the Two Great World Systems* of 1632, although other hints of related matters also appeared in his *Assayer* in 1623.

8

NOVELTY FROM EXPERIENCE

———◦◦◦———

Francis Bacon, Lord Chancellor of England, said that he took knowledge as his province—that is, as his department of government. The expression betrays his concern with bureaucratic organization to enable the creation of natural knowledge (Bacon's especial interest). By creating a division of cognitive labour, Bacon hoped to permit discoveries to a select elite at the head of this process, who could decide whether or not to share their knowledge with others, including the rulers of the people. The kind of knowledge that Bacon hoped to generate through his investigative procedures was aimed at producing unprecedented new phenomena, of a kind never before seen, yet which had lurked in the unrealized potential of matter. The wonders of our own age would have filled Bacon with satisfaction.

Sylva sylvarum contains ten so-called "centuries" of experimental or experiential items, that is, one hundred items per century. This format was also used for medical case histories, similarly empirical in form. Bacon's amount to a very miscellaneous collection of first-hand trials, tales from Pliny and other classical as well as modern authors, and traditional beliefs presented as subjects of further tests. The work, posthumously published in 1626, became very popular in England in the seventeenth century, and exemplified much of what was then understood as "Baconian." It accompanied Bacon's well known *New Atlantis*, a utopian tract that described a research institute for conducting many of the same sorts of inquiries as are to be found, in a much less systematic form, in the *Sylva*.

Source: Francis Bacon, *Sylva sylvarum* (London, 1626), paras.14–16, 143–153, 326, 328, 795, 812–815, 886, 998.

Paras. 14–16:

Take a *Glasse* with a *Belly* and a long *Nebb*;[1] fill the *Belly* (in part) with *Water*. Take also another Glasse, whereinto put *Claret Wine* and *Water* mingled; Reverse the first *Glasse*, with the *Belly* upwards, Stopping the *Nebb* with your finger; Then dipp the Mouth of it within the Second *Glasse*, and remove your Finger: Continue it in that posture for a time; And it will unmingle the *Wine* from the *Water*: The *Wine* ascending and settling in the topp of the upper *Glasse*; And the *Water* descending and settling in the bottom of the lower *Glasse*. The passage is apparent to the Eye; For you shall see the *Wine*, as it were, in a small veine, rising through the *Water*. For handsomnesse sake (because the Working requireth some small time) it were good you hang the upper *Glasse* upon a Naile. But as soone as ther is gathered so much pure and unmixed *water* in the Bottome of the Lower *Glasse*, as that the Mouth of the upper *Glasse* dippeth into it, the *Motion* ceaseth.

Let the Upper *Glasse* be *Wine*, and the Lower *Water*, ther followeth no *Motion* at all. Lett the Upper *Glasse* be *Water* pure, the Lower *Water* coloured; or contrariwise; ther followeth no *Motion* at all. But it hath been tried, that though the Mixture of *Wine* and *Water*, in the Lower *Glasse*, be three parts *Water*, and but one *Wine*; yet it doth not dead the *Motion*. This *Separation* of *Water* and *Wine* appeareth to be made by *Weight*; for it must be of *Bodies* of unequal *Weight*, or ells it worketh not; And the Heavier *Body* must ever be in the upper *Glasse*. But then note withal, that the *Water* being made pensile, and ther being a great *Weight* of *Water* in the *Belly* of the *Glasse*, sustained by a small Pillar of *Water* in the Neck of the *Glasse*; It is that, which setteth the *Motion* on worke: for *Water* and *Wine* in one *Glasse*, with long standing, will hardly sever.[2]

This *Experiment* would be Extended from Mixtures of several *Liquors*, to *Simple Bodies*, which Consist of severall Similare Parts: Try it therefore with *Broyne* or *Salt water*, and *Fresh water*; Placing the *Salt water* (which is the heavier) in the upper *Glasse*; And see whether the *Fresh* will come above. Try it also with *Water thick Sugred* and *Pure water*; and see whether the *water* which commeth above, will loose his Sweetnes: For which purpose it were good ther were a little Cock made in the Belly of the upper *Glasse*.

...

---

1 Neck.
2 This experiment seems to have been fairly well known. It is discussed in the Neapolitan Giambattista della Porta's much-translated work of 1558 called *Magiae naturalis libri XX*, translated into English (from a later edition) a century later as *Natural Magick* (London, 1658), on p. 383, and is also discussed by others, including Galileo, in Galileo, *Discourses and Demonstrations Concerning Two New Sciences*, trans. Stillman Drake (Madison: University of Wisconsin Press, 1974), pp. 74–75.

Paras. 143–153:

Sounds are better heard, and further off, in an *Evening*, than at the *Noone*, or in the *Day*. The *Cause* is, for that in the *Day*, when the *Aire* is more Thin, (no doubt) the *Sound pierceth* better; But when the *Aire* is more Thicke, (as in the *Night*) the *Sound* spendeth and spreadeth abroad lesse: And so it is a Degree of *Enclosure*. As for the *Night*, it is true also, that the Generall Silence helpeth.

There be two Kinds of *Reflexions* of *Sounds*; The one at a *Distance*, which is the *Eccho*; Wherein the *Originall* is heard distinctly, and the *Reflexion* also distinctly; Of which we shall speake hereafter: The other in *Concurrence*; When the *Sound* Reflecting (the *Reflexion* being neare at hand) returneth immediately upon the *Originall*, and so iterateth it not, but amplifieth it. Therefore we see, that *Musicke* is better in Chambers Wainscotted, than Hanged.

The *Strings* of a Lute, or Violl, or Virginalls, doe give a far greater *Sound*, by reason of the *Knot*, and *Board*, and *Concave* underneath, than if there were nothing but onely the *Flat* of a *Board*, without that *Hollow* and *Knot*, to let in the Upper Aire into the Lower. The *Cause* is, the Communication of the Upper Aire with the Lower; And Penning of both from Expence, or Dispersing.

An *Irish Harpe* hath Open Aire on both sides of the *Strings*: And it hath the *Concave* or *Belly*, not along the *Strings*, but at the End of the *Strings*. It maketh a more Resounding *Sound*, than a *Bandora*, *Orpharion*, or *Citterne*, which have likewise *Wire-strings*. I judge the *Cause* to be, for that Open Aire on both Sides helpeth, so that there be a *Concave*; Which is therefore best placed at the End.

In a *Virginall*, when the *Lid* is downe, it maketh a more exile *Sound*, than when the *Lid* is open. The *Cause* is, for that all *Shutting in* of *Aire*, where there is no competent Vent, dampeth the *Sound*. Which maintaineth likewise the former *Instance*; For the *Belly* of the *Lute*, or *Violl*, doth pen the *Aire* somewhat.[3]

There is a Church at *Glocester*, (and as I have heard the like is in some other places;) where if you speake against a Wall, softly, another shall heare your *Voice* better a good way off, than neare hand. Enquire more particularly of the Frame of that Place.[4] I suppose there is some Vault, or Hollow, or Isle, behind the Wall, and some Passage to it towards the further end of that Wall, against which you speake; So as the *Voice* of him that speaketh, slideth along the Wall, and then entreth at some Passage, and communicateth with the *Aire* of the Hollow; For it is preserved somewhat by the plaine wall; but that is too weake to give a *Sound* Audible, till it hath communicated with the backe *Aire*.

---

3 Thus far, Bacon has provided statements about sounds of various kinds and their production. He has not adduced experimental trials to support his claims, or invited his readers to try things for themselves.

4 This reads like a note to himself reminding him to look further into the question; it exemplifies the unfinished nature of this text as a whole.

Strike upon a *Bowstring*, and lay the *Horne* of the *Bow* neare your Eare, and it will increase the *Sound*, and make a degree of a *Tone*.[5] The *Cause* is, for that the Sensory, by reason of the Close Holding, is percussed, before the Aire disperseth. The like is, if you hold the *Horne* betwixt your Teeth. But that is a plaine *Delation* of the *Sound*; from the Teeth, to the Instrument of Hearing; For there is a great Entercourse betweene those two Parts; As appeareth by this; That a Harsh *Grating Tune* setteth the Teeth on edge. The like falleth out, if the *Horne* of the *Bow* be put upon the Temples; But that is but the Slide of the *Sound* from thence to the Eare.

If you take a *Rod* of *Iron*, or *Brasse*, and hold the one end to your Eare, and strike upon the other, it maketh a far greater *Sound*, than the like Stroke upon the *Rod*, not so made Contiguous to the Eare. By which, and by some other *Instances*, that have beene partly touched, it should appeare; That *Sounds* doe not onely slide upon the Surface of a Smooth Body, but doe also communicate with the *Spirits*, that are in the Pores of the Body.

I remember in *Trinity Colledge* in *Cambridge*, there was an *Upper Chamber*, which being thought weake in the Roofe of it, was supported by a Pillar of Iron, of the bignesse of ones Arme, in the middest of the *Chamber*; Which if you had struck, it would make a little flat Noise in the *Roome* where it was struck; But it would make a great Bombe in the *Chamber* beneath.[6]

The *Sound* which is made by *Buckets* in a *Well*, when they touch upon the *Water*; Or when they strike upon the side of the *Well*; Or when two Buckets dash the one against the other; These *Sounds* are deeper, and fuller, than if the like Percussion were made in the *Open Aire*. The *Cause* is, the Penning and Enclosure of the Aire, in the Concave of the *Well*.

Barrells placed in a Roome under the Floare of a *Chamber*, make all *Noises* in the same Chamber, more Full and Resounding.

So that there be five ways (in general,) of Majoration of Sounds: Enclosure Simple; Enclosure with Dilatation; Communication; Reflexion Concurrent; *and* Approach *to the* Sensory.[7]

...

Para. 326:

The World hath beene much abused by the Opinion of *Making of Gold*: The *Worke* it selfe I judge to be possible; But the *Meanes* (hitherto propounded) to effect it, are, in the Practice, full of Errour and Imposture; And in the Theory, full of unsound Imaginations.[8] For to say, that *Nature* hath an Intention to

---

5   Another variant in Bacon's techniques for presenting experience: this time, he gives instructions, like a recipe, together with the asserted result.
6   This varies again, being a personally attested experience (what Bacon "remembers").
7   Notice how, throughout this and earlier discussions, Bacon often refers to the "causes" of the phenomena he presents, then merely asserts them without proof.
8   A reference, of course, to alchemy and its practitioners.

make all Metals *Gold*; And that, if she were delivered from all Impediments, she would performe her owne Worke; And that, if the Crudities, Impurities, and Leprosities of *Metals* were cured, they would become *Gold*; And that a little *Quantitie* of the *Medicine*, in the Works of *Projection*, will turne a Sea of the *Baser Metall* into *Gold*, by *Multiplying*: All these are but dreames: And so are many other Grounds of *Alchymy*. And to help the Matter, the *Alchymists* call in likewise many Vanities, out of *Astrologie*; *Naturall Magicke*; Superstitious Interpretations of *Scriptures*; Auricular *Traditions*; Faigned Testimonies of *Ancient Authors*; And the like. It is true, on the other side, they have brought to light not a few profitable *Experiments*, and thereby made the World some amends. But wee, when wee shall come to handle the *Version* and *Transmutation* of *Bodies*; And the *Experiments* concerning *Metalls* and *Minerals*; will lay open the true Wayes and Passages of *Nature*, which may leade to this great Effect. And wee commend the wit of the *Chineses*, who despaire of Making of *Gold*, but are Mad upon the Making of *Silver*: For certaine it is, that it is more difficult to make *Gold*, (which is the most Ponderous and Materiate amongst *Metalls*) of other *Metalls*, lesse Ponderous, and lesse Materiate; than (*via versa*) to make *Silver* of *Lead*, or *Quick-Silver*; Both which are more Ponderous than *Silver*; So that they need rather a further Degree of *Fixation*, than any *Condensation*. In the meane time, by Occasion of Handling the *Axiomes* touching *Maturation*, we will direct a *Triall* touching the *Maturing* of *Metalls*, and therby Turning some of them into *Gold*: For we conceive indeed, that a perfect good *Concoction*, or *Disgestion*, or *Maturation* of some *Metalls*, will produce *Gold*. And here we call to minde, that wee knew a *Dutch-man*, that had wrought himselfe into the beleefe of a great Person, by undertaking that he could make *Gold*: Whose discourse was, that *Gold* might be made; But that the *Alchymists* Over-fired the Worke: For (he said) the *Making* of *Gold* did require a very temperate *Heat*, as being in *Nature* a Subterrany worke, where little *Heat* commeth; But yet more to the *Making* of *Gold*, than of any other *Metall*; And therefore, that he would doe it with a great Lampe, that should carry a Temperature and Equall Heat: And that it was the *Worke* of many Moneths. The Device of the Lampe was folly; But the Over-firing now used; And the Equal Heat to be required; And the Making it a Worke of some good Time; are no ill Discourses.

...

Para. 328:

Gold hath these *Natures*: *Greatnesse of Weight*; *Closenesse of Parts*; *Fixation*; *Pliantnesse*, or *Softnesse*; *Immunity from Rust*; *Colour* or *Tincture of Yellow*. Therfore the Sure Way, (though most about,) to make *Gold*, is to know the *Causes* of the severall *Natures* before rehearsed, and the *Axiomes* concerning the same.

For if a Man can make a *Metall*, that hath all these *Properties*, Let Men dispute, whether it be *Gold*, or not.[9]

...

Para. 795:

Those *Effects*, which are wrought by the *Percussion* of the *Sense*, and by *Things* in *Fact*, are produced likewise, in some degree, by the *Imagination*. Therefore if a Man see another eat *Soure* or *Acide Things*, which set the *Teeth* on edge, this *Object* tainteth the *Imagination*. So that hee that seeth the *Thing* done by another, hath his owne *Teeth* also set on edge. So if a Man see another turne swiftly, and long; Or if he looke upon *Wheeles* that turne, Himselfe waxeth *Turne-sicke*. So if a Man be upon an *High Place*, without *Railes*, or good Hold, except he be used to it, he is Ready to Fall: For *Imagining* a *Fall*, it putteth his *Spirits* into the very *Action* of a *Fall*. So Many upon the *Seeing* of others *Bleed*, or *Strangled*, or *Tortured*, Themselves are ready to faint, as if they *Bled*, or were in *Strife*.

...

Paras. 812–15:

The *Predictions* likewise of *Cold* and *Long Winters*, and *Hot* and *Drie Summers*, are good to be knowne; As well for the *Discoverie* of the *Causes*, as for divers *Provisions*. That of *Plenty* of *Hawes*, and *Hops*, and *Briar-Berries*, hath beene spoken of before. If *Wainscast, or Stone*, that have used to Sweat, be more drie, in the Beginning of *Winter*; Or the *Drops* of the *Eaves* of *Houses* come more slowly downe, than they use; it portendeth a *Hard* and *Frostie Winter*. The *Cause* is, for that it sheweth an *Inclination* of the *Aire*, to *Drie Weather*; which in *Winter* is ever joined with *Frost*.

Generally, a *Moist* and *Coole Summer*, portendeth a *Hard Winter*. The *Cause* is, for that the *Vapours* of the *Earth*, are not dissipated in the *Summer*, by the *Sunne*; And so they rebound upon the *Winter*.

A *Hot* and *Drie Summer*, and *Autumne*, and especially if the *Heat* and *Drought* extend farre into *September*, portendeth and Open Beginning of *Winter*; and *Colds* to succeed, toward the latter Part of the *Winter*, and the beginning of the *Spring*: For till then, the former *Heat* and *Drought* beare the Sway; And the *Vapours* are not sufficiently Multiplied.

---

9 Bacon discusses such matters more theoretically elsewhere (as in his *Novum organum*, or *New Organon*, of 1620) in terms of the superinducing of so-called "simple natures" onto matter—in this case such properties as yellowness, heaviness, and pliability. From this perspective, the properties of a substance were not the marks of that substance's inner nature (as here, signs that the substance really is gold); instead, any substance possessing all those appropriate properties was by that very fact gold, as it were by definition—there was nothing more to it than that, much as with the appearance, walking, and quacking of a duck...

An *Open* and *Warme Winter* portendeth a *Hot* and *Drie Summer*: For the *Vapours* disperse into the *Winter Showres*; Whereas *Cold* and *Frost* keepeth them in, and transporteth them into the late *Spring*, and *Summer* following.

. . .

Para. 886:

It is reported, that amongst the *Leucadians*, in *Ancient* time, upon a Superstition, they did use to Precipitate a *Man*, from a *High Cliffe* into the *Sea*; Tying about him, with Strings, at some distance, many great *Fowles*; And fixing unto his *Body* divers *Feathers*, spred, to breake the *Fall*. Certainly many *Birds* of good *Wing*, (As *Kites*, and the like,) would beare up a good *Weight*, as they flie; And *Spreading* of *Feathers*, thinne, and close, and in great Bredth, will likewise beare up a great *Weight*; Being even laid, without Tilting upon the Sides. The further *Extension* of this *Experiment* for *Flying* may be thought upon.

. . .

Para. 998:

It is constantly Received, and Avouched, that the *Anointing* of the *Weapon*, that maketh the *Wound*, will heal the *Wound* it selfe.[10] In this *Experiment*, upon the Relation of *Men* of *Credit*, (though my selfe, as yet, am not fully inclined to believe it,) you shall note the *Points* following. First, the *Ointment*, wherewith this is done, is made of Divers *Ingredients*; whereof the Strangest and Hardest to come by, are the *Mosse* upon the *Skull* of a *dead Man*, *Unburied*; And the *Fats* of a *Boare*, and a *Beare*, killed in the *Act* of *Generation*. These two last I could easily suspect to be prescribed as a Starting Hole; That if the *Experiment* proved not, it might be pretended, that the *Beasts* were not killed in the due Time; For as for the *Mosse*, it is certaine, there is great Quantitie of it in *Ireland*, upon *Slaine Bodies*, laid on *Heaps*, *Unburied*.

. . .

10 The famous "weapon salve."

9

MAKING EXPERIMENTAL
KNOWLEDGE

The seventeenth century witnessed the development of new ways of making knowledge about the natural behaviours of material bodies. Galileo taught about the motion of heavy bodies in the vicinity of the Earth's surface, arguing that freely falling bodies accelerate from rest with their speed of fall increasing in proportion to the time elapsed. He asserted that the truth of this claim could be known from experimental tests using balls rolling down inclined planes and the careful measurement of the times elapsed during their traversal of particular distances. Such experimental demonstrations depended on ways of converting assertions of experimental results into universally applicable knowledge-claims. Similar practical questions of knowledge-making were soon afterwards confronted by the French mathematician Blaise Pascal when he tried to establish doctrines concerning air pressure and water pressure (work involving barometric tubes and siphons), and by the English natural philosopher Robert Boyle with his experiments using an air-pump.

Source: Galileo Galilei, *Discourses and Demonstrations Concerning Two New Sciences* (Italian, with Latin passages, 1638), English trans. Henry Crew and Alfonso de Salvio (New York: Macmillan, 1914), extracts from Second Day, pp.109–117.

SECOND DAY[1]

Sagredo: While Simplicio and I were awaiting your arrival we were trying to recall that last consideration which you advanced as a principle

---

1   The style of Galileo's *Discourses* is worthy of note: a conversation takes place over four days between three fictionalised interlocutors, Salviati (Galileo's spokesman), Simplicio (a conventional Aristotelian philosopher) and Sagredo (an intelligent man-in-the-middle who perhaps stands in for the reader); these are the same three participants as those of Galileo's earlier *Dialogue Concerning the Two Great World*

and basis for the results you intended to obtain; this consideration dealt with the resistance which all solids offer to fracture and depended upon a certain cement which held the parts glued together so that they would yield and separate only under considerable pull [*potente attrazzione*]. Later we tried to find the explanation of this coherence, seeking it mainly in the vacuum; this was the occasion of our many digressions which occupied the entire day and led us far afield from the original question which, as I have already stated, was the consideration of the resistance [*resistenza*] that solids offer to fracture.

Salviati: I remember it all very well. Resuming the thread of our discourse, whatever the nature of this resistance which solids offer to large tractive forces [*violenta attrazzione*] there can at least be no doubt of its existence; and though this resistance is very great in the case of a direct pull, it is found, as a rule, to be less in the case of bending forces [*nel violentargli per traverso*]. Thus, for example, a rod of steel or of glass will sustain a longitudinal pull of a thousand pounds while a weight of fifty pounds would be quite sufficient to break it if the rod were fastened at right angles into a vertical wall. It is this second type of resistance which we must consider, seeking to discover in what proportion it is found in Prismes and cylinders of the same material, whether alike or unlike in shape, length, and thickness. In this discussion I shall take for granted the well-known mechanical principle which has been shown to govern the behavior of a bar, which we call a lever, namely, that the force bears to the resistance the inverse ratio of the distances which separate the fulcrum from the force and resistance respectively.

Simplicio: This was demonstrated first of all by Aristotle, in his *Mechanics*.[2]

Systems, Ptolemaïc and Copernican of 1632, which had, because of its clear pro-Copernican stance, resulted in Galileo's trial and his condemnation to house arrest for life. In the *Discourses*, the conversation is interrupted by text understood to have been written by Galileo himself, and which appears in the original work in Latin, the usual language of formal mathematical texts. The discussions themselves were in Italian (the Tuscan dialect of Florence, by this time a well accepted language of considerable cultural status). Galileo thus combines the formal acceptability of a mathematical text with informal, discursive consideration of the premises and assumptions that the mathematical reasoning employed. In the material presented here, practical engineering knowledge receives a philosophical–mathematical treatment designed both to increase accuracy and to raise the cultural standing of engineering know-how.

2   The *Mechanics*, or *Mechanical Problems*, is now believed to date from a little after Aristotle's own time, but to have been written by someone of his school.

Salv.: Yes, I am willing to concede him priority in point of time; but as regards rigor of demonstration the first place must be given to Archimedes, since upon a single proposition proved in his book on *Equilibrium* depends not only the law of the lever but also those of most other mechanical devices.[3]

Sagr.: Since now this principle is fundamental to all the demonstrations which you propose to set forth would it not be advisable to give us a complete and thorough proof of this proposition unless possibly it would take too much time?

Salv.: Yes, that would be quite proper, but it is better I think to approach our subject in a manner somewhat different from that employed by Archimedes, namely, by first assuming merely that equal weights placed in a balance of equal arms will produce equilibrium—a principle also assumed by Archimedes—and then proving that it is no less true that unequal weights produce equilibrium when the arms of the steelyard have lengths inversely proportional to the weights suspended from them; in other words, it amounts to the same thing whether one places equal weights at equal distances or unequal weights at distances which bear to each other the inverse ratio of the weights.

In order to make this matter clear imagine a Prisme or solid cylinder, AB, suspended at each end to the rod [*linea*] HI, and supported by two threads HA and IB; it is evident that if I attach a thread, C, at the middle point of the balance beam HI, the entire Prisme AB will, according to the principle assumed, hang in equilibrium since one-half its weight lies on one side, and the other half on the other side, of the point of suspension C. Now suppose the Prisme to be divided into unequal parts by a plane through the line D, and let the part DA be the larger and DB the smaller: this division having been made, imagine a thread ED, attached at the point E and supporting the parts AD and DB, in order that these parts may remain in the same position relative to line HI: and since the relative position of the Prisme and the beam HI remains unchanged, there can be no doubt but that the Prisme will maintain its former state of equilibrium. But circumstances would remain the same if that part of the Prisme which is now held up, at the ends, by the threads AH and DE were supported at the middle by a single thread GL; and likewise the other part DB would not change position if held by a thread FM placed at its middle point. Suppose now

---

3   Archimedes's treatise known as *On the Equilibrium of Planes* concerns centres of gravity.

the threads HA, ED, and IB to be removed, leaving only the two GL and FM, then the same equilibrium will be maintained so long as the suspension is at C. Now let us consider that we have here two heavy bodies AD and DB hung at the ends G and F, of a balance beam GF in equilibrium about the point C, so that the line CG is the distance from C to the point of suspension of the heavy body AD, while CF is the distance at which the other heavy body, DB, is supported. It remains now only to show that these distances bear to each other the inverse ratio of the weights themselves, that is, the distance GC is to the distance CF as the Prisme DB is to the Prisme DA—a proposition which we shall prove as follows: Since the line GE is the half of EH, and since EF is the half of EI, the whole length GF will be half of the entire line HI, and therefore equal to CI: if now we subtract the common part CF the remainder GC will be equal to the remainder FI, that is, to FE, and if to each of these we add CE we shall have GE equal to CF: hence GE:EF=FC:CG. But GE and EF bear the same ratio to each other as do their doubles HE and EI, that is, the same ratio as the Prisme AD to DB. Therefore, by equating ratios we have, *convertendo,* the distance GC is to the distance CF as the weight BD is to the weight DA, which is what I desired to prove.

If what precedes is clear, you will not hesitate, I think, to admit that the two Prismes AD and DB are in equilibrium about the point C since one-half of the whole body AB lies on the right of the suspension C and the other half on the left; in other words, this arrangement is equivalent to two equal weights disposed at equal distances. I do not see how any one can doubt, if the two Prismes AD and DB were transformed into cubes, spheres, or into any other figure whatever and if G and F were retained as points of suspension, that they would remain in equilibrium about the point C, for it is only too evident that change of figure does not produce change of weight so long as the mass [*quantità di materia*] does not vary. From this we may derive the general conclusion that any two heavy

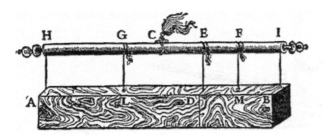

Figure 9.1 Demonstrating the law of the lever. From Galileo, *Two New Sciences.*

bodies are in equilibrium at distances which are inversely proportional to their weights.

This principle established, I desire, before passing to any other subject, to call your attention to the fact that these forces, resistances, moments, figures, etc., may be considered either in the abstract, dissociated from matter, or in the concrete, associated with matter. Hence the properties which belong to figures that are merely geometrical and non-material must be modified when we fill these figures with matter and therefore give them weight. Take, for example, the lever BA which, resting upon the support E, is used to lift a heavy stone D. The principle just demonstrated makes it clear that a force applied at the extremity B will just suffice to equilibrate the resistance offered by the heavy body D provided this force [*momento*] bears to the force [*momento*] at D the same ratio as the distance AC bears to the distance CB; and this is true so long as we consider only the moments of the single force at B and of the resistance at D, treating the lever as an immaterial body devoid of weight. But if we take into account the weight of the lever itself—an instrument which may be made either of wood or of iron—it is manifest that, when this weight has been added to the force at B, the ratio will be changed and must therefore be expressed in different terms. Hence before going further let us agree to distinguish between these two points of view; when we consider an instrument in the abstract, i.e., apart from the weight of its own material, we shall speak of "taking it in an absolute sense" [*prendere assolutamente*]; but if we fill one of these simple and absolute figures with matter and thus give it weight, we shall refer to such a material figure as a "moment" or "compound force" [*momento o forza composta*].

Sagr.: I must break my resolution about not leading you off into a digression; for I cannot concentrate my attention upon what is to follow until a certain doubt is removed from my mind, namely, you seem to compare the force at B with the total weight of the stone D, a part of which—possibly the greater part—rests upon the horizontal plane: so that...

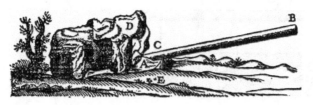

Figure 9.2 Levers and weights. From Galileo, *Two New Sciences*.

Salv.: I understand perfectly: you need go no further. However please observe that I have not mentioned the total weight of the stone; I spoke only of its force [*momento*] at the point A, the extremity of the lever BA, which force is always less than the total weight of the stone, and varies with its shape and elevation.

Sagr.: Good: but there occurs to me another question about which I am curious. For a complete understanding of this matter, I should like you to show me, if possible, how one can determine what part of the total weight is supported by the underlying plane and what part by the end A of the lever.

Salv.: The explanation will not delay us long and I shall therefore have pleasure in granting your request. In the accompanying figure, let us understand that the weight having its center of gravity at A rests with the end B upon the horizontal plane and with the other end upon the lever CG. Let N be the fulcrum of a lever to which the force [*potenza*] is applied at G. Let fall the perpendiculars, AO and CF, from the center A and the end C. Then I say, the magnitude [*momento*] of the entire weight bears to the magnitude of the force [*momento della potenza*] at G a ratio compounded of the ratio between the two distances GN and NC and the ratio between FB and BO. Lay off a distance X such that its ratio to NC is the same as that of BO to FB; then, since the total weight A is counterbalanced by the two forces at B and at C, it follows that the force at B is to that at C as the distance FO is to the distance OB. Hence, *componendo*, the sum of the forces at B and C, that is, the total weight A [*momento di tutto 'l peso A*], is to the force at C as the line FB is to the line BO, that is, as NC is to X: but the force [*momento della potenza*] applied at C is to the force applied at G as the distance GN is to the distance NC; hence it follows, *ex æquali in proportione perturbata,* that the entire weight A is to the force applied at G as the distance GN is to X. But the ratio of GN to X is compounded of the ratio of GN to NC and of NC to X, that is, of FB to BO; hence the weight A bears to the equilibrating force at G a ratio compounded of that of GN to NC and of FB to BO: which was to be proved.

Let us now return to our original subject; then, if what has hitherto been said is clear, it will be easily understood that,

Proposition I

A Prisme or solid cylinder of glass, steel, wood or other breakable material which is capable of sustaining a very heavy weight when applied longitudinally is, as previously remarked, easily broken by the transverse application of

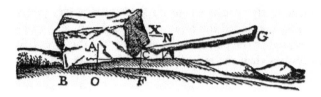

Figure 9.3 Levers and centres of gravity. From Galileo, *Two New Sciences.*

a weight which may be much smaller in proportion as the length of the cylinder exceeds its thickness.

Let us imagine a solid Prisme ABCD fastened into a wall at the end AB, and supporting a weight E at the other end; understand also that the wall is vertical and that the Prisme or cylinder is fastened at right angles to the wall. It is clear that, if the cylinder breaks, fracture will occur at the point B where the edge of the mortise acts as a fulcrum for the lever BC, to which the force is applied; the thickness of the solid BA is the other arm of the lever along which is located the resistance. This resistance opposes the separation of the part BD, lying outside the wall, from that portion lying inside. From the preceding, it follows that the magnitude [*momento*] of the force applied at C bears to the magnitude [*momento*] of the resistance, found in the thickness of the Prisme, i.e., in the attachment of the base BA to its contiguous parts, the same ratio which the length CB bears to half the length BA; if now we define absolute resistance to fracture as that offered to a longitudinal pull (in which case the stretching force acts in the same direction as that through which the body is moved), then it follows that the absolute resistance of the Prisme BD is to the breaking load placed at the end of the lever BC in the same ratio as the length BC is to the half of AB in the case of a Prisme, or the semi-diameter in the case of a cylinder. This is our first proposition. Observe that in what has here been said the weight of the solid BD itself has been left out of consideration, or rather, the Prisme has been assumed to be devoid of weight. But if the weight of the Prisme is to be taken account of in conjunction with the weight E, we must add to the weight E one half that of the Prisme BD: so that if, for example, the latter weighs two pounds and the weight E is ten pounds we must treat the weight E as if it were eleven pounds.

Simp.: Why not twelve?

Salv.: The weight E, my dear Simplicio, hanging at the extreme end C acts upon the lever BC with its full moment of ten pounds: so also would the solid BD if suspended at the same point exert its full moment of two pounds; but, as you know, this solid is uniformly distributed throughout

Figure 9.4 The strength of materials. From Galileo, *Two New Sciences*.

its entire length, BC, so that the parts which lie near the end B are less effective than those more remote.

Accordingly if we strike a balance between the two, the weight of the entire Prisme may be considered as concentrated at its center of gravity which lies midway of the lever BC. But a weight hung at the extremity C exerts a moment twice as great as it would if suspended from the middle: therefore if we consider the moments of both as located at the end C we must add to the weight E one-half that of the Prisme.

Simp.: I understand perfectly; and moreover, if I mistake not, the force of the two weights BD and E, thus disposed, would exert the same moment as would the entire weight BD together with twice the weight E suspended at the middle of the lever BC.

Salv.: Precisely so, and a fact worth remembering. Now we can readily understand.

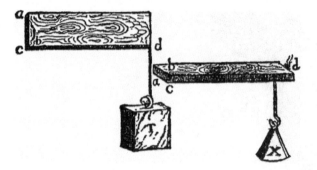

Figure 9.5 Resistance to fracture. From Galileo, *Two New Sciences.*

Proposition II

How and in what proportion a rod, or rather a Prisme, whose width is greater than its thickness offers more resistance to fracture when the force is applied in the direction of its breadth than in the direction of its thickness.

For the sake of clearness, take a ruler *ad* whose width is *ac* and whose thickness, *cb*, is much less than its width. The question now is why will the ruler, if stood on edge, as in the first figure, withstand a great weight T, while, when laid flat, as in the second figure, it will not support the weight X which is less than T. The answer is evident when we remember that in the one case the fulcrum is at the line *bc*, and in the other case at *ca*, while the distance at which the force is applied is the same in both cases, namely, the length *bd:* but in the first case the distance of the resistance from the fulcrum—half the line *ca*—is greater than in the other case where it is only half of *bc*. Therefore the weight T is greater than X in the same ratio as half the width *ca* is greater than half the thickness *bc*, since the former acts as a lever arm for *ca*, and the latter for *cb*, against the same resistance, namely, the strength of all the fibres in the cross-section *ab*. We conclude, therefore, that any given ruler, or Prisme, whose width exceeds its thickness, will offer greater resistance to fracture when standing on edge than when lying flat, and this in the ratio of the width to the thickness.

10

CASTING A HOROSCOPE

Astrology well into the seventeenth century remained an integral part of an astronomer's concerns.[1] Indeed, the entire complex of astronomical and astrological techniques has been dubbed for this period "the science of the stars,"[2] so as to emphasize the organic integration of what later became quite separate endeavours. The technical content of astrology depended on many of the same skills as were used in astronomy, and it is historically unremarkable, as a consequence, that famous astronomers such as Kepler and Tycho themselves took astrological prognostication very seriously (see Robert S. Westman, *The Copernican Question: Prognostication, Skepticism, and Celestial Order* [Berkeley: University of California Press, 2011]). In the following extract, a mid-seventeenth century English astrologer discusses some of his adventures in the period of the English Civil War, and shows the extent to which an astrologer could make a career for himself even at the centre of the Scientific Revolution.

Source: William Lilly, *Christian Astrology* (London, 1647), extracts from "To the Reader."

To the Reader.

I have oft in my former works hinted the many feares I had of that danger I was naturally like to be in in the yeer 1647, as any may read, either in my Epistle before the Conjunction of *Saturne* and *Jupiter*, printed 1644, or in page thereof 108, or in the Epistle of *Anglicus* 1645, where you shall find these words: *I have run over more dayes then fifteen thousand five hundred fifty and nine, before I am sixteen thousand four hundred twenty two days old, I shall be in grat hazard of my life, but that yeer which afflicts me will stagger a Monarch and*

---

1   See now Brendan Dooley, 'Astrology and Science', in Dooley (ed.), *A Companion to Astrology in the Renaissance* (Leiden: Brill, 2014), pp. 233–266, as well as other essays in the same volume.
2   The term preferred in Robert S. Westman, *The Copernican Question*.

Kingdome, &c. What concernes my selfe, hath almost in full measure proved true, in 1647. having in this untoward yeer been molested with palpitation of the Heart, with Hypocondry melancholy, a disaffected Spleen, the Scurvy, &c. and now at this present, viz. August 1647. when I had almost concluded this Treatise, I am shut up of the Plague, having the fourth of *August* buried one Servant thereof, and on the 28. of the same moneth another [...]

I thank almighty God, who hath prolonged my life to this present, and hath been so gracious unto me, as to spare me so long, whereby I have been enabled now at length to perfect that *Introduction* so oft by me promised, so earnestly desired by many wel-wishers unto this learning.

The latter part of my prediction concerning Monarchy, is now upon the stage and the eyes of millions attending what shall become of it: let me leave the event hereof unto God, who is hastening to require a strict accompt of some people entrusted in the Kingdomes affaires; *fiat Justitia; vivat Rex; floreat Parliamentum.*[3]

The Citizens of *London* make small reckoning of *Astrology*; there are in one of those Epistles of mine, words significant, and of which time will make them sensible (that they were not wrote in vaine) but now too late, *actum est.* To the work in hand, *viz.* the Book ensuing, which is divided into three Treatises; the first whereof doth with much facility, and after a new method, instruct the Student how to begin his work, *viz.* it teacheth him the use of an *Ephemeris*, of the Table of Houses, &c. it acquaints him how to erect a figure of heaven, how therein to place the Planets, how to rectifie their motions to the hour of his Figure; it unfolds the nature of the Houses, of the Planets, of the Signes of the *Zodiack*, their division, and subdivision, their severall properties, terms of Art, and whatever else is fit for the Learner to know before he enter upon judgment: unto whom and every one that will be studious this way, I give these cautions.

First, that he be very exact in knowing the use of his *Ephemeris*, and in setting a Scheame of Heaven for all the hours of the day or night, and in reducing the motions of the Planets to the hour thereof when need requireth, and to know their characters distinctly and readily.

Secondly, I would have the Student very perfect in knowing the nature of the Houses, that he may the better discover from what house to require judgment upon the question propounded, lest for want of true understanding he mistake one thing for another.

---

3   This tag reflects Lilly's desire to avoid committing himself too firmly to one side or the other in the ongoing English civil war between monarchists and parliamentarians. At this stage (1647) it was by no means clear that the king would be executed and a non-monarchical republican rule be established, as subsequently happened. Praising a theoretical status quo in which both the monarch and parliament played central roles in the commonwealth was the safest course for Lilly to take.

Thirdly, I would have him ready in, and well to understand the Debilities and Fortitudes of every Planet, both Essentiall and Accidentall.

Fourthly, he must be well-versed in discovering the Nature of the Significator, what he signifies naturally, what accidentally, and how to vary his signification, as necessity shall require.

Fiftly, let him well understand the nature of the Signes, their properties and qualities, and what forme, shape and conditions they give of themselves naturally, and what by the personall existence of a Planet in any of them.

...

I have with all uprightnesse and sincerity of heart, plainly and honestly delivered the Art, and have omitted nothing willingly, which I esteemed convenient or fit, or what might any thing assist, the yong Students herein; I have refused the Methods of all former Authors, and framed this *De Novo*, which I have ever found so easie and successful, that as yet I never undertook the instruction of any, whom I have not abundantly satisfied, and made very capable of the *Art*, in lesse time then any could expect; for although I am not yet six and forty yeers of age compleat, and have studied this *Science* but since 1632. and have lived six yeers since that time in the Country, yet I know I have made more Schollers in this Profession, then all that Professe this *Art* in *England*. It remaines, that I give every Author his due, and deale plainly, unto which of them I am engaged for such matter as they have assisted me with in the *Introductory part*: verily the Method is my owne, it's no translation; yet have I conferred my owne notes with *Dariot, Bonatus, Ptolomey, Haly, Etzler, Dietericus, Naibod, Hasfurtus, Zael, Tanstettor, Agrippa, Ferriers, Duret, Maginus, Origanus, Argol.*[4]

...

Had I respected my owne private lucre, I need not to have wrote at all; who could have compelled me? my owne fortune is competent: but this thing we call the publick good, was ever, and shall be my maxime to guide me in such like actions: how shall I my selfe expect truth in any Author, if I my selfe, being an Author, play the knave in the same kind: *Quod non vis tibi, ne facias alteri.*[5]

...

Having been of late traduced by some halfe-witted fooles, I deliver my selfe to Posterity who I am, and of what profession; I was borne at *Diseworth* in *Leicestershire May 1602.* in an obscure Village, and bred a Grammer Scholler at *Ashby*, and intended for *Cambridge*, &c. 1618. and 1619. my Father decayed his Estate so much, that he was not capable of sending me thither; those two

---

4   A list of writers both ancient and modern. The most fundamental of all is Ptolemy, the second-century AD Greco-Roman astronomer and astrologer, who taught students of the stars how to do their work for a millennium and a half.

5   An equivalent of the maxim "do unto others as you would have them do unto you."

yeers I lived in some penury and discontent; in 1620. an Atturney sent me up unto *London* to wait on a Gentleman, one *Gilbert Wright*, who lived and dyed in the House I now live in; he never was of any Profession, but had sometimes attended the Lord Chancellour *Egerton*, and then lived privately. 1624. his wife dyed of a cancer in her left brest. 1625. I lived in London where I now doe, daring all that great Sicknesse, God be praised I had it not. February 1626. my master married againe; he dyed May 22 1627. having before setled twenty pounds *per annum* of me during my life, which to this day I thanke God I enjoy; nor did I ever live so freely as when I was his servant. Ere the yeer 1627. was quite run out my Mistris was pleased to accept of me for her husband. During some yeers of her life I passed my time privately and with much obscurity, yet we lived exceeding lovingly together; but in 1632 I was strangely affected to *Astrology*, and desirous to study it, onely to see if there were any verity in it, there being at that time some Impostors, that set out Bils publiquely what they could doe. I met with a Master I confesse, but such a one, as of all was the veriest Knave: This gave me small encouragement; after six weekes I cast him off, nor to this day doe we converse together. I was then forced to study hard, for rather then to entangle my selfe with another coxcombe, I was resolved to lay all aside; but by diligence and hard study, and many times conference with some as ignorant as my selfe, I at last became capable of knowing truth from falshood, and perceived the vulgar *Astrologer* that meerly lived of the Art, was a Knave.

In September 1633. my wife dyed, not knowing any one in the world that had any affinity unto her; she left me a competent fortune; and this I shall acquaint Posterity with, that having some Lands to dispose of, rather then she would suffer me to be at twenty Nobles charges to convey it unto me, she gave me the whole money, and sold it for 20l.

In November 1634. I married againe. In 1635. I was oppressed with the *Hypocondryak Melancholly* so surely, that I was enforced to leave *London*, and removed into *Surrey* 1636. where untill *September* 1641. I lived amongst such whom I may name the most rurall of all men living. I then came for *London*, staggering in my judgement in point of Church-government; and knowing that it is necessary, I ever loved Monarchy, I but still thought without a Parliament preserved in their just rights, it would vanish to nothing.[6] I was nothing knowne then, or taken notice of by any; time produced me acquaintance, and amongst these a good Lady in 1643. about *February*, desired I would give judgement upon a most noble Gentlemans Urine a Councellor at Law, who then was not well; I consented, the Urine was brought, my judgement returned; I visited him, whom I no sooner beheld, but I knew there was aboundance of gallantry in the man; for indeed he is all Gentleman and a friend in very great earnest; my visit of him was the happiest day I ever

---

6 Again, careful political positioning by Lilly.

saw in my whole life; for by his alone generosity and countenance, I am what I am, and *Astrology* is in despight of her enemies restored, and must call him her Restaurator.

Being by his goodnesse admitted to visit him, I presented him with a small Manuscript of my *Astrologicall Judgment* of the yeer 1644. wherein I was free in delivering my opinion modestly of that yeers affaires; it pleased him to communicate it, Copies were obtained and dispersed; so that by his alone commendation of that poore Manuscript unto his private friends, this noble *Art* at first had respect amongst our Worthies in the Parliament; since which time, the Judicious of the whole Kingdome had it in a better esteem; therefore let his name live unto Posterity in an honourable esteem, that upon so slender acquaintance with the Author, with the Art, hath been so advantagious unto both.

...

Corner House over against Strand-bridge, *August 21. 1647.*

11

SEEING NEW THINGS

Just as the telescope revealed hitherto unsuspected novelties on the grand scale of the heavens, so a similar optical instrument, the microscope, proved capable of revealing novelties at the level of the very small. Although the principle of the microscope had already been discussed by Galileo in 1623 in his *The Assayer*, it was in 1665 that the first real classic in microscopical observation appeared. Robert Hooke's *Micrographia* garnered much attention for its lavish illustrations (some perhaps done by Christopher Wren), but Hooke's work also promoted the idea that empirical research in the natural sciences could be improved by devising instruments to assist the senses in general, not only that of vision. In these views Hooke echoed Francis Bacon, who also anticipated means of improving the senses. Indeed, Hooke, who was employed by the Royal Society as its "curator of experiments," responsible for trying experiments when ordered, and for entertaining the Society's meetings with experimental demonstrations of his own, frequently invoked Bacon's name as a guide to the right way to go about doing experimental natural philosophy.

Source: Robert Hooke, *Micrographia* (London, 1665). The preface with omission of some detailed descriptions of instruments.

The preface

It is the great prerogative of Mankind above other Creatures, that we are not only able to *behold* the works of Nature, or barely to *sustein* our lives by them, but we have also the power of *considering, comparing, altering, assisting,* and *improving* them to various uses. And as this is the peculiar priviledge of humane Nature in general, so is it capable of being so far advanced by the helps of Art, and Experience, as to make some Men excel others in their Observations, and Deductions, almost as much as they do Beasts. By the addition of such *artificial Instruments* and *methods*, there may be, in some manner, a reparation made for the mischiefs, and imperfection, mankind has drawn upon it self, by negligence, and intemperance, and a wilful and superstitious deserting the Prescripts and Rules of Nature, whereby every man, both from a deriv'd corruption, innate and born with him,[1] and from his breeding and converse with men, is very subject to slip into all sorts of errors.

The only way which now remains for us to recover some degree of those former perfections, seems to be, by rectifying the operations of the *Sense*, the *Memory*, and *Reason*, since upon the evidence, the *strength*, the *integrity*, and the *right correspondence* of all these, all the light, by which our actions are to be guided is to be renewed, and all our command over things it to be establisht.

It is therefore most worthy of our consideration, to recollect their several defects, that so we may the better understand how to supply them, and by what assistances we may *inlarge* their power, and *secure* them in performing their particular duties.

As for the actions of our *Senses*, we cannot but observe them to be in many particulars much outdone by those of other Creatures, and when at best, to be far short of the perfection they seem capable of: And these infirmities of the Senses arise from a double cause, either from the *disproportion of the Object to the Organ*, whereby an infinite number of things can never enter into them, or else from *error in the Perception*, that many things, which come within their reach, are not received in a right manner.

The like frailties are to be found in the *Memory*; we often let many things *slip away* from us, which deserve to be retain'd, and of those which we treasure up, a great part is either *frivolous* or *false*; and if good, and substantial, either in tract of time *obliterated*, or at best so *overwhelmed* and buried under more frothy notions, that when there is need of them, they are in vain sought for.

The two main foundations being so deceivable, it is no wonder, that all the succeeding works which we build upon them, of arguing, concluding, defining, judging, and all the other degrees of Reason, are lyable to the same imperfection, being, at best, either vain, or uncertain: So that the errors of the *understanding* are answerable to the two other, being defective both in the quantity and goodness of its knowledge; for the limits, to which our thoughts are confin'd, are small in respect of the vast extent of Nature it self; some parts of it are *too large* to be comprehended, and some *too little* to be perceived. And from thence it must follow, that not having a full sensation of the Object, we must be very lame and imperfect in our conceptions about it, and in all the proportions which we build upon it; hence, we often take the *shadow* of things for the *substance*, small *appearances* for good *similitudes*, *similitudes* for *definitions*; and even many of those, which we think, to be the most solid definitions,

---

1   This is an allusion to the Christian doctrine of Original Sin, a major trope in the seventeenth century: Peter Harrison, *The Fall of Man and the Foundations of Science* (Cambridge: Cambridge University Press, 2007).

are rather expressions of our own misguided apprehensions then of the true nature of the things themselves.

The effects of these imperfections are manifested in different ways, according to the temper and disposition of the several minds of men, some they incline to *gross ignorance* and stupidity, and others to a *presumptuous imposing* on other mens Opinions, and a *confident dogmatizing* on matters, whereof there it no assurance to be given.

Thus all the uncertainty, and mistakes of humane actions, proceed either from the narrowness and wandring of our *Senses*, from the slipperiness or delusion of our *Memory*, from the confinement or rashness of our *Understanding*, so that 'tis no wonder, that our power over natural causes and effects is so slowly improv'd, seeing we are not only to contend with the obscurity and *difficulty of the things* whereon we work and think, but even the *forces of our own minds* conspire to betray us.[2]

These being the dangers in the process of humane Reason, the remedies of them all can only proceed from the *real*, the *mechanical*, the *experimental* Philosophy, which has this advantage over the Philosophy of *discourse* and *disputation*, that whereas that chiefly aims at the subtilty of its Deductions and Conclusions, without much regard to the first ground-work, which ought to be well laid on the Sense and Memory; so this intends the right ordering of them all, and the making them serviceable to each other.

The first thing to be undertaken in this weighty work, is a *watchfulness over the failings* and an *inlargement of the dominion*, of the Senses.

To which end it is requisite, first, That there should be a *scrupulous* choice, and a *strict examination*, of the reality, constancy, and certainty of the Particulars that we admit: This is the first rise whereon truth is to begin, and here the most severe, and most impartial diligence, must be imployed; the storing up of all, without any regard to evidence or use, will only tend to darkness and confusion. We must not therefore esteem the riches of our Philosophical treasure by the *number* only, but chiefly by the *weight*; the most *vulgar* Instances are not to be neglected, but above all, the most *instructive* are to be entertain'd; the footsteps of Nature are to be trac'd, not only in her *ordinary course*, but when she seems to be put to her shifts, to make many *doublings* and *turnings*, and to use some kind of art in indeavouring to avoid our discovery.

The next care to be taken, in respect of the Senses, is a supplying of their infirmities with *Instruments*, and, as it were, the adding of *artificial Organs* to the *natural*; this in one of them has been of late years accomplisht with prodigious benefit to all sorts of useful knowledge, by the invention of Optical Glasses. By the means of *Telescopes*, there is nothing so *far distant* but may be represented to our view; and by the help of *Microscopes*, there is nothing so

---

2   These are all Baconian themes, discussed in Bacon's *New Organon* of 1620 in terms of the "Idols" of the understanding.

small, as to escape our inquiry; hence there is a new visible World discovered to the understanding. By this means the Heavens are open'd, and a vast number of new Stars, and new Motions, and new Productions appear in them, to which all the ancient Astronomers were utterly Strangers. By this the Earth it self, which lyes so neer us, under our feet, shews quite a new thing to us, and in every *little particle* of its matter; we now behold almost as great a variety of Creatures, as we were able before to reckon up in the whole *Universe* it self.

It seems not improbable, but that by these helps the subtilty of the composition of Bodies, the structure of their parts, the various texture of their matter, the instruments and manner of their inward motions, and all the other possible appearances of things, may come to be more fully discovered; all which the ancient *Peripateticks*[3] were content to comprehend in two general and (unless further explain'd) useless words of *Matter* and *Form*. From whence there may arise many admirable advantages, towards the increase of the *Operative*, and the *Mechanick* Knowledge, to which this Age seems so much inclined, because we may perhaps be inabled to discern all the secret workings of Nature, almost in the same manner as we do those that are the productions of Art, and are manag'd by Wheels, and Engines, and Springs, that were devised by humane Wit.[4]

In this kind I here present to the World my imperfect Indeavours; which though they shall prove no other way considerable, yet, I hope, they may be in some measure useful to the main Design of a *reformation* in Philosophy, if it be only by shewing, that there it not so much requir'd towards it, any strength of *Imagination*, or exactness of *Method*, or depth of *Contemplation* (though the addition of these, where they can be had, must needs produce a much more perfect composure) as a sincere *Hand*, and a *faithful* Eye, to examine, and to record, the things themselves as they appear.

And I beg my Reader, to let me take the boldness to assure him, that in this present condition of knowledge, a man so qualified, as I have indeavoured to be, only with resolution, and integrity, and plain intentions of imploying his *Senses* aright, may venture to compare the reality and the usefulness of his services, towards the true Philosophy, with those of other men, that are of much stronger, and more acute *speculations*, that shall not make use of the same method by the Senses.

The truth is, the Science of Nature has been already too long made only a work of the *Brain* and the *Fancy*: It is now high time that it should return to the plainness and soundness of *Observations* on *material* and *obvious* things. It is said of great Empires, That *the best way to preserve them from decay, is to bring them back to the first Principles, and Arts, on which they did begin.* The same is undoubtedly true in Philosophy, that by wandring far away into *invisible Notions*, has almost quite

---

3 Followers of Aristotle's philosophy.
4 Another Baconian theme, the reduction of Nature to Art.

destroy'd it self, and it can never be recovered, or continued, but by returning into the same *sensible paths*, in which it did at first proceed.

If therefore the Reader expects from me any infallible Deductions, or certainty of *Axioms*, I am to say for my self, that those stronger Works of Wit and Imagination are above my weak Abilities; or if they had not been so, I would not have made use of them in this present Subject before me: Whenever he finds that I have ventur'd at any small Conjectures, at the causes of the things that I have observed, I beseech him to look, upon them only as *doubtful Problems*, and *uncertain ghesses*, and not as unquestionable Conclusions, or matters of unconfutable Science; I have produced nothing here, with intent to bind his understanding to an *implicit* consent; I am so far from that, that I desire him, not absolutely to rely upon these Observations of my eyes, if he finds them contradicted by the future Ocular Experiments of other and impartial Discoverers.[5]

As for my part, I have obtained my end, if these my small Labours shall be thought fit to take up some place in the large stock, of *natural Observations*, which so many hands are busie in providing. If I have contributed the *meanest foundations* whereon others may raise nobler *Superstructures*, I am abundantly satisfied; and all my ambition is, that I may serve to the great Philosophers of this Age, as the makers and the grinders of my Glasses did to me; that I may prepare and furnish them with some *Materials*, which they may afterwards *order* and *manage* with better skill, and to far greater advantage.

The next remedies in this universal cure of the Mind are to be applyed to the *Memory*, and they are to consist of such Directions as may inform us, what things are best to be *stor'd up* for our purpose, and which is the best way of so *disposing* them, that they may not only be *kept in safety*, but ready and convenient, to be at any time *produc'd* for use, as occasion shall require. But I will not here prevent my self in what I may say in another Discourse, wherein I shall make an attempt to propose some Considerations of the manner of compiling a Natural and Artificial History, and of so ranging and registring its Particulars into Philosophical Tables, as may make them most useful for the raising of *Axioms* and *Theories*.

The last indeed is the most hazardous Enterprize, and yet the most *necessary*; and that is, to take such care that the *Judgment* and the *Reason* of Man (which is the third Faculty to be repair'd and improv'd) should receive such assistance, as to avoid the dangers to which it is by nature most subject. The Imperfections, which I have already mention'd, to which it is lyable, do either belong to the *extent*, or the *goodness* of its knowledge; and here the difficulty is the greater, least that which may be thought a *remedy* for the one should prove *destructive* to the other, least by seeking to inlarge our Knowledge, we should

5   A rhetorical self-effacement typical of empiricists of the period.

render it weak, and uncertain; and least by being too scrupulous and exact about every Circumstance of it, we should confine and streighten it too much.

In both these the middle wayes are to be taken, nothing is to be *omitted*, and yet every thing to pass a *mature deliberation*: No *Intelligence* from Men of all Professions, and quarters of the World, to be *slighted*, and yet all to be so *severely examin'd*, that there remain no room for doubt or instability; much *rigour* in admitting, much *strictness* in comparing, and above all, much *slowness* in debating, and *shyness* in determining, is to be practised. The Understanding is to *order* all the inferiour services of the lower Faculties; but yet it is to do this only as a *lawful Master*, and not as a *Tyrant*. It must not *incroach* upon their Offices, nor take upon it self the employments which belong to either of them. It must *watch* the irregularities of the Senses, but it must not go before them, or *prevent* their information. It must *examine, range*, and *dispose* of the bank which it laid up in the Memory: but it must be sure to make *distinction* between the *sober* and *well collected heap*, and the *extravagant Ideas*, and *mistaken Images*, which there it may sometimes light upon. So many are the *links*, upon which the true Philosophy depends, of which, if any one be *loose*, or *weak*, the whole *chain* is in danger of being dissolv'd; it is to begin with the Hands and Eyes, and to *proceed* on through the Memory, to be *continued* by the Reason; nor is it to stop there, but to *come about* to the Hands and Eyes again, and so, by a *continual passage round* from one Faculty to another, it is to be maintained in life and strength, as much as the body of man it by the *circulation* of the blood through the several parts of the body, the Arms, the Feet, the Lungs, the Heart, and the Head.

If once this method were followed with diligence and attention, there is nothing that lyes within the power of human Wit (or which is far more effectual) of human Industry, which we might not compass; we might not only hope for Inventions to equalize those of *Copernicus, Galileo, Gilbert, Harvy*,[6] and of others, whose Names are almost lost, that were the Inventors of *Gun-powder*, the *Seamans Compass, Printing, Etching, Graving, Microscopes*, &c. but multitudes that may far exceed them: for even those discoveries seem to have been the products of some such method, though but imperfect; What may not be therefore expected from it if thoroughly prosecuted? *Talking* and *contention of Arguments* would soon be turn'd into *labours*; all the fine *dreams* of Opinions, and *universal metaphysical natures*, which the luxury of subtil Brains has devis'd, would quickly vanish, and give place to *solid Histories, Experiments* and *Works*. And as at first, mankind *fell* by *tasting* of the forbidden Tree of Knowledge,[7] so we, their Posterity, may be in part *restor'd* by the same

6   All figures represented in this book except for William Harvey, the English physician and anatomist who argued for the general circulation of the blood around the body.
7   Another reference to Original Sin, and the expulsion from the Garden of Eden.

way, not only by *beholding* and *contemplating*, but by *tasting* too those fruits of Natural knowledge, that were never yet forbidden.

From hence the World may be assisted with *variety* of Inventions, *new* matter for Sciences may be *collected*, the *old improv'd*, and their *rust* rubb'd away; and as it is by the benefit of Senses that we receive all our Skill in the works of Nature, so they also may be wonderfully benefited by it, and may be guided to an easier and more exact performance of their Offices; 'tis not unlikely, but that we may find out wherein our Senses are deficient, and as easily find wayes of repairing them.

The Indeavours of Skilful men have been most conversant about the assistance of the Eye, and many noble Productions have followed upon it; and from hence we may conclude, that there it a way open'd for advancing the operations, not only of all the other Senses, but even of the Eye it self; that which has been already done ought not to content us, but rather to incourage us to proceed further, and to attempt greater things in the same, and different wayes.

'Tis not unlikely, but that there may be yet invented several other helps for the eye, at much exceeding those already found, as those do the bare eye, such as by which we may perhaps be able to discover *living Creatures* in the Moon, or other Planets, the *figures* of the compounding Particles of matter, and the particular *Schematisms* and *Textures* of Bodies.

And as *Glasses* have highly promoted our *seeing*, so not improbable, but that there may be found many *Mechanical Inventions* to improve our other Senses, of *hearing, smelling, tasting, touching*. 'Tis not impossible to hear a *whisper* a *furlongs* distance, it having been already done; and perhaps the nature of the thing would not make it more impossible, though that furlong should be ten times multiply'd. And though some famous Authors have affirm'd it impossible to hear through the *thinnest plate* of Muscovy-glass; yet I know a way, by which 'tis easie enough to hear one speak through a *wall a yard thick*. It has not been yet thoroughly examin'd, how far *Otocousticons* may be improv'd, nor what other wayes there may be of *quickning* our hearing, or *conveying* sound through *other bodies* then the *Air*: for that that it not the only *medium*, I can assure the Reader, that I have, by the help of a *distended wire*, propagated the sound to a very considerable distance in an *instant*, or with as seemingly quick a motion as that of light, at least, incomparably swifter then that, which at the same time was propagated through the Air; and this not only in a straight line, or direct, but in one bended in many angles.[8]

Nor are the other three so perfect, but that *diligence, attention*, and many *mechanical contrivances*, may also highly improve them. For since the sense of *smelling* seems to be made by the *swift passage* of the *Air* (*impregnated* with the steams and *effluvia* of several odorous Bodies) through the grisly *meanders* of

---

8   Compare this paragraph with some of Bacon's remarks on sound in the *Sylva* (Chapter 8), above.

the Nose whose surfaces are cover'd with a very sensible *nerve*, and *moistned* by a *transudation* from the *processus mamillares* of the Brain, and some adjoyning *glandules*, and by the moist *steam* of the *Lungs*, with a Liquor convenient for the reception of those *effluvia* and by the adhesion and mixing of those steams with that liquor, and thereby affecting the nerve, or perhaps by insinuating themselves into the juices of the brain, after the same manner, as I have in the following Observations intimated, the parts of Salt to pass through the skins of Effs, and Frogs. Since, I say, smelling seems to be made by some such way, 'tis not improbable, but that some contrivance, for making a great quantity of Air pass quick through the Nose, might at much promote the sense of smelling, as the any wayes hindring that passage does dull and destroy it. Several tryals I have made, both of hindring and promoting this sense, and have succeeded in some according to expectation; and indeed to me it seems capable of being improv'd, for the judging of the constitutions of many Bodies. Perhaps we may thereby also judge (as other Creatures seem to do) what is wholsome, what poyson; and in a word, what are the specifick properties of Bodies.

There may be also some other mechanical wayes found out, of sensibly perceiving the *effluvia* of Bodies; several Instances of which, were it here proper, I could give of Mineral steams and exhalations; and it seems not impossible, but that by some such wayes improved, may be discovered, what Minerals lye buried under the Earth, without the trouble to dig for them; some things to confirm this Conjecture may be found in *Agricola*, and other Writers of Minerals, speaking of the Vegetables that are apt to thrive, or pine, in those steams.

Whether also those steams, which seem to issue out of the Earth, and mix with the Air (and so to precipitate some *aqueous* Exhalations, wherewith 'tis impregnated) may not be by some way detected before they produce the effect, seems hard to determine; yet something of this kind I am able to discover, by an Instrument I contriv'd to shew all the minute variations in the pressure of the Air; by which I constantly find, that before, and during the time of rainy weather, the pressure of the Air is less, and in *dry weather*, but especially when an *Eastern Wind* (which having past over vast tracts of Land is heavy with Earthy Particles) blows, it is much more, though these changes are varied according to very odd Laws.

...

But this is but one way of discovering the *effluvia* of the Earth mixt with the Air; there may be, perhaps many others, witness the *Hygroscope*, an Instrument whereby the watery steams volatile in the Air are discerned, which the Nose it self is not able to find. This I have describ'd in the following Tract in the Description of the Beard of a wild Oat. Others there, are, may be discovered both by the Nose, and by other wayes also. Thus the smoak of burning *Wood* is *smelt, seen*, and sufficiently *felt* by the eyes: The *fumes* of burning *Brimstone* are *smelt* and discovered also by the destroying the Colours of Bodies, as by the *whitening of a red Rose*: And who knows, but that the Industry of man, following this method, may find out wayes of improving this sense to as great a degree of perfection at it is in any Animal, and perhaps yet higher.

'Tis not improbable also, but that our *taste* may be very much improv'd either by *preparing* our taste for the Body, as, after eating *bitter* things, *Wine*, or other *Vinous liquors*, are more sensibly tasted; or else by *preparing* Bodies for our tast; as the dissolving of Metals with acid Liquors, make them tastable, which were before altogether insipid; thus *Lead* becomes *sweeter* then Sugar, and *Silver* more *bitter* then Gall, *Copper* and *Iron* of most *loathsome* tasts. And indeed the business of this sense being to discover the presence of dissolved Bodies in Liquors put on the Tongue, or in general to discover that a fluid body has some solid body dissolv'd in it, and what they are; whatever contrivance makes this discovery improves this sense. In this kind the mixtures of Chymical Liquors afford many Instances; as the sweet Vinegar that is impregnated with Lead may be discovered to be so by the affusion of a little of an *Alcalizate solution*: The bitter liquor of *Aqua fortis* and *Silver* may be discover'd to be charg'd with that Metal, by laying in it some plates of Copper: 'Tis not improbable also, but there may be multitudes of other wayes of discovering the parts dissolv'd, or dissoluble in liquors; and what is this discovery but a kind of *secundary tasting*.

'Tis not improbable also, but that the sense of *feeling* may be highly improv'd, for that being a sense that judges of the more *gross* and *robust motions* of the *Particles* of Bodies, seems capable of being improv'd and assisted very many wayes. Thus for the distinguishing of *Heat* and *Cold*, the *Weather-glass* and *Thermometer*, which I have describ'd in this following Treatise, do exceedingly perfect it; by each of which the least variations of heat or cold, which the most Acute sense is not able to distinguish, are manifested. This is oftentimes further promoted also by the help of *Burning-glasses*, and the like, which collect and unite the radiating heat. Thus the *roughness* and *smoothness* of a Body is made much more sensible by the help of a *Microscope*, then by the most *tender* and *delicate Hand*. Perhaps, a Physitian might, by several other tangible proprieties, discover the constitution of a Body as well as by the *Pulse*. I do but instance in these, to shew what possibility there may be of many others, and what probability and hopes there were of finding them, if this method were followed; for the Offices of the five Senses being to detect either the *subtil* and *curious Motions* propagated through all *pellucid* or perfectly *homogeneous* Bodies; Or the more *gross* and *vibrative Pulse* communicated through the *Air* and all other convenient *mediums*, whether fluid or solid: Or the *effluvia* of Bodies *dissolv'd* in the *Air*; Or the *particles* of bodies *dissolv'd* or *dissoluble* in *Liquors*, or the more *quick* and *violent shaking motion* of *heat* in all or any of these: whatsoever does any wayes promote any of these kinds of criteria, does afford a way of improving some one sense. And what a multitude of these would a diligent Man meet with in his inquiries? And this for the helping and promoting the *sensitive faculty* only.

Next, as for the *Memory*, or *retentive faculty*, we may be sufficiently instructed from the *written Histories* of *civil actions*, what great assistance may be afforded the Memory, in the committing to writing things observable in *natural operations*. If a Physitian be therefore accounted the more able in his Faculty, because he has had long experience and practice, the remembrance of which, though perhaps very imperfect, does regulate all his after actions: What ought to be thought of that man, that has not only a perfect *register* of his own experience, but is grown *old* with the experience of many hundreds of years, and many thousands of men.

And though of late, men, beginning to be sensible of this convenience, have here and there registred and printed some few *Centuries*[9], yet for the most part they are set down very lamely and imperfectly, and, I fear, many times not so truly, they seeming, several of them, to be design'd more for *Ostentation* then *publique use*: For, not to instance, that they do, for the most part, omit those Experiences they have made, wherein their Patients have miscarried, it is very easie to be perceiv'd, that they do all along *hyperbolically extol* their own Prescriptions, and vilifie those of others. Notwithstanding all which, these kinds of Histories are generally esteem'd useful, even to the ablest Physitian.

What may not be expected from the *rational* or *deductive Faculty* that is furnisht with such *Materials*, and those so readily *adapted*, and rang'd for use, that in a moment, as 'twere, thousands of Instances, serving for the *illustration*, *determination*, or *invention*, of almost any inquiry, may be *represented* even to the sight? How neer the nature of *Axioms* must all those *Propositions* be which are examin'd before so many *Witnesses*?[10] And how difficult will it be for any, though never so subtil an error in Philosophy, to *scape* from being discover'd, after it has indur'd the *touch*, and so many other *tryals*?

...

And this [i.e. the *Micrographia*] was undertaken in prosecution of the Design which the ROYAL SOCIETY has propos'd to it self. For the Members of the Assembly having before their eys so many *fatal* Instances of the errors and falshoods, in which the greatest part of mankind has so long wandred, because they rely'd upon the strength of humane Reason alone, have begun anew to correct all *Hypotheses* by sense, as Seamen do their *dead Reckonings* by *Coelestial Observations*; and to this purpose it has been their principal indeavour to *enlarge & strengthen* the *Senses* by *Medicine*, and by such outward *Instruments* as are proper for their particular works. By this means they find some reason to

---

9 This mention of "Centuries" recalls Bacon's use of Centuries as collections of a hundred empirical items in the *Sylva*; they were also a common form for gathering case histories in medicine.

10 An interesting attempt to accommodate empirical assertions to the status of mathematical premises, and thereby to elevate their practical certainty.

suspect, that those effects of Bodies, which have been commonly attributed to *Qualities*, and those confess'd to be *occult*, are perform'd by the small *Machines* of Nature, which are not to be discern'd without these helps, seeming the meer products of *Motion, Figure*, and *Magnitude*; and that the *Natural Textures*, which some call the *Plastick faculty*, may be made in *Looms*, which a greater perfection of Opticks may make discernable by these Glasses; so as now they are no more puzzled about them, then the vulgar are to conceive, how *Tapestry* or *flowred Stuffs* are woven. And the ends of all these Inquiries they intend to be the *Pleasure* of Contemplative minds, but above all, the *ease and dispatch* of the labours of mens hands. They do indeed neglect no opportunity to bring all the *rare* things of Remote Countries within the compass of their knowledge and practice. But they still acknowledg their *most useful* Informations to arise from *common* things, and from *diversifying* their most *ordinary* operations upon them. They do not wholly reject Experiments of meer *light* and *theory*; but they principally aim at such, whose Applications will *improve and facilitate* the present way of *Manual Arts*. And though some men, who are perhaps taken up about less honourable Employments, are pleas'd to censure their proceedings, yet they can shew more *fruits* of their first three years, wherein they have assembled, then any other *Society* in *Europe* can for a much larger space of time. 'Tis true, such undertakings as theirs do commonly meet with small incouragement, because men are generally rather taken with the *plausible* and *discursive*, then the *real* and the solid part of Philosophy; yet by the good fortune of their institution, in an Age of all others the most *inquisitive*, they have been assisted by the *contribution* and *presence* of very many of the chief *Nobility* and *Gentry*, and others who are some of the *most considerable* in their several Professions. But that that yet farther convinces me of the *Real esteem* that the more *serious* part of men have of this *Society*, is, that several *Merchants*, men who act in earnest (whose Object is *meum & tuum*, that great *Rudder* of humane affairs) have adventur'd considerable sums of *Money*, to put in practice what some of our Members have contrived, and have continued *stedfast* in their good opinions of such Indeavours, when not one of a hundred of the vulgar have believed their undertakings feasable. And it is also fit to be added, that they have one advantage peculiar to themselves, that very many of their number are *men of Converse and Traffick*; which is a good Omen, that their attempts will bring Philosophy from *words* to *action*, seeing the men of Business have had so great a share in their first foundation.

And of this kind I ought not to conceal one particular *Generosity*, which more nearly concerns my self. It is the *munificence* of *Sir John Cutler*, in endowing a Lecture for the promotion of *Mechanick Arts*, to be governed and directed by This *Society*.[11] This *Bounty* I mention for the *Honourableness* of the thing it self, and for the expectation which I have

11 Hooke himself benefitted as a presenter of "Cutlerian lectures," later published.

of the *efficacy* of the *Example*; for it cannot now be objected to them, that their Designs will be esteemed *frivolous* and *vain*, when they have such a *real Testimony* of the *Approbation* of a *Man* that is such an eminent *Ornament* of this renowned City, and one, who, by the *Variety*, and the *happy Success*, of his negotiations, has given evident proofs, that he is not easie to be deceiv'd. This Gentleman has well observ'd, that the *Arts* of life have been too long *imprison'd* in the dark shops of Mechanicks themselves, & there *hindred from growth*, either by ignorance, or self-interest: and he has bravely *freed* them from these *inconveniences*: He hath not only obliged *Tradesmen*, but *Trade* it self: He has done a work that is worthy of *London*, and has taught the chief City of Commerce in the world the right way how Commerce is to be improv'd. We have already seen many other great signs of Liberality and a large mind, from the same hand: For by his *diligence* about the *Corporation for the Poor*; by his honorable *Subscriptions* for the rebuilding of St. *Paul's*; by his chearful *Disbursment* for the replanting of *Ireland*, and by many other such *publick works*, he has shewn by what means he indeavours to *establish* his Memory; and now by this last gift he has done that, which became one of the *wisest Citizens* of our Nation to accomplish, seeing one of the *wisest of our Statesmen*, the *Lord Verulam*,[12] first propounded it.

...

After I had almost compleated these Pictures and Observations (having had divers of them ingraven, and was ready to send them to the Press) I was inform'd, that the Ingenious Physitian *Dr. Henry Power* had made several *Microscopical* Observations,[13] which had I not afterwards, upon our interchangably viewing each others Papers, found that they were for the most part differing from mine, either in the Subject it self, or in the particulars taken notice of; and that his design was only to print Observations without Pictures, I had even then *suppressed* what I had so far proceeded in. But being further *excited* by several of my Friends, in complyance with their opinions, that it would not be unacceptable to several inquisitive Men, and hoping also, that I should thereby discover something New to the World, I have at length cast in my Mite, into the vast Treasury of *A Philosophical History*. And it is my *hope*, as well as *belief*, that these my *Labours* will be no more comparable to the *Productions* of many other *Natural Philosophers*, who are now every where busie about *greater* things; then my *little Objects* are to be compar'd to the greater and more beautiful *Works of Nature*, A Flea, a Mite, a Gnat, to an Horse, an Elephant, or a Lyon.

---

12 A title held by Bacon.
13 Henry Power, *Experimental Philosophy* (London, 1664), largely consisting of descriptions of microscopical observations.

12

SYSTEMATIC DATA-GATHERING

Robert Boyle, as a leading figure in the Royal Society, was eager to use his institutional standing to assist in gathering together comparative and miscellaneous information from around the world concerning social and natural "matters of fact" to contribute to his, and the Society's, Baconian project. The use of standardised questionnaires had quickly become a usual practice with the Society; another early example is John Wilkins's attempt to test his own theory of the tides (adapted from an idea of Galileo's) by similar means, to coordinate varying tide-times in differing locations. These questionnaires were typically sent out to commercial functionaries of various kinds located in distant colonial trading posts. In practice these questionnaires were usually ignored; their response rate seems to have been so low that they turned out to be useless. The ambition behind them, however, reveals a desire to create useful generalisations concerning natural and social phenomena that would assist the very enterprises of the colonial trading companies whose employees were targets of the questionnaires. Knowing more about the natural resources of various lands, with the aim of developing improved ways of exploiting them as part of the Royal Society's own brief, could assist trading companies themselves, and indirectly the Crown; greater knowledge of the inhabitants of those lands might also assist their integration into those colonial enterprises: Boyle himself was keenly interested in projects to convert the heathens of other lands to Christianity, which might serve to save their souls (Boyle's first concern), but would also promote the colonial enterprise.

Source: [Robert Boyle], "General Heads for a Natural History of a Countrey, Great or small, imparted likewise by Mr. Boyle." *Philosophical Transactions* 1 (1665–66), pp. 186–189.

It having been already intimated (*Num.* 8. of *Phil. Transac.* p. 140. 141.) that divers *Philosophers* aime, among other things, at the Composing of a good Natural History, to superstruct, in time, a *Solid* and *Useful* Philosophy upon;[1] and it being of no slight importance, to be furnisht with pertinent Heads, for the direction of Inquirers; that lately named *Benefactour to Experimental Philosophy*, has been pleased to communicate, for the ends abovesaid, the following *Articles*, which (as himself did signifie) belong to one of his *Essays* of the unpublisht part of the Usefulness of Nat. and Experimen. Philosophy.[2]

But first he premises, that what follows, is design'd only to point at the more *General* heads of Inquiry, which the proposer ignores not to be Divers of them very comprehensive, in so much, that about some of the *Subordinate* subjects, perhaps too, not the most fertile, he has drawn up *Articles* of inquisition about particulars, that take up near as much room, as what is here to be deliver'd of this matter.

The *Heads* themselves follow;

The things, to be observ'd in such a History, may be variously (and almost at pleasure) divided: As, into *Supraterraneous*, *Terrestrial*, and *Subterraneous*; and otherwise: but we will at present distinguish them into those things, that respect the *Heavens*, or concern the *Air*, the *Water*, or the *Earth*.

1. To the *First* sort of Particulars, belong the Longitude and Latitude of the Place (that being of moment in reference to the observations about the Air *&c.*) and consequently the length of the longest and shortest days and nights, the Climate, parallels *&c.* what fixt starrs are and what not seen there: What Constellations 'tis said to be subject to? Whereunto may be added other Astrological matters, if they be thought worth mentioning.

2. About the *Air* may be observ'd, its Temperature, as to the first four Qualities (commonly so call'd) and the Measures of them: its Weight, Clearness, Refractive power: its Subtlety or Grossness: its abounding with, or wanting an *Esurine* Salt: its variations according to the seasons of the year, and the times of the day; What duration the several kinds of Weather usually have; What *Meteors* it is most or least wont to breed; and in what order they are generated; and how long they usually last: Especially, what Winds it is subject to; whether any of them be stated and ordinary, *&c.* What diseases are Epidemical, that are supposed to flow from the Air: What other diseases, wherein *that* hath a share, the *Countrey* is subject to; the Plague and Contagious sicknesses: What is the usual salubrity or insalubrity of the Air; and with what Constitutions it agrees better or worse, than others.

1 Once again, the Baconian project.
2 The published text was Robert Boyle's *Some Considerations Touching the Usefulnesse of Experimental Naturall Philosophy*, two parts, 1663 and 1671.

3. About the *Water*, may be observ'd, the Sea, its Depth, degree of Saltiness, Tydes, *&c.* Next, Rivers, their Bigness Length, Course, Inundations, Goodness, Levity (or their Contraries) of Waters, *&c.* Then, Lakes, Ponds, Springs, and especially Mineral waters, their Kinds, Qualities, Vertues, and how examined. To the *Waters* belong also *Fishes*, what kinds of them (whether Salt or Fresh-water fish) are to be found in the Country; their Store, Bigness, Goodness, Seasons, Haunts, Peculiarities of any kind, and the wayes of taking them, especially those that are not purely *Mechanical*.[3]
4. In the *Earth*, may be observed,
    1. *It self.*
    2. Its *Inhabitants* and its *Productions*, and these *External*, and *Internal*.

First, in the Earth *it self*, may be observ'd, its dimensions, scituation, East, West, North, and South: its Figure, its Plains, and Valleys, and their Extents, its Hills and *Mountains*, and the height of the tallest, both in reference to the neighbouring Valleys or Plains, and in reference to the Level of the Sea: As also, whether the Mountains lye scattered, or in ridges, and whether those run North and South, or East and West, *&c.* What Promontories, fiery or smoaking Hills, *&c.* the Country has, or hath not: Whether the Country be coherent, or much broken into Ilands. What the Magnetical Declination is in several places, and the Variations of that Declination in the same place (and, if either of those be very considerable, then, what circumstances may assist one to guess at the Reason as Subterraneal fires, the Vicinity of Iron-mines, *&c.*)[4] what the Nature of the Soyle is, whether Clays, Sandy, &c. or good Mould; and what Grains, Fruits, and other Vegetables, do the most naturally agree with it: As also, by what particular Arts and Industries the Inhabitants improve the Advantages, and remedy the Inconveniences of their Soyl: What hidden qualities the Soyl may have (as that of *Ireland*, against Venomous Beasts, *&c.*)

Secondly, above the ignobler *Productions* of the Earth, there must be a careful account given of the *Inhabitants* themselves, both *Natives* and *Strangers*, that have been long settled there: And in particular, their Stature, Shape, Colour, Features, Strength, Agility, Beauty (or the want of it) Complexions, Hair, Dyet, Inclinations, and Customs that seem not due to Education. As to their Women (besides the other things) may be observed their Fruitfulness or Barrenness; their hard or easy Labour, *&c.* And both in Women and Men must be taken notice of what diseases they are subject to, and in these whether there be any symptome, or any other Circumstance, that is unusual and remarkable.

---

3   Evidently, means of catching fish beyond simply capturing them with nets or hooks.
4   On these terrestrial magnetic matters, see Gilbert extract (Chapter 6).

As to the *External* Productions of the Earth, the Inquiries may be such as these: What Grasses, Grains, Herbs, (Garden and Wild) Flowers, Fruit-trees, Timber-trees (especially any Trees, whose wood is considerable) Coppices, Groves, Woods, Forrests, &c. the Country has or wants: What peculiarities are observable in any of them: What Soyles they most like or dislike; and with what Culture they thrive best. What *Animals* the Country has or wants, both as to wild Beasts, Hawks, and other Birds of Prey; and as to Poultrey, and Cattle of all sorts, and particularly, whether it have any *Animals*, that are not common, or any thing, that is peculiar in those, that are so.

The *Internal* Productions or Concealments of the Earth are here understood to be, the riches that lay hid under the Ground, and are not already referr'd to other Inquiries.

Among these *Subterraneal* observations may be taken notice of, what sorts of Minerals of any kind they want, as well as what they have; *Then* what Quarries the Country affords, and the particular conditions both of the Quarries and the Stones: As also, how the Beds of Stone lye, in reference to North and South, &c. What Clays and Earths it affords, as Tobacco-pipe-clay, Marles, Fullers-earths, Earths for Potters wares, Bolus's and other medicated Earths: What other Minerals it yields, as Coals, Salt-Mines, or Salt-springs, Allom, Vitrial, Sulphur, &c. What Mettals the Country yields, and a description of the Mines, their number, scituation, depth, signs, waters, damps, quantities of ore, goodness of ore, extraneous things and ways of reducing their ores into Mettals, &c.

To these General Articles of inquiries (saith their *Proposer*) should be added; 1 *Inquiries* about *Traditions* concerning all particular things, relating to that Country, as either peculiar to it, or at least, uncommon elsewhere. 2 *Inquiries*, that require *Learning* or *Skill* in the Answerer: to which should be subjoyned *Proposals* of ways, to enable men to give Answers to these more difficult inquiries.

Thus far our Author, who, as he has been pleased to impart these *General* (but yet very *Comprehensive* and greatly *Directive*) Articles; so, 'tis hoped from his own late intimation, that he will shortly enlarge them with *Particular* and *Subordinate* ones. These, in the mean time, were thought fit to be publisht, that the Inquisitive and Curious, might, by such an Assistance, be invited not to delay their searches of matters, that are so highly conducive to the improvement of *True Philosophy*, and the wellfare of *Mankind*.

13

EXPERIMENTAL PHILOSOPHY

———◦◦◦◦———

In the later seventeenth century the term "experimental philosophy" became voguish in England, among the Fellows of the Royal Society and especially in the subsequent usage of Isaac Newton. The latter's adoption of the term ensured its longevity and its adoption elsewhere, and coupled experimental manipulations with mathematical formalisms and analysis. Newton's first publication, in 1672, displayed such an approach even before Newton adopted the term itself, but it nicely displays Newton's approach. Qualitative experimental approaches to phenomena of colours, augmented by simple measurements and geometrical inferences, are presented in such a way as to create the impression that substantive conclusions can be drawn about the phenomena under examination. More elaborate mathematical ideas are, in this work of Newton's, cloaked in Baconian descriptions.

Source: [Isaac Newton], "A Letter of Mr. Isaac Newton...containing his New Theory about Light and Colours," *Philosophical Transactions* 80 (February 19, 1671/72), extracts from pp. 3075–3079.

SIR,

To perform my late promise to you, I shall without further ceremony acquaint you, that in the beginning of the Year 1666 (at which time I applied myself to the grinding of Optick glasses of other figures than *Spherical*,) I procured me a Triangular glass-Prisme, to try therewith the celebrated *Phænomena* of *Colours*. And in order thereto having darkened my chamber, and made a small hole in my window-shuts, to let in a convenient quantity of the Suns light, I placed my Prisme at his entrance, that it might be thereby refracted to the opposite wall.[1] It was at first a pleasing divertissement, to view the vivid and intense colors produced thereby; but after a while applying my self to consider them more circumspectly, I became surprised to see them in

---

1 This initial historical narration sets up the paper as an only-somewhat mathematised version of a Baconian experiment.

an *oblong* form; which, according to the received laws of Refraction, I expected should have been *circular*.

They were terminated at the sides with streight lines, but at the ends, the decay of light was so gradual, that it was difficult to determine justly, what was their figure; yet they seemed *semicircular*.

Comparing the length of this coloured *Spectrum* with its breadth, I found it about five times greater; a disproportion so extravagant, that it excited me to a more then ordinary curiosity of examining, from whence it might proceed. I could scarce think, that the various *Thickness* of the glass, or the termination with shadow or darkness, could have any Influence on light to produce such an effect; yet I thought it not amiss, first to examine those circumstances, and so tried, what would happen by transmitting light through parts of the glass of divers thicknesses, or through holes in the window of divers bignesses, or by setting the Prisme without so, that the light might pass through it, and be refracted before it was terminated by the hole; But I found none of those circumstances material. The fashion of the colors was in all these cases the same.

Then I suspected, whether, by any *unevenness* in the glass, or other contingent irregularity, these colors might be thus dilated. And to try this, I took another Prisme like the former, and so placed it, that the light, passing through them both, might be refracted contrary ways, and so by the latter returned into that course, from which the former had diverted it. For by this means I thought, the *regular* effects of the first Prisme would be destroyed by the second Prisme, but the *irregular* ones more augmented, by the multiplicity of refractions. The event was, that the light, which by the first Prisme was diffused into an *oblong* form, was by the second reduced into an *orbicular* one with as much regularity, as when it did not at all pass through them. So that, what ever was the cause of that length, 'twas not any contingent irregularity.

I then proceeded to examin more critically what might be effected by the difference of the incidence of Rays coming from divers parts of the Sun; and to that end, measured the several lines and angles, belonging to the Image. Its distance from the hole or Prisme was 22 foot; its utmost length 13¼ inches; its breadth 2 5/8 ; the diameter of the hole ¼ of an inch; the angle, with the Rays, tending towards the middle of the image, made with those lines, in which they would have proceeded without refraction, was 44 deg. 15'. And the vertical Angle of the Prisme, 63 deg. 12'. Also the Refractions on both sides the Prisme, that is, of the Incident, and Emergent Rays, were as near, as I could make them, equal, and consequently about 54 deg. 4'. And the Rays fell perpendicularly upon the wall. Now subducting the diameter of the hole from the length and breadth of the Image, there remains 13 Inches the length, and 2 3/8 the breadth, comprehended by those Rays, which passed through the center of the said hole, and consequently the angle of the hole, which that breadth subtended, was about 31', answerable to the Suns Diameter; but the angle, which its length subtended, was more then five such diameters, namely 2 deg. 49'.

. . .

Then I began to suspect, whether the Rays, after their trajection through the Prisme, did not move in curve lines, and according to their more or less curvity tend to divers parts of the wall. And it increased my suspicion when I remembred that I had often seen a Tennis ball, struck with an oblique Racket, describe such a curve line. For, a circular as well as a progressive motion being communicated to it by that stroak, its parts on that side, where the motions conspire, must press and beat the contiguous Air more violently than on the other, and there excite a reluctancy and reaction of the Air proportionably greater. And for the same reason, if the Rays of light be globular bodies, and by their oblique passage out of one medium into another acquire a circular motion, they ought to feel the greater resistance from the ambient Aether, on that side, where the motions conspire, and thence be continually bowed to the other. But notwithstanding this plausible ground of suspition, when I came to examine it, I could observe no such curvity in them. And besides (which was enough for my purpose) I observed, that the difference 'twixt the length of the Image, and diameter of the hole, through which the light was transmitted, was proportionable to their distance.

The gradual removal of these suspitions at length led me to the *Experimentum Crucis*, which was this:I took two boards, and placed one of them close behind the Prisme at the window, so that the light might pass through a small hole, made in it for the purpose, and fall on the other board, which I placed at about 12 feet distance, having first made a small hole in it also, for some of that Incident light to pass through. Then I placed another Prisme behind this second board, so that the light, trajected through both the boards, might pass through that also, and be again refracted before it arrived at the wall. This done, I took the first Prisme in my hand, and turned it to and fro slowly about its *Axis*, so much as to make the several parts of the Image, cast on the second board, successively pass through the hole in it, that I might observe to what places on the wall the second Prisme would refract them. And I saw by the variation of those places, that the light, tending to that end of the Image, towards which the refraction of the first Prisme was made, did in the second Prisme suffer a Refraction considerably greater then the light tending to the other end. And so the true cause of the length of that Image was detected to be no other, then that *Light* consists of *Rays differently refrangible*, which, without any respect to a difference in their incidence, were, according to their degrees of refrangibility, transmitted towards divers parts of the wall.[2]

. . .

---

2   Newton continues now with a discussion that takes a more formalised mathematical approach, abandoning his historical narration for a summary of his general conclusions about light and colours. His Baconian set-up has concluded.

14

SOCIAL DATA

William Petty was involved, during the English Interregnum under Oliver Cromwell in the 1650s, with land surveying and management in Ireland, to which he returned in the 1660s, having become a Fellow of the Royal Society. In that same decade he applied the principles of numerical analysis to social data in his celebrated *Political Arithmetick* (published posthumously in 1690 — Petty died in 1687 — but dating from the 1670s). Closely contemporary with Petty's work, John Graunt published in 1662 a work based on the Bills of Mortality (annual records of deaths) for London, investigating demographic data and the statistical conclusions that might be drawn from them. In the present extract from Petty, Petty considers the population of London and its historical development, as well as of the nation as a whole, on the basis of available estimated data and principles of population increase.

Source: William Petty, *Another Essay in Political Arithmetick* (London, 1682), pp. 3–22.

The Principal Points of this Discourse.

1. THAT *London* doubles in forty years, and all *England* in Three hundred and sixty Years.
2. That there be, *Anno 1682*, about six hundred and seventy thousand Souls in London, and about seven Millions, four hundred Thousand in all *England* and *Wales*, and about twenty eight Millions of Acres of Land.
3. That the Periods of doubling the People, are found to be in all Degrees, from between Ten, to Twelve hundred Years.
4. That the Growth of *London* must stop of its self, before the Year 1800.
5. A Table helping to understand the *Scriptures*, concerning the Number of People mentioned in them.
6. That the *World* will be fully Peopled within the next two Thousand Years.
7. Twelve ways whereby to Try any Proposal, pretended for the Publick Good.
8. How the City of *London* may be made (Morally speaking) *invincible.*

9. An help to uniformity in Religion.
10. That 'tis possible to increase Mankind by Generation four times more than at present.
11. The Plagues of *London* is the Chief Impediment and Objection against the Growth of the City.
12. That an Exact Account of the People is Necessary in this Matter.

Of the Growth of the CITY of London: And of the Measures, Periods, Causes, and Consequences thereof.

BY the City of *London*, we mean the Housing within the Walls of the Old City, with the Liberties thereof, *Westminster*, the *Burrough of Southwark*, and so much of the built Ground in *Middlesex* and *Surrey*, whose Houses are contiguous unto, or within Call of those afore-mentioned. Or else we mean the Housing which stand upon the Ninety-seven Parishes within the Walls of *London*; upon the Sixteen Parishes next, without them; the Six Parishes of *Westminster*, and the Fourteen out-Parishes in *Middlesex* and *Surrey*, contiguous to the former, all which One hundred and thirty three Parishes are comprehended within the Weekly *Bills of Mortality*.

The Growth of this City is Measured. 1. By the Quantity of Ground, or Number of Acres upon which it stands. 2. By the Number of Houses, as the same appears by the Hearth-books and late *Maps*. 3. By the Cubical Content of the said Housing. 4. By the Flooring of the same. 5. By the Number of Days-work, or Charge of Building the said Houses. 6. By the Value of the said Houses, according to their Yearly Rent, and Number of Years Purchase. 7. By the Number of Inhabitants; according to which latter sense onely, we make our Computations in this Essay.

Till a better Rule can be obtained, we conceive that the Proportion of the People may be sufficiently Measured by the Proportion of the *Burials* in such Years as were neither remarkable for extraordinary Healthfulness or Sickliness.

That the City hath Increased in this latter sense, appears from the Bills of *Mortality* represented in the two following Tables, *viz.* One whereof is a continuation for Eighteen Years, ending 1682, of that Table which was Published in the 117th *pag.* of the Book of the Observations upon the *London Bills of Mortality*, Printed in the Year 1676. The other sheweth what Number of People dyed at a *Medium* of two Years, indifferently taken, at about Twenty Years distance from each other.

Wherein Observe, That the Number C. is double to A. and 806 over. That D. is double to B. within 1906. That C. and D. is double to A. B. within 293. That E. is double to C. within 1435. That D. and E. is double to B. and C. within 3341. And that C and D. and E. are double to A. and B. and C. within 1736. And that E. is above Quadruple to A. All which differences (every way considered) do allow the doubling of the People of *London* in forty Years, to be a sufficient estimate thereof in round Numbers, and without the

Table 14.1 Deaths in London I. From Petty, *Another Essay in Political Arithmetic*

A.D.	97 Parishes.	16 Parishes.	Out Parishes.	Buried in all.	Besides of the Plague.	Christened.
			The first of the said two Tables.			
1665	5,320	12,463	10,925	28,708	68,596	9,967
1666	1,689	3,969	5,082	10,740	1,998	8,997
1667	761	6,405	8,641	15,807	35	10,938
1668	796	6,865	9,603	17,267	14	11,633
1669	1,323	7,500	10,440	19,263	3	12,335
1670	1,890	7,808	10,500	20,198		11,997
1671	1,723	5,938	8,063	15,724	5	12,510
1672	2,237	6,788	9,200	18,225	5	12,593
1673	2,307	6,302	8,890	17,499	5	11,895
1674	2,801	7,522	10,875	21,198	3	11,851
1675	2,555	5,986	8,702	17,243	1	11,775
1676	2,756	6,508	9,466	18,730	2	12,399
1677	2,817	6,632	9,616	19,065	2	12,626
1678	3,060	6,705	10,908	20,673	5	12,601
1679	3,074	7,481	11,173	21,728	2	12,288
1680	3,076	7,066	10,911	21,053		12,747
1681	3,669	8,136	12,166	23,971		13,355
1682	2,975	7,009	10,707	20,691		12,653

Table 14.2 Deaths in London II. From Petty, *Another Essay in Political Arithmetic*

According to which latter table there dyed as follows:—
THE LATTER OF THE SAID TWO TABLES.
There dyed in London at the medium between the years

1604 and 1605	5,135.	A.
1621 and 1622	8,527.	B.
1641 and 1642	11,883.	C.
1661 and 1662	15,148.	D.
1681 and 1682	22,331.	E.

trouble of Fractions. We also say, that 669930 is near the Number of People now in *London*, because the Burials are 22331. which Multiplied by 30, (one dying yearly out of 30, as appears in the 94 *pag.* of the aforementioned Observations) maketh the said Number; and because there are 84 Thousand Tenanted Houses (as we are Credibly informed) which at 8 in each, makes 672 Thousand Souls; the said two Accounts differing inconsiderably from each other.

We have thus pretty well found out in what Number of Years (*viz.* in about 40) that the City of *London* hath doubled, and the present Number of

Inhabitants to be about 670 Thousand. We must now also endeavour the same for the whole *Territory* of *England* and *Wales*. In Order whereunto, we

First say that the Assessment of *London* is about an Eleventh part of the whole Territory, and therefore that the People of the whole may well be Eleven times that of *London, viz.* about 7 Millions, 369 Thousand Souls; with which Account that of the *Poll-Money, Hearth-Money*, and the Bishops late Numbring of the *Communicants*, do pretty well agree; wherefore, although the said Number of 7 Millions, 369 Thousand, be not (as it cannot be) a *demonstrated Truth*, yet it will serve for a good *Supposition*, which is as much as we want at present.

As for the time in which the People double, it is yet more hard to be found: For we have good Experience (in the said 94 *pag.* of the afore-mentioned Observations) that in the Country, but one of fifty die *per Annum*; and by other late Accounts, that there have been sometimes but 24 *Births* for 23 *Burials*: The which two points, if they were universally, and constantly true, there would be colour enough to say, that the People doubled but in about 1200 years. As for Example: Suppose there be 600 People, of which let a fiftieth part die *per Annum*, then there shall die 12 *per Annum*; and if the Births be as 24 to 23, then the Increase of the People shall be somewhat above half a Man *per Annum*, and consequently the supposed Number of 600, cannot be doubled but in 1126 Years, which, to reckon in round Numbers, and for that the afore-mentioned Fractions were not exact, we had rather call 1200.

There are also other good *Observations*, That even in the Country, one in about 30, or 32 *per Annum* hath died, and that there have been five *Births* for four *Burials*. Now, according to this Doctrine, 20 will die *per Annum* out of the above 600, and 25 will be born, so as the *Increase* will be 5, which is a hundred and twentieth part of the said 600. So as we have two fair *Computations*, differing from each other as one to ten; and there are also several other good *Observations* for other *Measures*.

I might here Insert, that although the Births in this last Computation be 25 of 600, or a Twenty fourth part of the People; yet that in Natural possibility, they may be near thrice as many, and near 75. For that by some late *Observations*, the *Teeming* females between 15 and 44, are about 180 of the said 600, and the *Males* of between 18 and 59, are about 180 also, and that every Teeming *Woman* can bear a *Child* once in two Years; from all which it is plain, that the *Births* may be 90, (and abating 15 for *Sickness*, Young *Abortions*, and Natural *Barrenness*) there may remain 75 Births, which is an Eighth of the People, which by some Observations we have found to be but a *two and thirtieth part*, or but a *quarter* of what is thus shown to be Naturally possible. Now, according to this Reckoning, if the *Births* may be 75 of 600, and the *Burials* but 15, then the *Annual Increase* of the People will be 60; and so the said 600 People may double in 10 Years, which differs yet more from 1200, above-mentioned. Now to get out of this Difficulty, and to temper those vast disagreements, I took the *Medium* of 50 and 30 dying *per Annum*, and pitch'd upon 40; and I also took the *Medium* between 24 *Births* and 23 *Burials*, and 5 *Births* for 4 Burials, *viz.*, allowing about 10 *Births* for 9 *Burials*; upon which Supposition, there must die 15 *per Annum* out of the above-mentioned 600, and the *Births* must be 16 *and two thirds*, and the Increase 1, and two Thirds, or five Thirds of a Man, which Number compared with 1800 *Thirds*, or 600 Men, gives 360 Years for the time of doubling...

...

According to which Account or Measure of doubling, if there be now in *England* and *Wales*, 7 Millions 400 Thousand People, there were about 5 Millions 526 Thousand in the beginning of Queen *Elizabeths* Reign, *Anno* 1560, and about two Millions at the *Norman Conquest*, of which Consult the *Dooms-day Book*, and My Lord *Hale's Origination of Mankind*.[1]

Memorandum, That if the People double in 360 Years, that the present 320 Millions computed by some Learned Men, (from the Measures of all the Nations of the World, their degrees of being Peopled, and good Accounts of the People in several of them) to be now upon the face of the Earth, will within the next 2000 Years, so increase, as to give one Head for every two Acres of Land in the *Habitable* part of the *Earth*. And then, according to the *Prediction* of the *Scriptures*, there must be *Wars*, and great *Slaughter*, &c.[2]

Wherefore, as an *Expedient* against the above-mentioned difference between 10 and 1200 years, we do for the present, and in this Country admit of 360 Years to be the time wherein the People of *England* do double, according to the present *Laws* and *Practice* of *Marriages*.

Now, if the City double its People in 40 Years, and the present Number be 670 Thousand, and if the *whole Territory* be 7 Millions 400 Thousand, and double in 360 Years, as aforesaid, then by the underwritten Table it appears that *Anno* 1840 the People of the City will be 10718880, and those of the whole Country but 10917389, which is but inconsiderably more. Wherefore it is certain and necessary that the *Growth* of the City must stop before the said year 1840; and will be at its utmost height in the next preceding Period, *Anno* 1800, when the Number of the City will be Eight times its present Number, *viz.* 5 Millions 359 Thousand. And when (besides the said Number) there will be 4 Millions 466 Thousand to perform the *Tillage*, *Pasturage*, and other Rural Works necessary to be done without the said City, as by the following Table, *viz.*

Now, when the People of *London* shall come to be so near the people of all *England*, Then it follows, that the *Growth* of *London* must stop before the said

---

1   A reference to Matthew Hale, the prominent judge and legal theorist (died 1676).
2   Scriptural correlations and references were usual ingredients of scholarly discourse on world history in this period; Biblical prophecy and Biblical chronology were important parts of Isaac Newton's work.

Table 14.3 Projected population. From Petty, *Another Essay in Political Arithmetic*

A.D.	Burials.		People in London.	People in England.
1565	2,568		77,040	5,526,929
1605	5,135			
1642	11,883	[As in the former Table]		
1682	22,331		669,930	7,369,230
1722	44,662			
1762	89,324			
1802	178,648		5,359,440	9,825,650
1842	357,296		10,718,889	10,917,389

Year 1842, as aforesaid, and must be at its greatest height *Anno* 1800, when it will be eight times more than now, with above 4 Millions for the service of the *Countrey* and Ports, as aforesaid.

Of the afore-mentioned vast difference between 10 Years and 1200 Years for *doubling* the People, we make this use, *viz*. To justify the *Scriptures* and all other good *Histories* concerning the *Number* of the People in Ancient Time. For supposing the Eight *Persons* who came out of the *Ark, Increased* by a Progressive doubling in every 10 Years, might grow in the first 100 Years after the *Flood* from 8 to 8000, and that in 350 Years after the *Flood* (when abouts *Noah* died) to one Million, and by this time 1682, to 320 Millions (which by rational conjecture, are thought to be now in the World) it will not be hard to compute, how in the intermediate Years, the *Growths* may be made, according to what is set down in the following *Table* [Note: here omitted], wherein making the doubling to be 10 Years at first, and within 1200 Years at last, we take a discretionary liberty, but justifiable by Observations and the Scriptures for the rest, which Table we leave to be Corrected by *Historians*, who know the bigness of *Ancient Cities, Armies,* and *Colonies* in the respective *Ages* of the *World,* in the mean time affirming that without such difference in the *Measures* and Periods for doubling (the extreams whereof we have demonstrated to be real and true) it is impossible to solve what is written in the Holy *Scriptures* and other *Authentick Books.* For if we pitch upon any one Number throughout for this purpose, 150 Years is the fittest of all round Numbers; according to which, there would have been but 512 Souls in the whole World in *Moses's* time (being 800 Years after the Flood), when 603 Thousand *Israelites* of above 20 Years Old (besides those of other Ages, Tribes, and Nations) were found upon an exact Survey appointed by God, whereas our Table makes 12 Millions. And there would have been but 8000 in *David's* time, when were found 1100 Thousand of above 20 Years Old (besides others, as aforesaid) in *Israel,* upon the Survey instigated by Satan, whereas our Table makes 32 Millions. And there would have been but a quarter of a Million about the Birth of Christ, or *Augustus* his Time, when *Rome* and the *Roman* Empire were so great, whereas our Table makes 100 Millions. Where Note, that the *Israelites* in about 500 Years between their coming out of *Egypt* to *David's* Reign, increased from 603 Thousand to 1100 Thousand.[3]

3   The use of the Bible as a straightforward source of historical data on world history was common not only in the second half of the seventeenth century, but remained so until the nineteenth (see Jones extract, below).

15

TRADE AND THE PHYSICAL GLOBE

The expansion of European trade around the world that occurred during the sixteenth and seventeenth centuries was unparalleled in its extent and swiftness. And as the late seventeenth century began to see capitalist economic imperatives emerging, especially in Britain, to push for ever-greater rates of growth, the would-be utilitarian natural philosophers of the Royal Society saw the need to assist in making nautical trade ever more efficient. Detailed knowledge of trade winds was a desideratum that could make a huge difference to the return to Europe of ships laden with cargo from eastern Asia; unanticipated monsoons could delay a departure for many months. In the following extract, Edmond Halley, friend of Newton's and predictor of cometary orbits,[1] attempted to reduce global trading movements to order by making use of information, including that gleaned from oral sources (the seamen of London), regarding the winds and their annual schedules. In the age of sail, knowing how to get to a destination quickly depended on how to get there (the route best exploiting wind patterns) more than it relied on where somewhere was on a static map.

Source: Edmond Halley, "An Historical Account of the Trade Winds, and Monsoons, observable in the Seas between and near the Tropicks, with an attempt to assign the Phisical cause of the said Winds," *Philosophical Transactions* 16 (1686–1692), pp. 153–168.

An exact Relation of the constant and Periodical Winds, observable in several Tracts of the Ocean, is a part of Natural History not less desireable and useful, than it is difficult to obtain, and it's *Phænomena* hard to explicate: I am not Ignorant that several Writers have undertaken this subject, and although *Varenius* (*Lib. I. Chap. XXI. Geo. Gen*) seems to have endeavoured after the best information from *Voiagers*, yet cannot his accounts be admitted for accurate, by those that shall attentively consider and compare them togather

1   Alan Cook, *Edmond Halley: Charting the Heavens and the Seas* (Oxford: Oxford University Press, 1998).

[*sic*]; and some of them are most evident mistakes; which, as near as I can, I shall attempt to rectify, having had the opportunity of conversing with Navigators acquainted with all parts of *India*, and having lived a considerable time between the *Tropicks*, and there made my own remarks.

The substance of what I have collected is briefly as follows.

The Universal *Ocean* may most properly be divided into three parts *viz*. 1. The *Atlantick* and *Æthiopick*[2] Sea: 2. The *Indian Ocean*: 3. The Great *South Sea* or the *Pacifick Ocean*; and tho' these Seas do all communicate by the South, yet as to our present purpose of the *Trade Winds*, they are sufficiently separated by the interposition of great tracts of *Land*; the first lying between *Africa* and *America*, the second between *Africa*, and the *Indian Islands* and *Hollandia Nova*; and the last, between the *Philippine Isles*, *China*, *Japan* and *Hollandia Nova* on the *West*, and the Coast of *America* on the *East*. Now following this natural division of the Seas, so will we divide our History into three parts, in the same order.

I. In the *Atlantick* and *Æthiopick* Seas, between the *Tropicks*, there is a general *Easterly Wind*, all the Year long, without any considerable variation, excepting that it is subject to be deflected therefrom, some few points of the Compass towards the *North* or *South*, according to the position of the place. The Observations which have been made of these deflections, are the following.

1. That near the coast of *Africa*, as soon as you have passed the *Canary Isles* you are sure to meet a fresh Gale of *N.E.* Wind about the Latitude of 28. Degrees *North*, which seldom comes to the *Eastwards* of the *E.N.E.* or passes the *N.N.E.* This Wind accompanies those bound to the Southward, to the Latitude of 10 North, and about 100. Leagues from the *Guinea* Coast, where till the *4th* degree of North *Latitude*, they fall into calmes and *Tornadoes*, of which more hereafter.

2. That those bound to the *Caribbe Isles*, find, as they approach the *American* side, that the aforesaid *North-East Wind*, becomes still more and more *Easterly*, so as sometimes to be *East*, sometimes *East* by *South*, but yet most commonly to the *Northward* of the *East* a point or two, seldome more. 'Tis likewise observed, that the strength of these *Winds* does gradually decrease, as you saile to the *Westwards*.

3. That the limits of the *Trade* and *Variable Winds*, in this Ocean, are farther extended on the *American* side than the *African*: for whereas you meet not with this certain *Wind* till after you have passed the *Latitude* of 8 *degrees* on this side; on the *American* side it commonly holds to 30. 31 or 32 *degrees* of *Latitude*; and this is verified likewise to the *Southwards* of the

2   This was a term for that part of the Atlantic stretching south from the coast of west Africa.

Equinoctial, for near the *Cape* of *Good-Hope* the limits of the *Trade Winds*, are 3 or 4 *degrees* nearer the Line, than on the coast of *Brazile*.

4. That from the *Latitude* of 4 *degrees North*, to the aforesaid limits on the *South* side of the *Equator*, the *Winds* are generally and perpetually between the *South* and *East*, and most commonly between the *South-East* and *East*, observing always this Rule, that on the *African* side they are more *Southerly*, and the *Brasilian* more *Easterly*, so as to become almost due *East*, the little deflection they have being still to the *Southwards*. In this part of the Ocean it has been my fortune to pass a full year, in an employment that obliged me to regard more than ordinary the Weather, and I found the Winds constantly about the *South-East*, the most usual point *S E b E* [south east by east]; when it was *Easterly* it generally blew hard, and was gloomy, dark, and sometimes rainy weather; if it came to the *Southwards* it was generally Serene, and a small gale next to a Calme, but this not very common. But I never saw it to the *Westwards* of the *South*, or *Northwards* of the *East*.

5. That the season of the Year has some small effect on these *Trade Winds*, for that when the Sun is considerable [*sic*] to the *Northwards* of the *Equator*, the *South-East* Winds, especially in the straight of this Ocean (if I may so call it) between *Brasile* and the Coast of *Guinea*, do vary a point or two to the *Southwards*, and the *North-East* become more *Easterly*; and on the contrary when the Sun is towards the *Tropick* of [Capricorn symbol], the *South-Easterly Winds* become more *Easterly*, and the *North-easterly Winds* on this side the *Line vere* more to the *Northwards*.

6. That as there is no general Rule that admits not of some exception, so there is in this Ocean a tract of Sea wherein the *Southerly* and S. *West* Winds are perpetual, *viz.* all along the Coast of *Guinea*, for above 500. Leagues together, from *Sierra Leona* to the *Isle* of St. *Thomas*; for the *South-East* Trade-Wind having passed the *Line*, and approaching the Coast of *Guinea* within 80 or 100 *Leagues* inclines towards the shore, and becomes S.S.E., and by degrees, as you come nearer, it vears [*sic*] about to *South*, S. S. *West*, and in with the land *South-West*, and sometimes *West South-West*; which variation is better expressed in the *Mapp* hereto annexed, than it can well be in words. These are in Winds, which are observed on this coast when it blows true, but there are frequent Calms, Violent suddain Gusts, called *Tornado's*, from all points of the compass, and sometimes unwholesome foggy *Easterly Winds* called *Hermitaa* by the Natives, which to often infest the Navigation of these parts.

7. That to the *Northwards* of the Line, between 4 and 10 *degrees* of Latitude, and between the Meridians of *Cape Virde* [*sic*], and of the *Easternmost Islands* that bear that name, there is a tract of Sea wherein it were improper to say there is any *Trade Wind*, or yet a Variable [wind]; for it seems condemned to perpetual Calms, attended with terrible Thunder and Lightning, and

Rains so frequent, that our Navigators from thence call this part of the Sea the *Rains*: the little Winds that are, be only some suddain uncertain Gusts, of very little continuance and less extent; so that sometimes each hour you shall have a different Gale, which dies away into a Calme before another succeed; and in a fleet of Shipps in sight of one another, each shall have the Wind from a several point of the Compass; with these weak *Brizes* Shipps are obliged to make the best of their way to the *Southward* through the aforesaid six degrees, wherein 'tis reported some have been detained whole months for want of Wind.

From the three last observations is shewn the reason of two notable occurrents in the *East-Indies* and Guinea *Navigations*. The one is, why notwithstanding the narrowest part of the Sea between *Guinea* and *Brasile* be about 500 leagues over, yet Shipps bound to the *Southward* sometimes, especially in the months of *July* and *August*, find a great difficulty to pass it. This happens because of the *South-east Winds*, at that time of the year commonly extending some degrees beyond the ordinary limit of 4 *degrees North Lat.* and withal they come so much *Southerly*, as to be sometimes *South*, sometimes a point or two to the *West*; there remains then only to plié [turn] to Wind-ward, and if on the one side they stand away W.S.W. they gain the Wind still more and more *Easterly*, but there is danger of not weathering the *Brasilian* shore, or at least the shoals upon that Coast. But if upon the other tack they go away E.S.E, they fall into the neighberhood [sic] of the Coast of *Guinea*, from which there is no departing without running *Easterly*, as far as the *Isle* of St. *Thomas*, which is the constant practice of all the *Guiny Shipps*, and which may seem very strang without the consideration of the sixth remark, which shews the reason of it. For being in with the Coast, the Wind blows generally at S.W. and W.S.W., with which Winds they cannot go to the *Northward* for the Land, and on the other tack they can lie no nearer the Wind than S.S.E. or *South*; with these courses they run off the shore, but in so doing they alwaies find the *Winds* more and more contrary; so that when near the shore they could lie near the *South*, at a greater distance they can make their way no better than S.E. and afterwards E.S.E., with which courses they fetch commonly the Isle of St. *Thomas* and Cape *Lopez*, where finding the Winds to the *Eastward* of the *South*, they keep them favourable by running away to the *Westward* in the *South Lat.* of 3 or 4 *degrees*, where the *S.E. Winds* are perpetual.

For the sake of these general *Winds*, all those that use the *West-Indian Trade*, even those bound to *Virginia*, count it their best course to get as soon as they can, to the *Southwards*, that so they may be certain of a fair and fresh gale to runn before it to the *Westwards*; and for the same reason those homewards bound from *America*, endeavor to gain the Latitude of 30 *degrees*, as soon as possible, where they first find the Winds begin to be Variable; though the most ordinary Winds in the *Northern* part of the *Atlantick* Ocean come from between the *South* and the *West*.

As to those furious storms called *Hurricanes*, which are as it were peculiar to the *Caribbe Isles*; and which so dreadfully afflict them in the month of *August*, or not much before or after, they do not so properly belong to this place, both by reason of their small continuance and extent, as likewise because they are not Anniversary [annual], some years having more than one, and sometimes for several years togeather there being none at all. But their Violence is so unconceivable, and their other *Phænomena* so surprising, that they merit well to be considered apart.

...[similar section on the Indian Ocean]...

By reason of the shifting of these Winds, all those that sail in these Seas, are obliged to observe the seasons proper for their Voiages, and so doing they fail not of a fair wind and speedy passage; but if so be they chance to out-stay their time, till the contrary *Monsoon* set in, as it frequently happens, they are forced to give over the hopes of accomplishing their intended Voiages, and either return to the port from whence they came, or else put in to some other Harbour, there to spend the time till the Winds shall come favourable.

...[similar section on the Pacific Ocean]...

What the *Spanish* Authors say of the Winds they find in their Courses, and what is confirmed by the old Accounts of *Drake* and *Candish*,[3] and since by *Schooten*, who sailed the whole breadth of this Sea in the Southern Latitude of 15 or 16 degrees, is, that there is a great conformity between the Winds of this Sea, and those of the *Atlantick* and *Æthiopick*; that is to say, that to the Northwards of the *Equator*, the predominant Wind is between the *East* and *North-East*, and to the *Southwards* thereof there is a constant steady gale between the *East* and *South-East*, and that on both sides the *Line* with so much constance, that they scarce ever need to attend the Sails, and strength, that it is rare to fail of crossing this vast Ocean in ten weeks time, which is about 13 miles *per diem*; besides 'tis said that *Stormes* and Tempests are never known in these parts: So that here is the very best of Sailing; no want of a fresh fair Wind, and yet no danger of having too much: Wherefore some have thought it might be as short a Voiage to *Japan* and *China*, to go by the Streights of *Magellan*, is by the *Cape of Good-hope*.

...

Thus far matter of Fact, wherein if the information I have received be not in all parts Accurate, it has not been for want of inquiry from those I conceived best able to instruct me; and I shall take it for a very great kindness if any Master of a Ship, or any other person, well informed of the Nature of the Winds, in any of the aforementioned parts of the World, shall please to communicate their Observations thereupon; that so what I have here collected may be either confirmed or amended, or by the addition of some material Circumstances enlarged. It is not the work of one, nor of few, but of a

---

3   Thomas Cavendish, Elizabethan navigator and contemporary of Francis Drake.

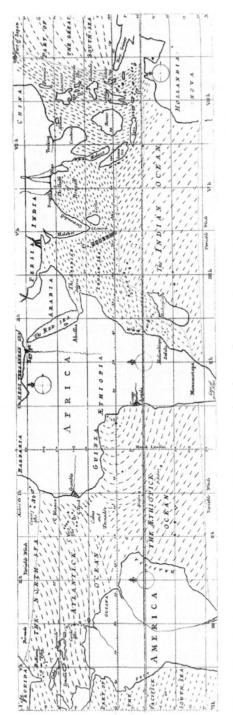

Figure 15.1 Trade winds. From Halley, "An Historical Relation."

multitude of Observers, to bring togather the experience requisite to compose a perfect and compleat History of these Winds; however I am not much doubtful that I have erred in, or omitted any of the principal Observables, whatever lesser particulars may have escaped my knowledg.]

To help the conception of the reader in a matter of so much difficulty, I believed it necessary to adjoyn a Scheme, shewing at one view all the various Tracts and Courses of these Winds; whereby 'tis possible the thing may be better understood, than by any verbal description whatsoever.[4]

The limits of these several Tracts, are designed every where by prickt lines, as well as in the *Atlantick* and *Æthiopick*, where they are the boundaries of the Trade and Variable Winds, as in the *Indian* Ocean, where they also shew the extent of the several *Monsoons*. I could think of no better way to design the course of the Winds on the Mapp, than by drawing rows of stroaks in the same line that a Ship would move going always before it; the sharp end of each little stroak pointing out that part of the *Horizon*, from whence the Wind continually comes; and where there are *Monsoons* the rows of the stroaks run alternately backwards and forwards, but which means they are thicker there than elsewhere. As to the great South Sea, considering its vast extent, and the little Variety there is in its Winds, and the great *Analogy* between them, and those of the *Atlantick* and *Æthiopick* Oceans, besides that the greatest part thereof is wholly unknown to us; I thought it unnecessary to lengthen the Mapp therewith.

...[attempts to explain some of the constancies of these phenomena of winds]...

These are particulars that merit to be considered more at Large, and furnish a sufficient Subject for a just Volume; which will be a very commendable Task for such, who being used to Philosophick Contemplation, shall have leasure to apply their serious thoughts about it.

4   The map is generically reminiscent of a map of global ocean currents produced by the Roman Jesuit scholar Athanasius Kircher in his *Mundus subterraneus* (1665).

16

FINDING NEW PHENOMENA: ELECTRICAL EFFECTS

In the early eighteenth century new experimental phenomena came to the fore that concerned electrical effects. "Electricity" was a word coined in 1600 by the Englishman William Gilbert, and it originally denoted the attraction that light objects, such as bits of straw, exhibited to pieces of the resin amber when a lump of the latter in their vicinity was rubbed by something like a cloth: the straw would then spontaneously jump to the nearby amber. A century later, little had been added to this electrical phenomenon than examples of some additional materials, including glass, that could also be used to attract light bodies. But in the opening years of the eighteenth century, the Royal Society's "curator of experiments," Francis Hauksbee, displayed to the Fellows of the Society much more powerful and spectacular electrical effects than those seen hitherto. Hauksbee multiplied the magnitude of the effects in his new pieces of apparatus, enabling more precision in characterising the phenomena involved, and popularising the study of electricity as a result. Other natural philosophers in England, France, and Germany followed his lead in electrical research, discovering new aspects of the phenomena and new electrical properties. Charles Dufay's work from 1733–1734 took especially seriously the sequence of earlier investigations by others in setting up the historical context of his own experimental work, which incorporated interpretive descriptions derived from Cartesian talk of vortices of subtle matter as means of making intelligible the distance forces involved in electrical attraction and repulsion.

Source: Charles Dufay, "First memoir on electricity," *Mémoires de l'Académie Royale des Sciences* (1733), trans. Peter Dear, extracts from pp. 23–35; "Fourth memoir on electricity," extracts from pp. 457–459.

Electricity is a common property of several materials, and consists of attracting light bodies of every kind placed at a certain distance from the electric body, after it has received a preparation that is nothing but rubbing it with wool, paper, cloth, the hand, etc.

The name that was given to this property shows that it is in amber [Gr. *elektron*] that it was first recognized, it is indeed very manifest there, but there are several materials in which it is as considerable, and even some where it is greatly superior.

If I wanted to speak here of all those who have treated of electricity, I would have to cite all the authors who have written on Physics; there are few who have not paused at this phenomenon, and who haven't tried to find its explanation each in his [own] system; others have applied themselves to examining more particularly this property, and to make experiments, as much on the different materials that are susceptible of it as on the circumstances particular to each electric body. So as only to stop at those who have written on this subject with the greatest intelligence, or who have made some considerable discovery concerning it, and with the exactitude on which one can most rely, I will begin with Gilbert, who added to the number of electric bodies an infinity of materials in which this virtue hadn't at all been recognized. Since there were some in which it was very weak, he thought, to render it more sensible, to make use of a needle of whatever metal concerned, suspended on a pivot like a magnetic needle [i.e. compass needle]; if an electric body approached one of the ends of this needle, it drew it more or less strongly according to the force of its electricity. By this means he recognized that not only amber and jet possessed this property, but that it is common to most precious stones, like diamond, sapphire, ruby, opal, amethyst, aquamarine, rock crystal; that it is found also in glass, belemnite, sulphur [...]
...

He remarks that all electric bodies lack any [attractive] virtue if they are not rubbed, and that it was not enough that they be heated, whether by fire, the sun, or otherwise, even when they were burnt or melted. He adds several other observations on the alteration that attends the interposition of different bodies, but we will deepen this matter in what follows much more than he did. We pass by in silence, for the same reason, some very curious remarks that he made on the effect that electric bodies have on fire, flame, smoke, the air, etc.

Some time later Otto von Guericke made several experiments on a sulphur globe which ought to have carried knowledge of electricity a lot further, but it doesn't seem that anyone tried to follow them up, since there is no mention of them in the authors who have since treated the same things with greater detail; they are found in the collection of Magdeburg experiments,

p. 147.[1] The chief ones are these: a big ball of Sulphur, like a child's head, is turned on its axis using a crank. This ball being moved rapidly, if a hand is placed on it, it becomes electric, and attracts light bodies that are presented to it; if it is separated from the machine on which it's balanced so as to turn it, and it is held in the hand by the axle, not only will it attract a feather, but it will afterwards repel it, and will only attract something new if the feather had not touched any other body...The abridged statement of these experiments shows the basis and principle of all those that have been made since with the tube and the glass globe,[2] and one cannot help but be surprised that they remained forgotten for so long, or at least that no one thought it advisable to repeat them, and to try to carry them further.

At around the same time, the famous Boyle made some experiments on electricity. It was difficult [unfortunate] that so curious a subject did not take its turn as the object of the researches of a man who had traversed with such exactitude all the parts of Physics, and to whom we are obliged for so many beautiful discoveries. He reports several observations that he had made on this subject. Some Physicists had proposed that amber and the other electric bodies heated in fire became capable of attracting; others were confident that it was only by rubbing that this virtue could be excited. Mr. Boyle took the latter part, but he remarked that amber having been heated in fire acquired more virtue by a single application of friction than rubbing four times longer could produce when it was cold.

...

One finds in the *Philosophical Transactions* #308 & 309 many experiments by Mr. Hauksbee concerning the electricity of glass; the same author having continued his researches, has considerably augmented the number of his experiments, and details can be found in various places in the *Philosophical Transactions*: he next brought together all his discoveries in a single work, as much on electricity as on light, and on the difference of these phenomena in a vacuum or in air; it's from this book...that we have taken what we will report in a few words to continue the idea that we have begun to give of the progress of this discovery.

...[Account of Hauksbee's experiments with glass tubes and glass globes (the latter evacuable of air)]...[account of Stephen Gray's experiments published in *Philosophical Transactions* on communication of electricity]...

Thus, more or less, the advances made up until the present on this matter, and, so to speak, the abridged history of electricity. I will not repeat that my intention has not at all been to make mention of all those who have treated it; it's easily seen that my purpose has only been to mention those who have made some singular discovery in it, and who have contributed to carrying

1   Otto von Guericke, *Nova experimenta (ut vocantur) Magdeburgica* (Amsterdam, 1672).
2   Apparatus famously used by Francis Hauksbee.

the knowledge that we have about it to the point where they are today; I cannot avoid making this summary, so as to put before the reader's eyes the current state of this part of Physics, which was all the more necessary since none of the authors whom I've mentioned has spoken of the discoveries of his predecessors; it even seems that they have been unaware of them, and one can see that they have sometimes given, as new observations, things that have been noted by their predecessors, which is why I have undertaken to report as succinctly as I can the most important things that have been written on this matter up to the present, before coming to the experiments that I have made, and the details of which I will give in the following memoirs.

Fourth Memoir on Electricity (extract, pp. 457–459):

On the Attraction and Repulsion of Electric Bodies.

Up to now we have always considered electric virtue in general, and by this word has been understood not only the virtue of electric bodies to attract, but also that of repelling the bodies that they have attracted. This repulsion is not always constant, and it is subject to varieties that I have taken it upon myself to examine carefully, and I believe that I have discovered some very simple yet unsuspected principles that make sense of all these varieties in such a way that I so far know of no experiment that doesn't fit them very naturally.

I had observed that light bodies were not ordinarily repelled by the tube except when some body of a fairly considerable volume approached them, and this made me think that these bodies were rendered electric by the approach of the tube, and that they then attracted in their turn the down, or the gold leaf, and thus it was always attracted, whether by the tube or by neighbouring bodies, but that there was never real repulsion.

An experiment to which M. Reaumur[3] directed me opposed this explication; it consists of putting on the edge of a card a small heap of powder used to put on writing,[4] this heap of powder is approached by an electrified stick made of Spanish wax, and one sees very clearly that it chases the particles of powder from the card, with no suspicion that they were attracted by another neighbouring body.

Another experiment, just as simple and even more evident, succeeded in showing to me that my conjecture was false. If some pieces of gold leaf are put on a mirror, and the tube is approached from below, the pieces of leaf are driven upwards without falling back on the mirror, and this movement certainly cannot be explained by the attraction of some other neighbouring body. The same thing happens through coloured gauze and other bodies

---

3   French natural philosopher and naturalist; inventor of the Réaumur temperature scale.
4   That is, powder to sprinkle on a page to dry wet ink.

that allow the electric flow to pass through, in such a way that it cannot be doubted that there was no real repulsion in the action of electric bodies.

Finally, having reflected on how bodies less electric in themselves are attracted more vigorously than the rest, I thought that the electric body perhaps attracted all those that are not at all [electric], and repelled all those that have become electric by their approach, and by the communication of their virtue.

Otto von Guericke reports an experiment that I have cited in my first memoir, but to which I had not been able to return; it consists of leading a feather into a room by means of an electrified sulphur ball, without the feather approaching the ball: the small success that I had had, stemming either from the experiment not having been adequately described, or from my not having understood well. Hauksbee also speaks of this experiment, which he made with a glass tube; it's in this way that I have succeeded, and it will be seen that it is sufficiently singular as to make it worth giving some attention to.

The tube is given a good rub to make it electric, and the tube being placed horizontally, a scrap of gold foil is let fall; this foil usually goes edge on, if the tube is well electrified, because in this way it cuts the air more easily, and as soon as it has touched the tube, it is repelled perpendicularly upwards to a distance of eight or ten inches, it remains almost immobile in this position, and if one approaches it with the tube during the elevation, it rises also in such a way that it maintains itself always at the same distance, and such that it is impossible to touch it: it can be led wherever one wishes, because it will always flee the tube.

If the experiment is made to last five or six minutes, the foil will insensibly approach the tube, and finally it will fall down, but as soon as it touches it, it will move away from it with renewed force, and will continue the same game as much as when the tube retains all its electricity. It should be observed that the extent of the electric vortex can be judged by the distance by which the foil holds itself distant from the tube, and that conducting the foil about all parts of the tube, whether in turning it on its axis or in putting it in a vertical position, one can shape the image of the limits of the vortex, or rather that of the layer of the vortex that has sufficient force to resist the weight of the foil, for, if very small fragments of it are taken, it is seen that they support themselves at a much greater distance than the others.

17

ELECTRICITY: BALANCING
THE BOOKS

———⊃⊙○⊙⊂———

Benjamin Franklin's work on electricity was epochal. He invented the concepts of positive and negative electricity, and the associated idea of electrical charge, and he did this in connection with exemplary experiments. The idea of electrical charges and their equilibration in discharge set the stage for Franklin's later identification, in the 1750s, of lightning with electrical discharge of just the sort seen in experimental set-ups. This balancing of the electrical books played a central role in his grand theorising about electricity, the atmosphere, and the earth as part of a system governing global meteorological phenomena.

Source: Benjamin Franklin, letter to Peter Collinson about Philadelphia experiments. From Collinson's *Experiments and Observations on Electricity* (1751), Letter II (July 11, 1747), pp. 13–16.

We had for some time been of opinion, that the electrical fire was not created by friction, but collected, being really an element diffus'd among, and attracted by other matter, particularly by water and metals. We had even discovered and demonstrated its afflux to the electrical sphere, as well as its efflux, by means of little light windmill wheels made of stiff paper vanes, fixed obliquely and turning freely on fine wire axes. Also by little wheels of the same matter, but formed like water wheels. Of the disposition and application of which wheels, and the various phænomena resulting, I could, if I had time, fill you a sheet. The impossibility of electrising one's self (tho' standing on wax) by rubbing the tube and drawing the fire from it; and the manner of doing it by passing the tube near a person or thing standing on the floor, &c. had also occurred to us some months before Mr *Watson's* ingenious *Sequel*[1] came to hand, and these were some of the new things I intended to

---

1   William Watson was an electrical experimenter in London, a Fellow of the Royal Society, who came up with the notion of the earth as an electrical reservoir.

have communicated to you.—But now I need only mention some particulars not hinted in that piece, with our reasonings thereupon; though perhaps the latter might well enough be spared.

1. A person standing on wax, and rubbing the tube, and another person on wax drawing the fire; they will both of them, (provided they do not stand so as to touch one another) appear to be electrised, to a person standing on the floor; that is, he will perceive a spark on approaching each of them with his knuckle.
2. But if the persons on wax touch one another during the exciting of the tube, neither of them will appear to be electrised.
3. If they touch one another after exciting the tube, and drawing the fire as aforesaid, there will be a stronger spark between them, than was between either of them and the person on the floor.
4. After such strong spark, neither of them discover any electricity.

These appearances we attempt to account for thus: We suppose as aforesaid, that electrical fire is a common element, of which every one of the three persons abovementioned has his equal share, before any operation is begun with the Tube. A, who stands on wax and rubs the tube collects the electrical fire from himself into the glass; and his communication with the common stock being cut off by the wax, his body is not again immediately supply'd. B, (who stands on wax likewise) passing his knuckle along near the tube, receives the fire which was collected by the glass from A; and his communication with the common stock being likewise cut off, he retains the additional quantity received.—To C, standing on the floor, both appear to be electrised: for he having only the middle quantity of electrical fire, receives a spark upon approaching B, who has an over quantity; but gives one to A, who has an under quantity. If A and B approach to touch each other, the spark is stronger, because the difference between them is greater; after such touch there is no spark between either of them and C, because the electrical fire in all is reduced to the original equality. If they touch while electrising, the equality is never destroy'd, the fire only circulating. Hence have arisen some new terms among us: we say, B, (and bodies like circumstanced) is electrised *positively*; A, *negatively*. Or rather, B is electrised *plus*; A, *minus*. And we daily in our experiments electrise bodies *plus* or *minus* as we think proper.—To electrise *plus* or *minus*, no more needs to be known than this, that the parts of the tube or sphere that are rubbed, do, in the instant of the friction attract the electrical fire, and therefore take it from the thing rubbing: the same parts immediately, as the friction upon them ceases, are disposed to give the fire they have received, to any body that has less. Thus you may circulate it, as Mr *Watson* has shewn; you may also accumulate or substract it upon or from any body, as you connect that body with the rubber or with the receiver, the communication with the common stock being cut off. We think that ingenious gentleman was deceived, when he imagined (in his *Sequel*) that the electrical fire came down the wire from the cieling [*sic*] to the gun-barrel, thence to the sphere, and so electrised the machine and the man turning the wheel, *&c*. We suppose it was *driven off*, and not brought on thro' that wire; and that the machine and man, *&c*. were electrised *minus*; *i.e.* had less electrical fire in them than things in common.[2]

2   There was no way of telling which kind of electrification counted as "plus" and which "minus"; in fact, by today's reckoning Franklin got it the wrong way around. Ultimately, this is the reason why we now describe the charge on an electron as negative.

18

HOW TO MAKE SENSE OF
DIVERSITY IN NATURE

⸺◦◦◦⸺

An important practical form of natural knowledge was that of knowing and distinguishing among various types of natural objects: taxonomic knowledge, or classification. Naturalists typically devoted much of their time both to describing the products of nature and to cataloguing them according to their perceived similarities and differences. However, the meaning of such categorisations remained obscure. Associating particular species of plant together in the same category, as a supposedly natural "genus," conveyed little beyond the point that all those species had certain features in common; what those commonalities signified was less clear. A French zoologist, Georges-Louis Leclerc, later ennobled as the comte de Buffon, criticised the rising star of natural history, Carl Linnaeus, for his adherence to this conventional practice, and instead advocated (at least for zoology) a kind of natural history that eschewed elaborate systems of classification in favour of detailed descriptions that focused not only on the physical structure of a particular species' individual members (their morphology), but also on their ways of life. His arguments against the type of classification practiced by Linnaeus cut to the heart of the contemporary naturalist's approaches to nature, and interrogated the kind of knowledge that the naturalist could hope to acquire. Botanical knowledge was not a focus for Buffon as it was for Linnaeus, however: he tended to disregard the advantages of Linnaeus's kind of classification, which amounted to a kind of practical cataloguing system, for botanists concerned with plants and their identification, properties and uses throughout the world. The following extract focuses on integrating natural historical knowledge into natural philosophy more broadly.

Source: Georges-Louis Leclerc, comte de Buffon, *Histoire naturelle*, vol. 1 (1749), trans. Peter Dear, pp. 49–55.

We have said that the faithful recounting and exact description of each thing are the only two objects that one ought initially to propose to oneself in the study of Natural History. The Ancients fulfilled well the first, and are perhaps as much above the Moderns in this first part as the latter are above them in the second; for the Ancients treated very well the history of the life and behavior of animals, of the cultivation and uses of plants, of the properties and employment of minerals, and at the same time they seem to have purposely neglected the description of each thing: it isn't that they were not perfectly capable of doing it, but they apparently disdained to write of things that they regarded as useless, and this way of thinking held for things in general and was not as unreasonable as one might believe, and perhaps they could scarcely think otherwise. First they sought to be brief and only to put in their works essential and useful facts, because they did not have, as we do, the ease of copying books, and of lengthening them with impunity. In the second place, they turned all sciences towards utility, and afforded much less than we do to vain curiosity; everything that wasn't of interest for society, for health, for [technical] arts, was neglected, they related everything to the moral man, and they did not believe that useless things were worthy of their attention; a useless insect whose behavior our observers admire, a plant without medicinal value whose stamens our botanists observe, were only for them an insect or a plant: for example, Book 27 of Pliny's *Reliqua herbarum genera*, where he places together all the plants for which he doesn't make a large category, and which he is content to name by letters of the alphabet, in indicating only some one of their general characters and their medical uses. All of that came from the scant taste that the Ancients had for Physics, or, to speak more exactly (for they had no idea of what we call "particular and experimental Physics"), they did not think that one can draw any advantage from the scrupulous examination and exact description of all the parts of a plant or small animal, and they did not see the relations that that could have with the explication of the phenomena of Nature.[1]

However, this is the most important goal, and one cannot imagine, even today, that in the study of Natural History one should limit oneself solely to making exact descriptions and assuring oneself of particular facts. In truth, and as we have said, it is the essential goal that one ought to propose to oneself at the outset; but one must try to rise up to something greater and still more worthy of our attention, that is, to combine observations, to generalize facts, to arrange them together by the force of analogies, and attempt to arrive at that high degree of knowledge where one can judge that the particular effects depend on more general effects, where we can compare Nature with herself

---

1   *La Physique* meant in Buffon's time the general science of nature, including the study of living things. This more capacious meaning of the word "physics" than we use nowadays corresponds to Aristotle's category *phusis*, which had often been rendered in Latin as *physica* and is the source of the equivalent, more specialized terms in modern English and French.

in her great operations, and whence we can at length open to ourselves ways to perfect the different parts of Physics. A capacious memory, assiduity and attention suffice to arrive at the first goal; but something more is needed here: general views, an eye that takes things in at a glance, and reasoning formed still more by reflection than by study; finally, we need that quality of mind that makes us grasp distant relationships, puts them back together, and forms from them a body of rational ideas, after having appreciated rightly the verisimilitudes and having weighed their probabilities.

It is here where one has need of method to guide the mind, not that of which we have spoken, which only serves to arrange words arbitrarily, but that method which undertakes the very order of things, which guides our reasoning, which illuminates our views, extends them and prevents us from misleading ourselves.

The greatest philosophers have felt the need for this method, and they have even wished to give us principles and essays about it;[2] but some have only left us the history of their thoughts, and others the fantasy of their imagination; and if some have elevated themselves to that high point of Metaphysics from whence can be seen the principles, relations and the totality of the Sciences, no one has on this matter communicated his ideas to us, no one has given us his advice, and the method of conducting well one's mind in the Sciences[3] is still to be found: in place of precepts, examples have been substituted; in place of principles, definitions have been used; in place of avowed facts, arbitrary suppositions.

In this century itself, where the Sciences seem to be carefully cultivated, I believe that it is easy to perceive that Philosophy is neglected, and perhaps more so than in any other century. The arts that people are pleased to call scientific have taken its place; the methods of calculus and geometry, those of botany and natural history, in a word formulas and dictionaries preoccupy almost everyone. People imagine that they know more because of having increased the number of symbolic expressions and learned phrases, and pay no attention to the fact that all these arts are nothing but scaffolding for achieving knowledge [*la science*], and not knowledge itself—scaffolding that should only be used when one can't do without it, and that we should watch to make sure it doesn't let us down when we want to use it for the building.

Truth, that metaphysical being of which everyone believes he has a clear idea, seems to me to confound together so many different objects to which one applies the name, that I am not surprised that one can hardly recognize it. Prejudices and false applications multiply themselves in proportion as our hypotheses have been more learned, more abstract, and more perfected; it is therefore more difficult than ever to recognize what we can know, and to

2 A clear allusion to Descartes.
3 An allusion to the full title of Descartes's *Discours de la méthode* (1637).

distinguish it clearly from what we ought to ignore. The following reflections will serve at least as advice on this important subject.

The word truth only generates a vague idea, it's never had precise definition, and the definition itself taken in a general and absolute sense is only an abstraction which exists solely by virtue of some supposition; in place of seeking to give a definition of truth, let us therefore seek to give an enumeration, let us see at close hand what are commonly called truths, and try to form from them some clear ideas.

There are several species of truths, and mathematical truths are usually put in the first rank; these are however only truths of definition. These definitions certainly incorporate simple, but abstract, postulates,[4] and all truths of this kind are only consequences, but always abstract, composed of these definitions. We have made the postulates, we have combined them in all ways, this body of combinations is the science of mathematics; there is therefore nothing in this science except what we have put there, and the truths that are drawn from it can only be different expressions under which the postulates that we have used present themselves; thus mathematical truths are only exact repetitions of definitions or postulates. The final consequence is only true because it is identical with that which preceded it, where the latter is identical with its own precedent, and so on in turn in returning to the first postulate; and as definitions are the sole principles on which the whole is established, and as they are arbitrary and relative, all the consequences that can be drawn from them are equally arbitrary and relative. What one calls mathematical truths thus reduce to identities of ideas and have no reality; we postulate, we reason on our postulates, we draw consequences from them, we conclude, the conclusion or final consequence is a true proposition relative to our postulate, but this truth isn't any more real that the postulate itself. This is not the place to expound upon the uses of the mathematical sciences, any more than on the abuses that we can make of them; it's enough to have proved that mathematical truths are only truths of definition, or, if you prefer, different expressions of the same thing, and that they are only truths relative to these same definitions that we have made; this is why they have the advantage of always being exact and demonstrative, but abstract, intellectual, and arbitrary.

Physical truths, on the contrary, are not at all arbitrary and are independent of us in the sense of being founded on postulates that we had made. They only rest on facts; a group of similar facts or, if you prefer, a frequent repetition and uninterrupted succession of the same events, form the essence of physical truth: what one calls physical truth is therefore nothing but probability, but a probability so great that it is tantamount to certitude. In Mathematics

---

4   Literally "suppositions," the Latin version of the Greek mathematical term literally translated into English as "postulates."

one postulates, in Physics one posits and establishes; in the former there are definitions, in the latter facts; one goes from definitions to definitions in the abstract sciences, one proceeds from observations to observations in the solid [*réelle*] sciences; in the former one arrives at evidentness, in the latter at certitude. The word "truth" includes both, and consequently corresponds to two different ideas; its signification is vague and composite, and it was not possible therefore to define it generally; it was necessary, as we have done, to distinguish its kinds so as to form a clear idea.

19

BUILDING A NEWTONIAN UNIVERSE

————◦◦◦◦◦————

John Michell was a clergyman and Fellow of the Royal Society whose interest in natural philosophy centred on the stellar heavens.[1] Michell interpreted what he saw with his telescopes in the terms of the then-dominant Newtonian picture of the universe, in which all material bodies, including the distant stars, attracted each other by inverse-square gravitational force—universal gravitation. This was the generally accepted picture by the middle of the eighteenth century, yet no direct evidence could yet be adduced for the existence of gravity among the stars; all direct evidence of gravitating bodies concerned those that could be seen moving within the confines of the solar system and in the vicinity of the earth's surface. Michell attempted to develop empirical evidence for the action of gravity among the stars through creative arguments concerning telescopic evidence that was already known but which had not been analysed in the ways that Michell advocated, as well as through experimental/observational techniques premised on Newtonian theories about the behaviour and nature of light.

Source: John Michell, "On the Means of Discovering the Distance, Magnitude, &c. of the Fixed Stars...," *Philosophical Transactions* 74 (1784), extracts from pp. 51–57.

The Diminution of the velocity of light, in case it should be found to take place in any of the fixed stars, is the principal phænomenon whence it is proposed to discover their distance, &c. Now the means by which we may find what this diminution amounts to, seems to be supplied by the difference which would be occasioned in consequence of it, in the refrangibility of the light, whose velocity should be so diminished. For let us suppose with Sir Isaac Newton (see his *Optics*, prop. vi. paragr. 4 and 5) that the refraction of light

---

1 See now Russell McCormmach, *Weighing the World: The Reverend John Michell of Thornhill* (Dordrecht: Springer, 2012).

is occasioned by a certain force impelling it towards the refracting medium, an hypothesis which perfectly accounts for all the appearances.[2] Upon this hypothesis the velocity of light in any medium, in whatever direction it falls upon it, will always bear a given ratio to the velocity it had before it fell upon it, and the sines of incidence and refraction will, in consequence of this, bear the same ratio to each other with these velocities inversely. Thus, according to this hypothesis, if the sines of the angles of incidence and refraction, when light passes out of air into glass, are in the ratio of 31 to 20, the velocity of light in the glass must be to its velocity in air in the same proportion of 31 to 20. But because the areas, representing the forces generating these velocities, are as the squares of the velocities, see art. 5. and 6. these areas must be to each other as 961 to 400. And if 400 represents the area which corresponds to the force producing the original velocity of light, 561, the difference between 961 and 400, must represent the area corresponding to the additional force, by which the light was accelerated at the surface of the glass.

31. In art. 19. we supposed, by way of example, the velocity of the light of some particular star to be diminished in the ratio of 19 to 20, and it was there observed, that the area representing the remaining force which would be necessary to generate the velocity 19, was therefore properly represented by 361/400dth parts of the area, that should represent the force that would be necessary to generate the whole velocity of light, when undiminished. If then we add 561, the area representing the force by which the light is accelerated at the surface of the glass, to 361, the area representing the force which would have generated the diminished velocity of the star's light, the square root of 922, their sum, will represent the velocity of the light with the diminished velocity, after it has entered the glass. And the square root of 922 being 30,364, the sines of incidence and refraction of such light out of air into glass will consequently be as 30,364 to 19, or what is equal to it, as 31,96[2] to 20 instead of 31 to 20, the ratio of the sines of incidence and refraction, when the light enters the glass with its velocity undiminished.

32. From hence a prism, with a small refracting angle, might perhaps be found to be no very inconvenient instrument for this purpose: for by such a prism, whose refracting angle was of one minute, for instance, the light with its velocity undiminished would be turned out of its way 33", and with the diminished velocity 35",88 [Michell seems to mean 35".88'''] nearly, the difference between which being almost 2".53''', would be the quantity by which the light, whose velocity was diminished, would be turned out of its way more than that whose velocity was undiminished.

---

2   Michell's reasoning, in other words, is based on Newton's assumptions about the material character of light, whereby light rays are interpreted as streams of special particles that respond to applied forces. In particular, Michell himself assumes that these particles are accelerated by gravitational forces.

33. Let us now be supposed to make use of such a Prism to look at two stars, under the same circumstances as the two stars in the example above-mentioned, the central one of which should be large enough to diminish the velocity of its light one twentieth part, whilst the velocity of the light of the other, which was supposed to revolve about it as a satellite, for want of sufficient magnitude in the body from whence it was emitted, should suffer no sensible diminution at all. Placing then the line, in which the two faces of the Prism would intersect each other, at right angles to a line joining the two stars; if the thinner part of the Prism lay towards the same point of the heavens with the central star, whose light would be most turned out of its way, the apparent distance of the stars would be increased 2".53'" and consequently become 3".53'" instead of 1". only, the apparent distance supposed above in art. 21. On the contrary, if the Prism should be turned half way round, and its thinner part lye towards the same point of the heavens with the revolving star, their distance must be diminished by a like quantity, and the central star therefore would appear 1".53'" distant from the other on the opposite side of it, having been removed from its place near three times the whole distance between them.[3]

34. As a Prism might be made use of for this purpose, which should have a much larger refracting angle than that we have proposed, especially if it was constructed in the achromatic way, according to Mr. Dollond's principles,[4] not only such a diminution, as one part in twenty, might be made still more distinguishable; but we might probably be able to discover considerably less diminutions in the velocity of light, as perhaps a hundredth, a two-hundredth, a five-hundredth, or even a thousandth part of the whole, which, according to what has been said above, would be occasioned by spheres, whose diameters should be to that of the sun, provided they were of the same density, in the several proportions nearly of 70, 50, 30, and 22 to 1 respectively.

35. If such a diminution of the velocity of light, as that above supposed, should be found really to take place, in consequence of its gravitation towards the bodies from whence it is emitted, and there should be several of the fixed stars large enough to make it sufficiently sensible, a set of observations upon this subject might probably give us some considerable information with regard to many circumstances of that part of the universe, which is visible

---

3   The hope here is that the double star is not merely an optical double (where the two stars appear very close together in the sky but are in fact at vastly different distances from one another), but are a gravitationally linked binary where the apparently faint-er star is in fact a much smaller (less massive) star than its companion, and will there-fore slow its own emitted light to a much lesser degree than the larger of the two.

4   John Dollond, the eighteenth-century English inventor of achromatic lenses, which reduced the amount of the chromatic aberration in telescope lenses, a smearing of the image resulting from the different degrees of refraction undergone by different colours of light.

to us. The quantity of matter contained in many of the fixed stars might from hence be judged of, with a great degree of probability, within some moderate limits; for though the exact quantity must still depend upon their density, yet we must suppose the density most enormously different from that of the sun, and more so, indeed, than one can easily conceive to take place in fact, to make the error of the supposed quantity of matter very wide of the truth, since the density, as has been shewn above in art. 11. and 12. Which is necessary to produce the same diminution in the velocity of light, emitted from different bodies, is as the square of the quantity of matter contained in those bodies inversely.

36. But though we might possibly from hence form some reasonable guess at the quantity of matter contained in several of the fixed stars; yet, if they have no luminous satellites revolving about them, we shall still be at a loss to form any probable judgment of their distance, unless we had some analogy to go upon for their specific brightness, or had some other means of discovering it; there is, however, a case that may possibly occur, which may tend to throw some light upon this matter.

37. I have shewn in my Enquiry into the probable Parallax, &c. of the Fixed Stars, published in the Philosophical Transactions for the year 1767, the extremely great probability there is, that many of the fixed stars are collected together into groups; and that the Pleiades in particular constitute one of these groups. Now of the stars which we there see collected together, it is highly probable, as I have observed in that paper, that there is not one in a hundred which does not belong to the group itself; and by far the greatest part, therefore, according to the same idea, must lye within a sphære, a great circle of which is of the same size with a circle, which appears to us to include the whole group. If we suppose, therefore, this circle to be about 2°. in diameter, and consequently only about a thirtieth part of the distance at which it is seen, we may conclude, with the highest degree of probability, that by far the greatest part of these stars do not differ in their distances from the sun by more than about one part in thirty, and from thence deduce a sort of scale of the proportion of the light which is produced by different stars of the same group or system in the Pleiades at least; and, by a somewhat probable analogy, we may do the same in other systems likewise. But having yet no means of knowing their real distance, or specific brightness, when compared either with the sun or with one another, we shall still want something more to form a farther judgment from.

38. If, however, it should be found, that amongst the Pleiades, or any other like system, there are some stars that are double, triple, &c. of which one is a larger central body, with one or more satellites revolving about it, and the central body should likewise be found to diminish the velocity of its light; and more especially, if there should be several such instances met with in the same system; we should then begin to have a kind of measure both of the distance of such a system of stars from the earth, and of their mutual

distances from each other. And if several instances of this kind should occur in different groups or systems of stars, we might also, perhaps, begin to form some probable conjectures concerning the specific density and brightness of the stars themselves, especially if there should be found any general analogy between the quantity of the diminution of the light and the distance of the system deduced from it; as, for instance, if those stars, which had the greatest effect in diminishing the velocity of light should in general give a greater distance to the system, when supposed to be of the same density with the sun, we might then naturally conclude from thence, that they are less in bulk, and of greater specific density, than those stars which diminish the velocity of light less, and *vice versa*. In like manner, if the larger stars were to give us in general a greater or less quantity of light in proportion to their bulk, this would give us a kind of analogy, from whence we might perhaps form some judgment of the specific brightness of the stars in general; but, at all adventures, we should have a pretty tolerable measure of the comparative brightness of the sun and those stars, upon which such observations should be made, if the result of them should turn out agreeable to the ideas above explained.

39. Though it is not improbable, that a few years may inform us, that some of the great number of double, triple stars, &c. which have been observed by Mr. Herschel,[5] are systems of bodies revolving about each other, especially if a few more observers, equally ingenious and industrious with himself could be found to second his labors; yet the very great distance at which it is not unlikely many of the secondary stars may be placed from their principals, and the consequently very long periods of their revolutions, leave very little room to hope that any very great progress can be made in this subject for many years, or perhaps for some ages to come; the above outlines, therefore, of the use that may be made of the observations upon the double stars, &c. provided the particles of light should be subject to the same law of gravitation with other bodies, as in all probability they are, and provided also that some of the stars should be large enough sensibly to diminish their velocity, will, I hope, be an inducement to those, who may have it in their power, to make these observations for the benefit of future generations at least, how little advantage soever we may expect from them ourselves; and yet very possibly some observations of this sort, and such as may be made in a few years, may not only be sufficient to do something, even at present, but also to shew, that much more may be done hereafter, when these observations shall become more numerous, and have been continued for a longer period of years.

---

5   William Herschel, maker of reflecting telescopes, the discoverer of the planet Uranus, indefatigable observer along with his sister Caroline Herschel, and great theoriser of the structure of the stellar heavens.

20

CHARLES'S BALLOON ASCENT

———⊃o∘o⊂———

The next extract is the official deposition of Jacques-Alexandre-César Charles concerning his ascent in a hydrogen balloon in 1783, emulating the sensational recent achievements of the provincial Montgolfier brothers, Étienne and Joseph, who had recently put on shows of hot-air balloons that quickly grew to carry human aeronauts. When word of the first Montgolfier demonstration had originally reached Paris, the reports were ambiguous about the kind of air that filled the Montgolfier's balloons; the scientifically literate assumed that it must be the recently identified "inflammable air" (hydrogen) that was known to be lighter than common air. Charles was a Parisian public lecturer in experimental natural philosophy—an exponent of elaborate and sometimes spectacular demonstration apparatus. He engaged the brothers Robert, manufacturers of scientific instruments, to make two hydrogen balloons for him, one with no payload and then one designed to carry human cargo. On the first flight of the latter, Charles, as one of the two initial passengers, attempted a second stage alone to see how high he might reasonably ascend. The following is the original report of his adventure.[1]

Source: Barthélemy Faujas de Saint-Fond, *Première suite de la description des expériences aérostatiques* (Paris, 1784), trans Peter Dear, pp. 44–47.

---

1 For more on early ballooning, see Charles C. Gillispie, *The Montgolfier Brothers and the Invention of Aviation, 1783–1784* (Princeton: Princeton University Press, 1983); Richard Holmes, *The Age of Wonder: How the Romantic Generation Discovered the Beauty and Terror of Science* (New York: Pantheon, 2008), Chap. 3; and Mi Gyung Kim, *The Imagined Empire: Balloon Enlightenments in Revolutionary Europe* (Pittsburgh: University of Pittsburgh Press, 2016).

Copy of the statement [*procès-verbal*] written and prepared by M. Charles

"We the undersigned, Charles, Robert, Jean Burgatet, vicar of Nesles, and Charles Philippot, vicar of Fresnoy, Thomas Hutin, perpetual syndic of the said parish, and l'Heureux, vicar of Hédouville, certify that the aerostatic machine descended between Nesles and Hédouville (about nine leagues from Paris) in the meadow of Nesles, at 3:45. In testimony whereof we have signed this statement, written in the aerostatic car by me, Charles." There follow the signatures of the persons named above.

Monseigneur the Duke of Chartres and M. the Duke of Fitz-James, who arrived at the moment of the descent of the machine, honoured the statement with their signature, as did M. Farer, an English gentleman.

The statement being signed, and M. Robert having left the car, which produced a specific lightness of 130 pounds, M. Charles, who hadn't in the least forgotten that the journey that he had announced ought to profit Physics, courageously decided to depart by himself, inasmuch as enthusiasm raised the man above himself, and by itself produced great things.

The persons who held the car released it at an arranged signal, and the balloon rose with such speed that in ten minutes it was carried more than 1500 toises[2] according to M. Charles, who could no longer make out terrestrial objects from that height. "I saw no more," he said, "than the great masses of nature."

The sudden passage from temperate air to frigid air wasn't at all intolerable for the intrepid observer; and the effervescence that then animated him, far from being weakened by a cold that forced the mercury to drop to five degrees above freezing, did nothing but increase, and gave way to sensations of a new kind, expressed in a manner as energetic as it was new, in a discourse read publicly several days afterwards, which earned him many admirers, and which we would be justly reproached for passing by here in silence.

"The cold was keen and dry, but not at all insupportable: I interrogated placidly all my sensations; I heard myself living, as it were, and I can affirm that in the first moment, I experienced nothing disagreeable in this sudden traversal of pressure and temperature...I lay in the middle of the car, and abandoned myself to the spectacle afforded me by the immensity of the horizon. At my departure from the meadow, the sun was set for the inhabitants of the valleys. Soon it rose for me alone, and came once more to make golden with its rays the balloon and the car; I was the only illuminated body in the horizon, and I saw all the rest of nature plunged in shadow. In the midst of an inexpressible ravishment, and in this contemplative ecstasy, I was recalled to myself by a very extraordinary distress that I felt in my right ear

---

2 A *toise* was an Old Régime unit of length equal to about two yards.

and in the maxillary glands; I attributed it to the dilation of air contained in the cellular tissue of the organism, as much as to the cold of the surrounding air, &c."

Finally, M. Charles, perceiving at this great height that there were seven or eight minutes during which he had not risen, that he even began to descend, "by the condensation of the interior inflammable air,"[3] and recalling the promise that he had made to M. the Duke of Chartres to return to earth at the end of a half-hour, accelerated his descent, in opening from time to time the upper valve, and "came to descend gently onto the very wasteland that he had, so to speak, chosen," near the woods of the *Tour du Lay*, having made in thirty-five minutes a trip that can be reckoned at more than three leagues, owing to the frequent deviations that the balloon underwent in the air.

Thus ended this celebrated journey, which will long be an honour to the courage and talents of M. Charles and of MM. Robert who have played such a part in this experiment. The modesty of these latter [i.e. the brothers Robert], who constructed the machine with all the precision, taste, and intelligence possible, has prevented them from giving their own memoir, which will certainly be done with as much consideration as wisdom: they cannot be exhorted too much, in the name of true savants, to publish their observations, which will surely be received with as much interest as recognition.

---

3   That is, the hydrogen in the balloon.

21

LAVOISIER'S WORK ON WATER

Lavoisier's famous "chemical revolution" proclaimed its character as being rooted in experience, and especially in analysis and synthesis as a way of coordinating that experience. Perhaps the classic instance of his approach is that concerning the compound character of water, previously taken to be a simple elementary constituent of the material world.

Source: Antoine Lavoisier, "Sur la formation et la decomposition de l'eau" ("On the Formation and Decomposition of Water"), *Histoire de l'Académie Royale des Sciences, 1781* (Paris, 1784), trans. Peter Dear, pp. 21–25.

An experiment made by M. Macquer in 1776, and which he reports in his *Dictionary*, could create the suspicion that water forms in the combustion of inflammable air[1] with common air.

In the month of June 1783, M. Lavoisier, who, following views based on a theory already confirmed by many experiments, had prepared an apparatus for burning in closed vessels inflammable air with vital air,[2] found that there resulted from this combustion a liquid that was nothing but very pure water, the weight of which was detectably equal to that of the two airs employed. Now, he learned that M. Cavendish had produced water by the same operation, and shortly afterwards, M. Monge, then at Mézières, had, in using another apparatus, made the same experiment on a larger scale, and had derived from it the same result, but in a still more precise, and consequently more certain, manner. This experiment proves that in the combustion of inflammable air and vital air, there forms a quantity of water equal to the weight of these airs considered in a pure state, since the small quantity of air of a different nature that afterwards remains completes what's lacking in the weight of the water.

---

1   Now called hydrogen.
2   That is, the kind of air that supports life, soon to be dubbed "oxygen."

Nothing is lost in this experiment but the light and heat that escape through the vessel.

It was natural to conclude from this experiment that it would be possible to decompose water, and to separate the inflammable air from the vital air.

Several experiments seemed to suggest it, and particularly that by which a mixture of iron filings and a little water, placed under a bell jar and over mercury by M. Lavoisier had produced a considerable quantity of inflammable air. Indeed, the weight of the iron filings was increased in this experiment, that of the water was diminished; and in putting it alongside the previous experiment, it was difficult not to conclude from it that the water was decomposed and that it had produced this obtained inflammable air separated, inasmuch as the vital air had united itself to the iron. However, every day there appeared new proofs of this composition of water. M. Priestley had rephlogisticated[3] metallic calxes by putting them in bell jars full of inflammable air, and placed over water, and in exposing them to the fire of a burning mirror. In this experiment the metals had lost weight, the inflammable air had disappeared, the vital air that made up part of the metallic calxes had thus united with this inflammable air and had produced water. M. Priestley had also revivified metallic calxes in aeriform volatile alkali,[4] and M. Lavoisier observed that it then formed a liquid the nature of which he proposed to examine, and on which he had already made a large number of experiments. The revivification also occurred, although in an incomplete manner, in aeriform sulphurous acid. The more these experiments multiplied, the more it became plausible that water was not a simple substance, and the hopes of decomposing it gained greater force.

It was in these circumstances that the discovery of aerostatic machines came to open a new field to physicists [*Physiciens*].[5] It became important to be able to produce easily and cheaply a large quantity of inflammable air, MM. Lavoisier and Meusnier thinking to try deriving it from water: to do so, they

---

3 The English chemist and political radical Joseph Priestley had worked on combustion with an understanding, at this time shared by most chemists, that the physical process of combustion involved the release from the burning substance of a material called "phlogiston." "Rephlogisticating" metallic calxes meant, in the terms soon to be developed by Lavoisier, reducing the oxide of a metal back to its original metal, a process here understood in terms of adding phlogiston back to the calx in order to reconstitute the calx's metal. Metals were thus understood by Priestley as composed of a metallic calx plus phlogiston.

4 Again, a reduction reaction.

5 Referring to the advent in 1783 of flying machines in the form of hot-air balloons (the Mongolfier brothers) and hydrogen balloons (J.-A.-C. Charles), a spectacular French innovation that quickly swept Europe (see Charles extract, Chapter 20). Note also that the English term "physicist" actually dates from the 1840s; the earlier French term *physicien* meant, more generally, a natural philosopher or student of the physical world.

made water fall drop by drop into an iron tube plunged in coals burning in such a manner as to remain constantly red, a flexible tube was attached at the other end, a jar received the water that escaped from this ordeal, and a tube conducted the generated aeriform fluid into an apparatus suitable for receiving it: by this means, a very great quantity of inflammable air was produced most promptly. The interior of the cannon [i.e. the iron tube] calcined [nowadays: oxidized] and became coated with a substance black, shining, unmalleable, and which, if it was reduced to a powder, looked like genuine "martial ethiops."[6] This experiment, although made on a very large scale, still failed to satisfy M. Lavoisier. It was necessary to know the weight of water that had escaped the decomposition, that of the inflammable air, and finally the increase in weight of the iron cannon, and the sum of these weights combined had to prove equal to the weight of the water used: but the outside part of the iron cannon could have been partially calcined, at least it could have been suspected, and in experiments meant, like these, to establish important facts, and to confirm new theories, one couldn't take too many precautions as far as the smallest preparations taken with so much eagerness. However, MM. Lavoisier and Meusnier tried to extract inflammable air from water, in plunging into it different bodies while ignited, and they found that among the metals zinc alone had, like iron, the property of disengaging inflammable air. Thus, in using a copper tube in place of an iron tube, and in putting in this tube precisely weighed bits of iron, one can determine the increase in weight that the iron acquired from the union with vital air: also, in repeating the experiment under this new form, M. Lavoisier found the equality that ought to occur between the weight of the inflammable air added to the increase of weight of the iron, and that of the decomposed water.

This theory of the decomposition of water explains several important phenomena. For example, experiment has proven that water alone suffices for the nutrition of plants; now, plants are combustible; moreover, we know from M. Ingenhouz's experiments that plants exhale an abundant quantity of vital air. Ought one not to conclude from this that the water by which they are nourished decomposes in [the process of] vegetation, and that the vital air that takes part in it disengages itself, inasmuch as the inflammable air unites itself with the vegetal, and serves in the formation of inflammable substances that form part of it?

Spirituous fermentation is another phenomenon where this decomposition can equally be observed. If spirit of wine is burned in an apparatus proper to collect the vapours disengaged from it, a quantity of pure water is obtained superior in weight to the portion of spirit of wine used up; this water is produced by the union of the vital air that serves for the combustion, with the

---

6   A particular calcined form of iron, now represented as Fe_3O_4, here referred to by its traditional alchemical name.

inflammable air furnished by the spirit of wine. It can therefore be supposed that, in the spirituous fermentation of a dissolving of sugar in water, for example, the vital air combining with the carbonic part of the sugar forms chalky or aeriform carbonic acid [now called carbon dioxide], which separates itself with such abundance in this fermentation, whereas inflammable air combined with this same portion form spirit of wine: indeed, the spirit of wine, in burning, and in consequence combining with the vital air, produces aeriform carbonic acid, proof that it contains the same substance that, in carbon, contributes to the formation of this acid.

The theory that M. Lavoisier has published on the formation and decomposition of water has not been generally adopted by chemists, and yet it can be said that few simpler and more conclusive chemical theories are applied to experiments. It cannot be denied that inflammable air and vital air do not give water, that water doesn't produce inflammable air and vital air: as it hasn't been neglected in this experiment that the light and heat that are either combined with the water or separated from aeriform substances by combustion, one must either recognize that water is formed by these two fluids, less the quantity of light and heat, which made of it perhaps one of the constituent parts, or that each of these fluids is only water combined with light and heat, in two different manners. Hitherto, no direct experiment destroyed or confirmed either of these two opinions, it seems that one ought to lean towards that of that two which seems the most natural, the simplest, and then ought not all the advantage be for that of M. Lavoisier?

Until these recent times it was supposed in chemistry that a body that one saw formed by the uniting of two substances, was a combination of them; it was regarded as a compound [un mixte] of which these two substances were the immediate elements: the new experiments have made this principle, so simple in itself, appear subject to some exceptions, the contrary principle which is a consequence of it, has been equally shaken; and chemistry could be compared, in its current situation, to those States which have never been closer to obtaining a good constitution, while they appear, by their internal dissensions, menaced by a dreadful reversal.

22

MAKING CHEMISTRY RATIONAL

Lavoisier presented his ideology of chemistry in his famous book *Traité élémentaire de chimie*, first published in French in 1789, by prefacing its practical chemical content, organised around apparatus and manipulative procedures, with remarks that integrated that content with a characteristically Enlightenment philosophy of empiricism. Chemical procedures were at the heart of many practical endeavours in the eighteenth century, such as dyeing, metallurgy, tanning, and the production of various pharmaceuticals. The importance of practical chemistry inevitably reflected on its theoretical understanding: Lavoisier wanted to be the vanguard of a "revolution" in chemistry that would restructure its basic concepts and its basic ingredients, and the practical importance of chemistry would guarantee the significance of that revolution. Lavoisier stressed the way in which sensory experience was the true source of our knowledge of the world, and how this knowledge was compiled in language. A well-formed language of chemistry would provide not only a useful catalogue of chemical substances, but also a means of construing chemical processes and possibilities through the correct use of its appropriate grammar. Any activity that employed chemical procedures would be subject to the discipline of Lavoisier's chemistry. And French chemistry would become the world's standard.

Source: Antoine Lavoisier, Preface to *Elements of Chemistry,* trans. Robert Kerr (Edinburgh, 1790), pp. xiii–xxxvii.

PREFACE OF THE AUTHOR.

When I began the following Work, my only object was to extend and explain more fully the Memoir which I read at the public meeting of the Academy of Sciences in the month of April 1787, on the necessity of reforming and completing the Nomenclature of Chemistry. While engaged in this employment, I perceived, better than I had ever done before, the justice of the following maxims of the Abbé de Condillac, in his System of Logic, and some other of his works.[1]

"We think only through the medium of words.—Languages are true analytical methods.—Algebra, which is adapted to its purpose in every species of expression, in the most simple, most exact, and best manner possible, is at the same time a language and an analytical method.—The art of reasoning is nothing more than a language well arranged."

Thus, while I thought myself employed only in forming a Nomenclature, and while I proposed to myself nothing more than to improve the chemical language, my work transformed itself by degrees, without my being able to prevent it, into a treatise upon the Elements of Chemistry.

The impossibility of separating the nomenclature of a science from the science itself, is owing to this, that every branch of physical science must consist of three things; the series of facts which are the objects of the science, the ideas which represent these facts, and the words by which these ideas are expressed. Like three impressions of the same seal, the word ought to produce the idea, and the idea to be a picture of the fact. And, as ideas are preserved and communicated by means of words, it necessarily follows that we cannot improve the language of any science without at the same time improving the science itself; neither can we, on the other hand, improve a science, without improving the language or nomenclature which belongs to it. However certain the facts of any science may be, and, however just the ideas we may have formed of these facts, we can only communicate false impressions to others, while we want words by which these may be properly expressed.[2]

To those who will consider it with attention, the first part of this treatise will afford frequent proofs of the truth of the above observations. But as, in the conduct of my work, I have been obliged to observe an order of arrangement essentially differing from what has been adopted in any other chemical work yet published, it is proper that I should explain the motives which have led me to do so.

It is a maxim universally admitted in geometry, and indeed in every branch of knowledge, that, in the progress of investigation, we should proceed from

1   Étienne Bonnot, Abbé de Condillac (1714–1780), was one of the most celebrated of the so-called *philosophes* of eighteenth-century France. The *philosophes* counted themselves adherents of the Englishmen Isaac Newton and John Locke, in that they stressed the primacy of the senses in providing the raw material by which knowledge of all kinds, but especially that of the natural world, was constructed by the human mind. Condillac in particular was concerned with the construction of language as the medium by which such foundational sensory data was managed.

2   Hence for Lavoisier, following Condillac, only when knowledge is communicated through a properly constructed language can it become an effective tool for collective belief and, more crucially, collective action; knowledge on this view is necessarily social.

known facts to what is unknown. In early infancy, our ideas spring from our wants; the sensation of want excites the idea of the object by which it is to be gratified. In this manner, from a series of sensations, observations, and analyses, a successive train of ideas arises, so linked together, that an attentive observer may trace back to a certain point the order and connection of the whole sum of human knowledge.

When we begin the study of any science, we are in a situation, respecting that science, similar to that of children; and the course by which we have to advance is precisely the same which Nature follows in the formation of their ideas. In a child, the idea is merely an effect produced by a sensation; and, in the same manner, in commencing the study of a physical science, we ought to form no idea but what is a necessary consequence, and immediate effect, of an experiment or observation. Besides, he that enters upon the career of science, is in a less advantageous situation than a child who is acquiring his first ideas. To the child, Nature gives various means of rectifying any mistakes he may commit respecting the salutary or hurtful qualities of the objects which surround him. On every occasion his judgments are corrected by experience; want and pain are the necessary consequences arising from false judgment; gratification and pleasure are produced by judging aright. Under such masters, we cannot fail to become well informed; and we soon learn to reason justly, when want and pain are the necessary consequences of a contrary conduct.

In the study and practice of the sciences it is quite different; the false judgments we form neither affect our existence nor our welfare; and we are not forced by any physical necessity to correct them. Imagination, on the contrary, which is ever wandering beyond the bounds of truth, joined to self-love and that self-confidence we are so apt to indulge, prompt us to draw conclusions which are not immediately derived from facts; so that we become in some measure interested in deceiving ourselves. Hence it is by no means to be wondered, that, in the science of physics in general [i.e. the physical sciences, including chemistry], men have often made suppositions, instead of forming conclusions. These suppositions, handed down from one age to another, acquire additional weight from the authorities by which they are supported, till at last they are received, even by men of genius, as fundamental truths.[3]

The only method of preventing such errors from taking place, and of correcting them when formed, is to restrain and simplify our reasoning as much as possible. This depends entirely upon ourselves, and the neglect of

---

3　This idea that older ideas, especially those inherited from classical antiquity, were wrongly believed on the grounds of the mere authority of those who had held them, was a standard complaint by innovators in the sciences throughout the eighteenth and nineteenth centuries.

it is the only source of our mistakes. We must trust to nothing but facts: These are presented to us by Nature, and cannot deceive. We ought, in every instance, to submit our reasoning to the test of experiment, and never to search for truth but by the natural road of experiment and observation. Thus mathematicians obtain the solution of a problem by the mere arrangement of data, and by reducing their reasoning to such simple steps, to conclusions so very obvious, as never to lose sight of the evidence which guides them.[4]

Thoroughly convinced of these truths, I have imposed upon myself, as a law, never to advance but from what is known to what is unknown; never to form any conclusion which is not an immediate consequence necessarily flowing from observation and experiment; and always to arrange the facts, and the conclusions which are drawn from them, in such an order as shall render it most easy for beginners in the study of chemistry thoroughly to understand them. Hence I have been obliged to depart from the usual order of courses of lectures and of treatises upon chemistry, which always assume the first principles of the science, as known, when the pupil or the reader should never be supposed to know them till they have been explained in subsequent lessons. In almost every instance, these begin by treating of the elements of matter, and by explaining the table of affinities, without considering, that, in so doing, they must bring the principal phenomena of chemistry into view at the very outset: They make use of terms which have not been defined, and suppose the science to be understood by the very persons they are only beginning to teach. It ought likewise to be considered, that very little of chemistry can be learned in a first course, which is hardly sufficient to make the language of the science familiar to the ears, or the apparatus familiar to the eyes. It is almost impossible to become a chemist in less than three or four years of constant application.

These inconveniencies are occasioned not so much by the nature of the subject, as by the method of teaching it; and, to avoid them, I was chiefly induced to adopt a new arrangement of chemistry, which appeared to me more consonant to the order of Nature. I acknowledge, however, that in thus endeavouring to avoid difficulties of one kind, I have found myself involved in others of a different species, some of which I have not been able to remove; but I am persuaded, that such as remain do not arise from the nature of the order I have adopted, but are rather consequences of the imperfection under which chemistry still labours. This science still has many chasms, which interrupt the series of facts, and often render it extremely difficult to reconcile them with each other: It has not, like the elements of geometry,

---

4   Much energy has been expended by philosophers over the past century and more
     in showing how hard it is to establish such unequivocal "facts" in the sciences. The
     project was, however, regarded as entirely feasible by many in the eighteenth and
     nineteenth centuries.

the advantage of being a complete science, the parts of which are all closely connected together: Its actual progress, however, is so rapid, and the facts, under the modern doctrine, have assumed so happy an arrangement, that we have ground to hope, even in our own times, to see it approach near to the highest state of perfection of which it is susceptible.

The rigorous law from which I have never deviated, of forming no conclusions which are not fully warranted by experiment, and of never supplying the absence of facts, has prevented me from comprehending in this work the branch of chemistry which treats of affinities, although it is perhaps the best calculated of any part of chemistry for being reduced into a completely systematic body. Messrs Geoffroy, Gellert, Bergman, Scheele, De Morveau, Kirwan, and many others, have collected a number of particular facts upon this subject, which only wait for a proper arrangement; but the principal data are still wanting, or, at least, those we have are either not sufficiently defined, or not sufficiently proved, to become the foundation upon which to build so very important a branch of chemistry. This science of affinities, or elective attractions, holds the same place with regard to the other branches of chemistry, as the higher or transcendental geometry does with respect to the simpler and elementary part; and I thought it improper to involve those simple and plain elements, which I flatter myself the greatest part of my readers will easily understand, in the obscurities and difficulties which still attend that other very useful and necessary branch of chemical science.

Perhaps a sentiment of self-love may, without my perceiving it, have given additional force to these reflections. Mr. de Morveau is at present engaged in publishing the article Affinity in the Methodical Encyclopædia; and I had more reasons than one to decline entering upon a work in which he is employed.[5]

It will, no doubt, be a matter of surprise, that in a treatise upon the elements of chemistry, there should be no chapter on the constituent and elementary parts of matter; but I shall take occasion, in this place, to remark, that the fondness for reducing all the bodies in nature to three or four elements, proceeds from a prejudice which has descended to us from the Greek Philosophers. The notion of four elements, which, by the variety of their proportions, compose all the known substances in nature, is a mere hypothesis, assumed long before the first principles of experimental philosophy or of chemistry had any existence. In those days, without possessing facts, they framed systems; while we, who have collected facts, seem determined to reject them, when they do not agree with our prejudices. The authority of these fathers of human philosophy still

---

5   The *Encyclopédie méthodique* was a massive and successful competitor of the celebrated *Encyclopédie* of Diderot and D'Alembert.

carry great weight, and there is reason to fear that it will even bear hard upon generations yet to come.

It is very remarkable, that, notwithstanding of the number of philosophical chemists who have supported the doctrine of the four elements, there is not one who has not been led by the evidence of facts to admit a greater number of elements into their theory. The first chemists that wrote after the revival of letters, considered sulphur and salt as elementary substances entering into the composition of a great number of substances; hence, instead of four, they admitted the existence of six elements. Beccher assumes the existence of three kinds of earth, from the combination of which, in different proportions, he supposed all the varieties of metallic substances to be produced. Stahl gave a new modification to this system; and succeeding chemists have taken the liberty to make or to imagine changes and additions of a similar nature. All these chemists were carried along by the influence of the genius of the age in which they lived, which contented itself with assertions without proofs; or, at least, often admitted as proofs the slighted degrees of probability, unsupported by that strictly rigorous analysis required by modern philosophy.

All that can be said upon the number and nature of elements is, in my opinion, confined to discussions entirely of a metaphysical nature. The subject only furnishes us with indefinite problems, which may be solved in a thousand different ways, not one of which, in all probability, is consistent with nature. I shall therefore only add upon this subject, that if, by the term elements, we mean to express those simple and indivisible atoms of which matter is composed, it is extremely probable we know nothing at all about them; but, if we apply the term elements, or principles of bodies, to express our idea of the last point which analysis is capable of reaching, we must admit, as elements, all the substances into which we are capable, by any means, to reduce bodies by decomposition. Not that we are entitled to affirm, that these substances we consider as simple may not be compounded of two, or even of a greater number of principles; but, since these principles cannot be separated, or rather since we have not hitherto discovered the means of separating them, they act with regard to us as simple substances, and we ought never to suppose them compounded until experiment and observation has proved them to be so.

The foregoing reflections upon the progress of chemical ideas naturally apply to the words by which these ideas are to be expressed. Guided by the work which, in the year 1787, Messrs de Morveau, Berthollet, de Fourcroy, and I composed upon the Nomenclature of Chemistry, I have endeavoured, as much as possible, to denominate simple bodies by simple terms, and I was naturally led to name these first. It will be recollected, that we were obliged to retain that name of any substance by which it had been long known in the world, and that in two cases only we took the liberty of making alterations; first, in the case of those which were but newly discovered, and had not yet obtained names, or at least which had been known but for a short time, and the names of which had not yet received the sanction of the public; and, secondly, when the names which had been adopted, whether by the ancients or the moderns, appeared to us to express evidently false ideas, when they confounded the substances, to which they were applied, with others possessed of different, or perhaps opposite qualities. We made no scruple, in this case, of substituting other names in their room, and the greatest number of these were borrowed from the Greek language. We endeavoured to frame them in such a manner as to express the most general and the most characteristic quality of the substances; and this was attended with the additional advantage both of assisting the memory of beginners, who find it difficult to remember a new word which has no meaning, and of accustoming them early to admit no word without connecting with it some determinate idea.

To those bodies which are formed by the union of several simple substances we gave new names, compounded in such a manner as the nature of the substances directed; but, as the number of double combinations is already very considerable, the only method by which we could avoid confusion, was to divide them into classes. In the natural order of ideas, the name of the class or genus is that which expresses a quality common to a great number of individuals: The name of the species, on the contrary, expresses a quality peculiar to certain individuals only.

These distinctions are not, as some may imagine, merely metaphysical, but are established by Nature. "A child," says the Abbé de Condillac, "is taught to give the name tree to the first one which is pointed out to him. The next one he sees presents the same idea, and he gives it the same name. This he does likewise to a third and a fourth, till at last the word tree, which he first applied to an individual, comes to be employed by him as the name of a class or a genus, an abstract idea, which comprehends all trees in general. But, when he learns that all trees serve not the same purpose, that they do not all produce the same kind of fruit, he will soon learn to distinguish them by specific and particular names." This is the logic of all the sciences, and is naturally applied to chemistry.

The acids, for example, are compounded of two substances, of the order of those which we consider as simple; the one constitutes acidity, and is common to all acids, and, from this substance, the name of the class or the genus ought to be taken; the other is peculiar to each acid, and distinguishes it from the rest, and from this substance is to be taken the name of the species. But, in the greatest number of acids, the two constituent elements, the acidifying principle, and that which it acidifies, may exist in different proportions, constituting all the possible points of equilibrium or of saturation. This is the case in the sulphuric and the sulphurous acids; and these two states of the same acid we have marked by varying the termination of the specific name.

Metallic substances which have been exposed to the joint action of the air and of fire, lose their metallic lustre, increase in weight, and assume an earthy appearance. In this state, like the acids, they are compounded of a principle which is common to all, and one which is peculiar to each. In the same way, therefore, we have thought proper to class them under a generic name, derived from the common principle; for which purpose, we adopted the term oxyd; and we distinguish them from each other by the particular name of the metal to which each belongs.

Combustible substances, which in acids and metallic oxyds are a specific and particular principle, are capable of becoming, in their turn, common principles of a great number of substances. The sulphurous combinations have been long the only known ones in this kind. Now, however, we know, from the experiments of Messrs Vandermonde, Monge, and Berthollet, that charcoal may be combined with iron, and perhaps with several other metals; and that, from this combination, according to the proportions, may be produced steel, plumbago, &c. We know likewise, from the experiments of M. Pelletier, that phosphorus may be combined with a great number of metallic substances. These different combinations we have classed under generic names taken from the common substance, with a termination which marks this analogy, specifying them by another name taken from that substance which is proper to each.

The nomenclature of bodies compounded of three simple substances was attended with still greater difficulty, not only on account of their number, but, particularly, because we cannot express the nature of their constituent principles without employing more compound names. In the bodies which form this class, such as the neutral salts, for instance, we had to consider, 1st, The acidifying principle, which is common to them all; 2d, The acidifiable principle which constitutes their peculiar acid; 3d, The saline, earthy, or metallic basis, which determines the particular species of salt. Here we derived the name of each class of salts from the name of the acidifiable principle common to all the individuals of that class; and distinguished each species by the name of the saline, earthy, or metallic basis, which is peculiar to it.

A salt, though compounded of the same three principles, may, nevertheless, by the mere difference of their proportion, be in three different states. The nomenclature we have adopted would have been defective, had it not expressed these different states; and this we attained chiefly by changes of termination uniformly applied to the same state of the different salts.

In short, we have advanced so far, that from the name alone may be instantly found what the combustible substance is which enters into any combination; whether that combustible substance be combined with the acidifying principle, and in what proportion; what is the state of the acid; with what basis it is united; whether the saturation be exact, or whether the acid or the basis be in excess. It may be easily supposed that it was not possible to attain all these different objects without departing, in some

143

instances, from established custom, and adopting terms which at first sight will appear uncouth and barbarous. But we considered that the ear is soon habituated to new words, especially when they are connected with a general and rational system.[6] The names, besides, which were formerly employed, such as powder of algaroth, salt of alembroth, pompholix, phagadenic water, turbith mineral, colcathar, and many others, were neither less barbarous nor less uncommon. It required a great deal of practice, and no small degree of memory, to recollect the substances to which they were applied, much more to recollect the genus of combination to which they belonged. The names of oil of tartar per deliquium, oil of vitriol, butter of arsenic and of antimony, flowers of zinc, &c. were still more improper, because they suggested false ideas: For, in the whole mineral kingdom, and particularly in the metallic class, there exists no such thing as butters, oils, or flowers; and, in short, the substances to which they give these fallacious names, are nothing less than rank poisons.

When we published our essay on the nomenclature of chemistry, we were reproached for having changed the language which was spoken by our masters, which they distinguished by their authority, and handed down to us. But those who reproach us on this account, have forgotten that it was Bergman and Macquer themselves who urged us to make this reformation. In a letter which the learned Professor of Upsal [Uppsala], M. Bergman,[7] wrote, a short time before he died, to M. de Morveau, he bids him *spare no improper names; those who are learned, will always be learned, and those who are ignorant will thus learn sooner*.

There is an objection to the work which I am going to present to the public, which is perhaps better founded, that I have given no account of the opinion of those who have gone before me; that I have stated only my own opinion, without examining that of others. By this I have been prevented from doing that justice to my associates, and more especially to foreign chemists, which I wished to render them. But I beseech the reader to consider, that, if I had filled an elementary work with a multitude of quotations; if I had allowed myself to enter into long dissertations on the history of the science, and the works of those who have studied it, I must have lost sight of the true object I had in view, and produced a work, the reading of which must have been extremely tiresome to beginners. It is not to the history of the science, or of the human mind, that we are to attend in an elementary treatise: Our

---

6   There were chemists who resented the new nomenclature because they thought that by its means Lavoisier was smuggling in his own theoretical ideas under the guise of a positivistic digest of solid chemical experience. See Jan Golinski, *Science as Public Culture: Chemistry and Enlightenment in Britain, 1760–1820* (Cambridge: Cambridge University Press, 1992), Chap. 5, which also shows British distrust of Lavoisier's precise quantitative measurements.

7   Torbern Bergman (1735–1784) was a chemist at the University of Uppsala in Sweden.

only aim ought to be ease and perspicuity, and with the utmost care to keep every thing out of view which might draw aside the attention of the student; it is a road which we should be continually rendering more smooth, and from which we should endeavour to remove every obstacle which can occasion delay. The sciences, from their own nature, present a sufficient number of difficulties, though we add not those which are foreign to them. But, besides this, chemists will easily perceive, that, in the first part of my work, I make very little use of any experiments but those which were made by myself: If at any time I have adopted, without acknowledgment, the experiments or the opinions of M. Berthollet, M. Fourcroy, M. de la Place, M. Monge, or, in general, of any of those whose principles are the same with my own, it is owing to this circumstance, that frequent intercourse, and the habit of communicating our ideas, our observations, and our way of thinking to each other, has established between us a sort of community of opinions, in which it is often difficult for every one to know his own.

The remarks I have made on the order which I thought myself obliged to follow in the arrangement of proofs and ideas, are to be applied only to the first part of this work. It is the only one which contains the general sum of the doctrine I have adopted, and to which I wished to give a form completely elementary.

The second part is composed chiefly of tables of the nomenclature of the neutral salts. To these I have only added general explanations, the object of which was to point out the most simple processes for obtaining the different kinds of known acids. This part contains nothing which I can call my own, and presents only a very short abridgment of the results of these processes, extracted from the works of different authors.

In the third part, I have given a description, in detail, of all the operations connected with modern chemistry. I have long thought that a work of this kind was much wanted, and I am convinced it will not be without use. The method of performing experiments, and particularly those of modern chemistry, is not so generally known as it ought to be; and had I, in the different memoirs which I have presented to the Academy, been more particular in the detail of the manipulations of my experiments, it is probable I should have made myself better understood, and the science might have made a more rapid progress. The order of the different matters contained in this third part appeared to me to be almost arbitrary; and the only one I have observed was to class together, in each of the chapters of which it is composed, those operations which are most connected with one another. I need hardly mention that this part could not be borrowed from any other work, and that, in the principal articles it contains, I could not derive assistance from any thing but the experiments which I have made myself.

I shall conclude this preface by transcribing, literally, some observations of the Abbé de Condillac, which I think describe, with a good deal of truth, the state of chemistry at a period not far distant from our own. These observations were made on a different subject; but they will not, on this account, have less force, if the application of them be thought just.

"Instead of applying observation to the things we wished to know, we have chosen rather to imagine them. Advancing from one ill founded supposition to another, we have at last bewildered ourselves amidst a multitude of errors. These errors becoming prejudices, are, of course, adopted as principles, and we thus bewilder ourselves more and more. The method, too, by which we conduct our reasonings is as absurd; we abuse words which we do not understand, and call this the art of reasoning. When matters have been brought this length, when errors have been thus accumulated, there is but one remedy by which order can be restored to the faculty of thinking; this is, to forget all that we have learned, to trace back our ideas to their source, to follow the train in which they rise, and, as my Lord Bacon says, to frame the human understanding anew.

"This remedy becomes the more difficult in proportion as we think ourselves more learned. Might it not be thought that works which treated of the sciences with the utmost perspicuity, with great precision and order, must be understood by every body? The fact is, those who have never studied any thing will understand them better than those who have studied a great deal, and especially than those who have written a great deal.["]

At the end of the fifth chapter, the Abbé de Condillac adds: "But, after all, the sciences have made progress, because philosophers have applied themselves with more attention to observe, and have communicated to their language that precision and accuracy which they have employed in their observations: In correcting their language they reason better."

23

A NEW PHENOMENON: CURRENT ELECTRICITY

In the eighteenth century there had been no such thing as "static" electricity: what we call static electricity was simply "electricity"; it was the only kind. This picture changed with work at the end of the century by two Italians, Giuseppe Galvani and Alessandro Volta, who between them ended up convincing philosophers that there was an electrical fluid that *flowed*. In the following extract, Volta describes the use of the apparatus that generates and manifests the action of this propelled fluid.

Source: Alessandro Volta, *Phil. Trans*. 1800 Pt. II, dated 20th March, 1800; read to the Royal Society 26th June, 1800, pp. 403–409. English translation in *The Philosophical Magazine*, September 1800, pp. 289–311.

On the Electricity excited by the mere Contact of conducting Substances of different Kinds. In a Letter from Mr. Alexander Volta, F.R.S. Professor of Natural Philosophy in the University of Pavia, to the Right Hon. Sir Joseph Banks, Bart. K.B. P.R.S.

Como in the Milanese, March 20, 1800

After a long silence, for which I shall offer no apology, I have the pleasure of communicating to you, and through you to the Royal Society, some striking results I have obtained in pursuing my experiments on electricity excited by the mere mutual contact of different kinds of metal, and even by that of other conductors, also different from each other, either liquid or containing some liquid, to which they are properly indebted for their conducting power. The principal of these results, which comprehends nearly all the rest, is the construction of an apparatus having a resemblance in its effects (that is to say, in the shock it is capable of making the arms, &c. experience) to the Leyden flask[1], or, rather, to an electric battery weakly charged acting incessantly, which should charge itself after each explosion; and, in a word, which should have an inexhaustible charge, a perpetual action or impulse on the electric fluid; but which differs from it essentially both by this continual action, which is peculiar to it, and because, instead of consisting, like the common electric jars and batteries, of one or more insulating plates or thin strata of those bodies which are alone thought to be *electric*, armed with conductors, or bodies called *non-electric*, this new apparatus is formed merely of several of the latter bodies, chosen from among those which are the best conductors, and therefore the most remote, as has hitherto been believed, from the electric nature. The apparatus to which I allude, and which will, no doubt, astonish you, is only the assemblage of a number of good conductors of different kinds arranged in a certain manner. Thirty, forty, sixty, or more pieces of copper, or rather silver, applied each to a piece of tin, or zinc, which is much better, and as many strata of water, or any other liquid which may be a better conductor, such as salt water, ley,[2] &c. or pieces of pasteboard, skin, &c. well soaked in these liquids; such strata interposed between every pair or combination of two different metals in an alternate series, and always in the same order, of these three kinds of conductors, are all that is necessary for constituting my new instrument, which, as I have said, imitates the effects of the Leyden flask, or of electric batteries, by communicating the same shock as these do; but which, indeed, is far inferior to the activity of these batteries when highly charged, either in regard to the force and noise of the explosions, the spark, the distance at which the discharge may be effected, &c. as it equals only the effects of a battery very weakly charged, though of immense capacity: in other respects, however, it far surpasses the virtue and power of these batteries, as it has no need, like these, of being previously charged by means of foreign electricity, and as it is capable of giving a shock every time it is properly touched, however often it may be.

To this apparatus, much more similar at bottom, as I shall show, and even such as I have constructed it, in its form to the *natural electric organ* of the torpedo or electric eel, &c. than to the Leyden flask and electric batteries, I would wish to give the name of the *artificial electric organ*: and, indeed, is it not, like it, composed entirely of conducting bodies? Is it not also active of itself without any previous charge, without the aid of any electricity excited by any of the means hitherto known? Does it not act incessantly, and without intermission? And, in the last lace, is it not capable of giving every moment shocks of greater or less strength, according to circumstances—shocks which

1   The Leyden flask, or Leyden jar, was a kind of capacitor invented in the 1740s. It took the form of a glass jar filled with water, where the surfaces of the inside and outside of the jar acted like the plates of a parallel-plate capacitor to store charge.
2   Dishwater.

are renewed by each new touch, and which, when thus repeated or continued for a certain time, produce the same torpor in the limbs as is occasioned by the torpedo, &c.?[3]

I shall now give a more particular description of this apparatus and of others analogous to it, as well as of the most remarkable experiments made with them.

I provide a few dozens of small round plates or disks of copper, brass, or rather silver, an inch in diameter more or less (pieces of coin for example), and an equal number of plates of tin, or, what is better, of zinc, nearly of the same size and figure. I make use of the term *nearly*, because great precision is not necessary, and the size in general, as well as the figure of the metallic pieces, is merely arbitrary: care only must be taken that they may be capable of being conveniently arranged one above the other, in the form of a column. I prepare also a pretty large number of circular pieces of pasteboard, or any other spongy matter capable of imbibing and retaining a great deal of water or moisture, with which they must be well impregnated in order to ensure success in the experiments. These circular pieces of pasteboard, which I shall call moistened disks, I make a little smaller than the plates of metal, in order that, when interposed between them, as I shall hereafter describe, they may not project beyond them.

Having all these pieces ready in a good state, that is to say, the metallic disks very clean and dry, and the non-metallic ones well moistened with common water, or, what is much better, salt water, and slightly wiped that the moisture may not drop off, I have nothing to do but to arrange them, a matter exceedingly simple and easy.

I place then horizontally, on a table or any other stand, one of the metallic pieces, for example one of silver, and over the first I adapt one of zinc; on the second I place one of the moistened disks, then another plate of silver followed immediately by another of zinc, over which I place another of the moistened disks. In this manner I continue coupling a plate of silver with one of zinc, and always in the same order, that is to say, the silver below and the zinc above it, or *vice versa*, according as I have begun, and interpose between each of these couples a moistened disk. I continue to form, of several of these stories, a column as high as possible without any danger of its falling.

But, if it contain about twenty of these stories or couples of metal, it will be capable not only of emitting signs of electricity by Cavallo's electrometer, assisted by a condenser, beyond ten or fifteen degrees, and of charging this condenser by mere contact so as to make it emit a spark, &c. but of giving

---

3 On the torpedo comparison, see James Delbourgo, *A Most Amazing Scene of Wonders: Electricity and Enlightenment in Early America* (Cambridge, MA: Harvard University Press, 2006), Chap. 16; Giuliano Pancaldi, *Volta: Science and Culture in the Age of Enlightenment* (Princeton: Princeton University Press, 2003).

to the fingers with which its extremities (the bottom and top of the column) have been touched several small shocks, more or less frequent, according as the touching has been repeated. Each of these shocks has a perfect resemblance to that slight shock experienced from a Leyden flask weakly charged, or a battery still more weakly charged, or a torpedo in an exceedingly languishing state, which imitates still better the effects of my apparatus by the series of repeated shocks which it can continually communicate.

...[tips about using salt water for pasteboard, and warmer temperatures, as improving performance]...

But all these means and all these attentions have only a limited advantage, and will never occasion your receiving very strong shocks as long as the apparatus consists but of one column, formed only of twenty pair of plates, even though they may consist of the two metals properest for these experiments, *viz.* silver and zinc; for if they were silver and lead, or tin, or copper and tin, the half of the effect would not be produced, unless the weaker effect of each pair were supplied by a much greater number. What really increases the electric power of this apparatus, and to such a degree as to make it equal or surpass that of the torpedo or electric eel, is the number of plates arranged in such a manner, and with the attention before mentioned. If to the twenty pairs above described twenty or thirty others be added disposed in the same order, the shocks which may be communicated by a column lengthened in this manner will be much stronger, and extend to both arms as far as the shoulder; and especially of that, the hand of which has been immersed in the water: this hand, with the whole arm, will remain more or less benumbed, if by frequently renewing the touches these shocks be made to succeed each other rapidly, and without intermission. This will be the case if the whole hand, or the greater part of it, be immersed in the water of the bason [sic]; but if only one finger be immersed, either wholly or in part, the shocks being almost entirely concentrated in it alone, will become so much the more painful, and so acute as to be scarcely supportable.

It may readily be conceived that this column, formed of forty or fifty couples of metals, which gives shocks more than moderate to both the arms of one person, is capable of giving sensible shocks also to several persons, holding each other by the hands (sufficiently moist) so as to form an uninterrupted chain.

...[improvements and variants on the apparatus]...

...

From these experiments one might believe, that when the torpedo wishes to communicate a shock to the arms of a man or to animals which touch it, or which approach its body under the water (which shock is much weaker than what the fish can give out of the water), it has nothing to do but to bring together some of the parts of its electric organ in that place, where, by some interval, the communication is interrupted, to remove the interruptions from between the columns of which the said organ is formed, or from between its membranes in the form of thin disks, which lie one above the other from the bottom to the summit of each column: it has, I say, nothing to do but to remove these interruptions in one or more places, and to produce there the requisite contact, either by compressing these columns, or by making some moisture to flow in between the pellicles or diaphragms which have been separated, &c. This is what may be, and what I really conclude to be, the task of the torpedo when it gives a shock; for all the rest, the impulse and movement communicated to the electric fluid, is only a necessary effect of its singular organ, formed, as is seen, of a very numerous series of conductors, which I have every reason to believe sufficiently different from each other to be *exciters* of the electric fluid by their mutual contacts; and to suppose them ranged in a manner proper for impelling that fluid with a sufficient force from top to bottom, or from the bottom to the top, and for determining a current capable of producing the shock, &c. as soon and as often as all the necessary contacts and communications take place.

...[more technical tips]...

...

These cylinders are attended with this advantage, that they may be employed for experiments either in an erect, inclined, or lying position, according as you choose, or even immersed in water, provided the top of it be above the surface of the fluid: they might also give a shock when entirely immersed if they contained a greater number of plates, or if several of these cylinders were joined together, and if there were any interruption that could be removed at pleasure, &c. by which means these cylinders would have a pretty good resemblance to the electric eel; and, to have a better resemblance to it even externally, they might be joined together by liable metallic wires or screw-springs, and then covered with a skin terminated by a head and tail properly formed, &c.

...[effects on different senses]...

...

All the facts which I have related in this long paper in regard to the action which the electric fluid excited, and when moved by my apparatus, exercises on the different parts of our body which the current attacks and passes through;—an action which is not momentaneous, but which lasts, and is maintained during the whole time that this current can follow the chain not interrupted in its communications; in a word, an action the effects of which vary according to the different degrees of excitability in the parts, as has been seen;—all these facts, sufficiently numerous, and others which may be still discovered by multiplying and varying the experiments of this kind, will open a very wide field for reflection, and of views, not only curious, but particularly interesting to medicine. There will be a great deal to occupy the anatomist, the physiologist,[4] and the practitioner.

...

To what electricity then, or to what instrument ought the organ of the torpedo or electric eel, &c. to be compared? To that which I have constructed according to the new principle of electricity, discovered by me some years ago, and which my successive experiments, particularly those with which I am presently engaged, have so well confirmed, *viz.* that conductors are also, in certain cases, exciters of electricity in the case of the mutual contact of those of different kinds, &c. in that apparatus which I have named the *artificial electric organ*, and which being at bottom the same as the natural organ of the torpedo, resembles it also in its form, as I have advanced.

---

4   Notice the extent to which Volta represents these phenomena as intimately bound up with the organic tissue that registers them.

24

HUMAN SCIENCES: PHILOLOGY AND ANTHROPOLOGY

In 1783 Sir William Jones was appointed a judge in Calcutta, the capital of Bengal. Bengal was a British-controlled territory under the management of the East India Company, the joint-stock trading company based in London that ended up controlling most of the Indian subcontinent by the middle of the nineteenth century. Jones founded the Asiatick Society of Bengal in 1784 to pursue his interests in Sanskrit and antiquarian matters, and played a central role in establishing the concept of an Indo-European family of languages that united cultures across wide swathes of Europe and Asia. This philological approach became a widely used tool for classifying and distinguishing between human groups, and was later used as a model for historical filiations among varieties and species of organisms by Charles Darwin (see Stephen G. Alter, *Darwinism and the Linguistic Image*, 2002). Although strictly speaking the groupings used for language groups were independent of biological, genetic relationships among people, the two categories of linguistic and genetic relationships were often conflated in the nineteenth century by practitioners of what historians often call "scientific racism." Jones's use of comparative mythological accounts of ancient history to vindicate the biblical story of Noah's flood in the discourse presented below enabled him to associate different peoples with the various lines descended from Noah's sons. One is reminded of Mr. Casaubon's "key to all mythologies" in George Eliot's novel *Middlemarch*.

Source: William Jones, extract from *The Works of Sir William Jones*, 1807, vol. 3, pp. 185–204, Ninth Anniversary Discourse to the Asiatick Society, Calcutta.

DISCOURSE THE NINTH.
ON
THE ORIGIN AND FAMILIES OF NATIONS.
DELIVERED 23 FEBRUARY, 1792,
BY
THE PRESIDENT.

YOU have attended, gentlemen, with so much indulgence to my discourses on the five *Asiatick* nations, and on the various tribes established along their several borders or interspersed over their mountains,[1] that I cannot but flatter myself with an assurance of being heard with equal attention, while I trace to one centre the three great families, from which those nations appear to have proceeded, and then hazard a few conjectures on the different courses, which they may be supposed to have taken toward the countries, in which we find them settled at the dawn of all genuine history.

Let us begin with a short review of the propositions, to which we have gradually been led, and separate such as are morally certain, from such as are only probable: that the first race of *Persians* and *Indians*, to whom we may add the *Romans* and *Greeks*, the *Goths*, and the old *Egyptians* or *Ethiops*, originally spoke the same language and professed the same popular faith, is capable, in my humble opinion, of incontestable proof; that the *Jews* and *Arabs*, the *Assyrians*, or second *Persian* race, the people who spoke *Syriack*, and a numerous tribe of *Abyssinians*, used one primitive dialect wholly distinct from the idiom just mentioned, is, I believe, undisputed, and, I am sure, indisputable; but that the settlers in *China* and *Japan* had a common origin with the *Hindus*, is no more than highly probable; and, that all the *Tartars*, as they are inaccurately called, were primarily of a third separate branch, totally differing from the two others in language, manners, and features, may indeed be plausibly conjectured, but cannot, for the reasons alledged in a former essay, be perspicuously shown, and for the present therefore must be merely assumed. Could these facts be verified by the best attainable evidence, it would not, I presume, be doubted, that the whole earth was peopled by a variety of shoots from the *Indian, Arabian,* and *Tartarian* branches, or by such intermixtures of them, as, in a course of ages, might naturally have happened.

Now I admit without hesitation the aphorism of Linnæus, that "in the beginning God created one pair only of every living species, which has a diversity of sex;" but, since that incomparable naturalist argues principally from the wonderful diffusion of vegetables, and from an hypothesis, that the water on this globe has been continually subsiding, I venture to produce a shorter and closer argument in support of his doctrine. That *Nature*, of

---

1 That is, in previous anniversary discourses: Jones's five "Asiatick nations" he listed as Hindus, Arabs, Tartars, Persians, and Chinese.

which simplicity appears a distinguishing attribute, *does nothing in vain,*[2] is a maxim in philosophy; and against those, who deny maxims, we cannot dispute; but *it is vain* and superfluous *to do by many means what may be done by fewer,*[3] and this is another axiom received into courts of judicature from the schools of philosophers: *we must not,* therefore, says our great Newton, *admit more causes of things, than those, which are true, and sufficiently account for natural phenomena;*[4] but it is true, that one pair *at least* of every living species must at first have been created; and that one human pair was sufficient for the population of our globe in a period of no considerable length (on the very moderate supposition of lawyers and political arithmeticians,[5] that every pair of ancestors left on an average two children, and each of them two more), is evident from the rapid increase of numbers in geometrical progression, so well known to those, who have ever taken the trouble to sum a series of as many terms, as they suppose generations of men in two or three thousand years. It follows, that the Author of Nature (for all nature proclaims its divine author[6]) created but one pair of our species; yet, had it not been (among other reasons) for the devastations, which history has recorded, of water and fire, wars, famine, and pestilence, this earth would not now have had room for its multiplied inhabitants. If the human race then be, as we may confidently assume, of one natural species, they must all have proceeded from one pair; and if perfect justice be, as it is most indubitably, an essential attribute of GOD, that pair must have been gifted with sufficient wisdom and strength to be virtuous, and, as far as their nature admitted, happy, but intrusted with freedom of will to be vicious and consequently degraded: whatever might be their option, they must people in time the region where they first were established, and their numerous descendants must necessarily seek new countries, as inclination might prompt, or accident lead, them; they would of course migrate in separate families and clans, which, forgetting by degrees the language of their common progenitor, would form new dialects to convey new ideas, both simple and complex; natural affection would unite them at first, and a sense of reciprocal utility, the great and only cement of social

---

2   A maxim derived from medieval scholastic philosophy: *natura nihil frustra facit.* Maxims were an integral part of the English legal tradition, of which Jones, as a judge, was a part; Francis Bacon, also a lawyer, employed philosophical maxims (in the form of "aphorisms") in his natural philosophy.

3   This is best known as "Occam's razor," after the fourteenth-century English philosopher William of Ockham.

4   The first of Newton's rules of philosophising (*regulae philosophandi*) in his *Principia* (so called from the second edition of 1713 onward; original version labelled "hypotheses" in the first edition of 1687).

5   Writers such as William Petty (Chapter 14) and Thomas Malthus (Chapter 26).

6   An allusion to natural theology, which learned about God through reason and the study of nature rather than revelation.

union in the absence of publick honour and justice, for which in evil times it is a general substitute, would combine them at length in communities more or less regular; laws would be proposed by a part of each community, but enacted by the whole; and governments would be variously arranged for the happiness or misery of the governed, according to their own virtue and wisdom, or depravity and folly; so that, in less than three thousand years, the world would exhibit the same appearances, which we may actually observe on it in the age of the great *Arabian* impostor [Muhammed].

On that part of it, to which our united researches are generally confined, we see *five* races of men peculiarly distinguished, in the time of Muhammed, for their multitude and extent of dominion; but we have reduced them to *three*, because we can discover no more, that essentially differ in language, religion, manners, and other known characteristicks: now those three races, how variously soever they may at present be dispersed and intermixed, must (if the preceding conclusions be justly drawn) have migrated originally from a central country, to find which is the problem proposed for solution. Suppose it solved; and give any arbitrary name to that centre: let it, if you please, be *Iràn.* The three primitive languages, therefore, must at first have been concentrated in *Iràn,* and there only in fact we see traces of them in the earliest historical age; but, for the sake of greater precision, conceive the whole empire of *Iràn,* with all its mountains and valleys, plains and rivers, to be every way infinitely diminished; the first winding courses, therefore, of all the nations proceeding from it by land, and nearly at the same time, will be little right lines, but without intersections, because those courses could not have thwarted and crossed one another: if then you consider the seats of all the migrating nations as points in a surrounding figure, you will perceive, that the several rays, diverging from *Iràn,* may be drawn to them without any intersection; but this will not happen, if you assume as a centre *Arabia,* or *Egypt; India, Tartary,* or *China:* it follows, that *Iràn,* or *Persia* (I contend for *the meaning, not the name),* was the central country, which we sought. This mode of reasoning I have adopted, not from any affectation (as you will do me the justice to believe) of a scientifick diction, but for the sake of conciseness and variety, and from a wish to avoid repetitions; the substance of my argument having been detailed in a different form at the close of another discourse; nor does the argument in any form rise to demonstration, which the question by no means admits: it amounts, however, to such a proof, grounded on written evidence and credible testimony, as all mankind hold sufficient for decisions affecting property, freedom, and life.

Thus then have we proved, that the inhabitants of *Asia,* and consequently, as it might be proved, of the whole earth, sprang from three branches of one stem: and that those branches have shot into their present state of luxuriance in a period comparatively short, is apparent from a fact universally acknowledged, that we find no certain monument, or even probable tradition, of nations planted, empires and states raised, laws enacted, cities built, navigation improved, commerce encouraged, arts invented, or letters contrived, above twelve or at most fifteen or sixteen centuries before the birth of Christ, and from another fact, which cannot be controverted, that seven hundred or a thousand years would have been fully adequate to the supposed propagation, diffusion and establishment of the human race.

The most ancient history of that race, and the oldest composition perhaps in the world, is a work in *Hebrew*, which we may suppose at first, for the sake of our argument, to have no higher authority than any other work of equal antiquity, that the researches of the curious had accidentally brought to light: it is ascribed to Musah ; for so he writes his own name, which, after the *Greeks* and *Romans*, we have changed into Moses; and, though it was manifestly his object to give an historical account of a single family, he has introduced it with a short view of the primitive world, and his introduction has been divided, perhaps improperly, into *eleven* chapters.[7] After describing with awful sublimity the creation of this universe, he asserts, that one pair of every animal species was called from nothing into existence; that the human pair were strong enough to be happy, but free to be miserable; that, from delusion and temerity, they disobeyed their supreme benefactor, whose goodness could not pardon them consistently with his justice; and that they received a punishment adequate to their disobedience, but softened by a mysterious promise to be accomplished in their descendants. We cannot but believe, on the supposition just made of a history uninspired, that these facts were delivered by tradition from the first pair, and related by Moses in a figurative style; not in that sort of allegory, which rhetoricians describe as a mere assemblage of metaphors, but in the symbolical mode of writing adopted by eastern sages, to embellish and dignify historical truth; and, if this were a time for such illustrations, we might produce the same account of the *creation* and the *fall*, expressed by symbols very nearly similar, from the *Puránas* themselves, and even from the *Veda*, which appears to stand next in antiquity to the five books of Moses.

The sketch of antediluvian history, in which we find many dark passages, is followed by the narrative of a *deluge*, which destroyed the whole race of man, except four pairs; an historical fact admitted as true by every nation, to whose literature we have access, and particularly by the ancient *Hindus*, who have allotted an entire *Purána* to the detail of that event, which they relate,

---

7   Jones deliberately treats the Pentateuch (the first five books of the Bible) as if it were on a par with any other text from antiquity rather than being (as he at length admits) divinely inspired. This enables his comparative methodology, whereby he collates a variety of ancient sources, to stand independent of claims to a special status for the Bible. It paved the way for subsequent nineteenth-century literary criticism of the Bible itself (known as "Higher Criticism" and first developing in a significant way among German scholars) that treated it from an entirely secular standpoint and caused much controversy for its apparent impiety.

as usual, in symbols or allegories. I concur most heartily with those, who insist, that, in proportion as any fact mentioned in history seems repugnant to the course of nature, or, in one word, miraculous, the stronger evidence is required to induce a rational belief of it;[8] but we hear without incredulity, that cities have been overwhelmed by eruptions from burning mountains, territories laid waste by hurricanes, and whole islands depopulated by earthquakes: if then we look at the firmament sprinkled with innumerable stars; if we conclude by a fair analogy, that every star is a sun, attracting, like ours, a system of inhabited planets; and if our ardent fancy, soaring hand in hand with sound reason, waft us beyond the visible sphere into regions of immensity, disclosing other celestial expanses and other systems of suns and worlds on all sides without number or end, we cannot but consider the submersion of our little spheroïd as an infinitely less event in respect of the immeasureable universe, than the destruction of a city or an isle in respect of this habitable globe. Let a general flood, however, be supposed improbable in proportion to the magnitude of so ruinous an event, yet the concurrent evidences of it are completely adequate to the supposed improbability; but, as we cannot here expatiate on those proofs, we proceed to the fourth important fact recorded in the *Mosaick* history; I mean the first propagation and early dispersion of mankind *in separate families* to separate places of residence.

Three sons of the just and virtuous man, whose lineage was preserved from the general inundation, travelled, we are told, as they began to multiply, in *three* large divisions variously subdivided: the children of YA'FET seem, from the traces of *Sklavonian* names, and the mention of their being *enlarged*, to have spread themselves far and wide, and to have produced the race, which, for want of a correct appellation, we call *Tartarian*; the colonies, formed by the sons of HAM and SHEM, appear to have been nearly simultaneous; and, among those of the latter branch, we find so many names incontestably preserved at this hour in *Arabia*, that we cannot hesitate in pronouncing them the same people, whom hitherto we have denominated *Arabs*; while the former branch, the most powerful and adventurous of whom were the progeny of CUSH, MISR, and RAMA (names remaining unchanged in *Sanscrit*, and highly revered by the *Hindus*), were, in all probability, the race, which I call *Indian*, and to which we may now give any other name, that may seem more proper and comprehensive.

The general introduction to the *Jewish* history closes with a very concise and obscure account of a presumptuous and mad attempt, by a particular colony, to build a splendid city and raise a fabrick of immense height, independently of the divine aid, and, it should seem, in defiance of the divine power; a project, which was baffled by means appearing at first view inadequate to the purpose, but ending in violent dissention among the projectors, and in

8   An observation reflecting the famous argument of David Hume against miracles.

the ultimate separation of them: this event also seems to be recorded by the ancient *Hindus* in two of their *Puránas*; and it will be proved, I trust, on some future occasion, that *the lion bursting from a pillar to destroy a blaspheming giant*, and *the dwarf, who beguiled and held in derision* the magnificent Beli, are one and the same story related in a symbolical style.

Now these primeval events are described as having happened between the *Oxus* and *Euphrates*, the mountains of *Caucasus* and the borders of *India*, that is, within the limits of *Iràn*; for, though most of the *Mosaick* names have been considerably altered, yet numbers of them remain unchanged: we still find *Harràn* in *Mesopotamia*, and travellers appear unanimous in fixing the site of ancient *Babel*.

Thus, on the preceding supposition, that the first eleven chapters of the book, which it is thought proper to call *Genesis*, are merely a preface to the oldest civil history now extant, we see the truth of them confirmed by antecedent reasoning, and by evidence in part highly probable, and in part certain; but the *connection* of the *Mosaick* history with that of the Gospel by a chain of sublime predictions unquestionably ancient, and apparently fulfilled, must induce us to think the *Hebrew* narrative more than human in its origin, and consequently true in every substantial part of it, though possibly expressed in figurative language; as many learned and pious men have believed, and as the most pious may believe without injury, and perhaps with advantage, to the cause of revealed religion. If Moses then was endued with supernatural knowledge, it is no longer probable only, but absolutely certain, that the whole race of man proceeded from *Iràn*, as from a centre, whence they migrated at first in three great colonies; and that those three branches grew from a common stock, which had been miraculously preserved in a general convulsion and inundation of this globe.[9]

...[omitting section from pp. 197–201 on the perils of comparative linguistics]

From the testimonies adduced in the six last annual discourses, and from the additional proofs laid before you, or rather opened, on the present occasion, it seems to follow, that the only human family after the flood established themselves in the northern parts of *Iràn*; that, as they multiplied, they were divided into three distinct branches, each retaining little at first, and losing the whole by degrees, of their common primary language, but agreeing severally on new expressions for new ideas; that the branch of Ya'fet was *enlarged* in many scattered shoots over the north of *Europe* and Asia, diffusing of themselves as far as the western and eastern seas, and, at length in the infancy of navigation, beyond them both: that they cultivated no liberal arts, and had no use of letters, but formed a variety of dialects, as their tribes were variously ramified; that, secondly, the children of Ham, who founded

9   Jones finally trumps all his arguments with the certainty of divine revelation.

in *Iràn* itself the monarchy of the first *Chaldeans*, invented letters, observed and named the luminaries of the firmament, calculated the known *Indian* period of *four hundred and thirty-two thousand years*, or an *hundred and twenty* repetitions of the *saros*, and contrived the old system of Mythology, partly allegorical, and partly grounded on idolatrous veneration for their sages and lawgivers; that they were dispersed at various intervals and in various colonies over land and ocean; that the tribes of Misr, Cush, and Rama settled in *Africk* and *India*; while some of them, having improved the art of sailing, passed from *Egypt*, *Phenice*, and *Phrygia*, into *Italy* and *Greece*, which they found thinly peopled by former emigrants, of whom they supplanted some tribes, and united themselves with others; whilst a swarm from the same hive moved by a northerly course into *Scandinavia*, and another, by the head of the *Oxus*, and through the passes of *Imaus*, into *Cashghar* and *Eighùr*, *Khatá* and *Khoten*, as far as the territories of *Chín* and *Tancút*, where letters have been used and arts immemorially cultivated; nor is it unreasonable to believe, that some of them found their way from the eastern isles into *Mexico* and *Peru*, where traces were discovered of rude literature and Mythology analogous to those of *Egypt* and *India*; that, thirdly, the old *Chaldean* empire being overthrown by the *Assyrians* under Cayu'mers,[10] other migrations took place, especially into *India*, while the rest of Shem's progeny, some of whom had before settled on the Red Sea, peopled the whole *Arabian* peninsula, pressing close on the nations of *Syria* and *Phenice*; that, lastly, from all the three families were detached many bold adventurers of an ardent spirit and a roving disposition, who disdained subordination and wandered in separate clans, till they settled in distant isles or in deserts and mountainous regions; that, on the whole, some colonies might have migrated before the death of their venerable progenitor, but that states and empires could scarce have assumed a regular form, till fifteen or sixteen hundred years before the *Christian* epoch, and that, for the first thousand years of that period, we have no history unmixed with fable, except that of the turbulent and variable, but eminently distinguished, nation descended from Abraham.

My design, gentlemen, of tracing the origin and progress of the five principal nations, who have peopled *Asia*, and of whom there were considerable remains in their several countries at the time of Muhammed's birth, is now accomplished; succinctly, from the nature of these essays; imperfectly, from the darkness of the subject and scantiness of my materials, but clearly and comprehensively enough to form a basis for subsequent researches: you have seen, as distinctly as I am able to show, *who* those nations originally were, *whence* and *when* they moved toward their final stations; and, in my future annual discourses, I propose to enlarge on the *particular advantages* to our

---

10 Evidently a form of "Hammurabi," or "Khammurabi," the ancient Babylonian king famous for his legal code.

country and to mankind, which may result from our sedulous and united inquiries into the history, science, and arts, of these *Asiatick* regions, especially of the *British* dominions in *India*, which we may consider as the centre (not of the human race, but) of our common exertions to promote its true interests; and we shall concur, I trust, in opinion, that the race of man, to advance whose manly happiness is our duty and will of course be our endeavour, cannot long be happy without virtue, nor actively virtuous without freedom, nor securely free without rational knowledge.

25

SCIENCE AND INDUSTRY

Coal gas gave rise to an illustrious progeny in the nineteenth century. William Murdoch, in the extract below, speaks of the uses of this coal by-product, created from the heating of coal, for the purposes of illumination, a use that was very rapidly adopted for lighting both for private premises and for public street lamps. Economic uses of industrial by-products were becoming an important concern in this early period of the industrial revolution in Britain; the production of coal gas itself spawned an immensely consequential industry and theoretical developments in organic chemistry after mid-century with the investigation of "coal tar," the sludge left behind by the production of coal gas by destructive distillation of coal. Investigation by German chemists such as Justus Liebig, and especially by his student August Wilhelm Hofmann, spawned structural organic chemistry, and at the same time produced the aniline dye industry, a landmark in the growth of science-based industry (see Anthony S. Travis, *The Rainbow Makers* [Bethlehem, PA: Lehigh University Press, 1993]). William Murdoch was a Scottish engineer in the employ of Bolton and Watt, and thus at the centre of the industrial revolution; his paper on the uses of coal gas for lighting was an important early stage of this hugely significant episode in the industrialisation of academic science.[1]

Source: William Murdoch, "An Account of the Application of the Gas from Coal to Economical Purposes," *Philosophical Transactions* 98 (1808), extracts from pp. 124–132.

---

1   For the broader context of Murdoch's work on artificial illumination, see Simon Werrett, "From the Grand Whim to the Gas Works: 'Philosophical Fireworks' in Georgian England," in Lissa Roberts, Simon Schaffer, and Peter Dear (eds.), *The Mindful Hand: Inquiry and Invention from the Late Renaissance to Early Industrialisation* (Amsterdam: Koninklijke Nederlandse Akademie van Wetenschappen, 2007), pp. 325–347; more broadly, Wolfgang Schivelbusch, *Disenchanted Night: The Industrialization of Night in the Nineteenth Century* (Berkeley: University of California Press, 1995).

The facts and results intended to be communicated in this Paper, are founded upon observations made, during the present winter, at the cotton manufactory of Messrs. Philips and Lee at Manchester, where the light obtained by the combustion of the gas from coal is used upon a very large scale; the apparatus for its production and application having been prepared by me at the works of Messrs. Boulton, Watt, and Co. at Soho.

The whole of the rooms of this cotton mill, which is, I believe, the most extensive in the United Kingdom, as well as its counting-houses and store-rooms, and the adjacent dwelling-house of Mr. Lee, are lighted with the gas from coal. The total quantity of light used during the hours of burning, has been ascertained, by a comparison of shadows, to be about equal to the light which 2500 mould candles of six in the pound would give; each of the candles, with which the comparison was made consuming at the rate of 4/10ths of an ounce (175 grains) of tallow per hour.

The quantity of light is necessarily liable to some variation, from the difficulty of adjusting all the flames, so as to be perfectly equal at all times; but the admirable precision and exactness with which the business of this mill is conducted, afforded as excellent an opportunity of making the comparative trials I had in view, as is perhaps likely to be ever obtained in general practice. And the experiments being made upon so large a scale, and for a considerable period of time, may, I think, be assumed as a sufficiently accurate standard for determining the advantages to be expected from the use of the gas lights under favourable circumstances.

It is not my intention, in the present Paper, to enter into a particular description of the apparatus employed for producing the gas; but I may observe generally, that the coal is distilled in large iron retorts, which during the winter season are kept constantly at work, except during the intervals of charging; and that the gas, as it rises from them, is conveyed by iron pipes into large reservoirs, or gazometers, where it is washed and purified, previous to its being conveyed through other pipes, called mains, to the mill. These mains branch off into a variety of ramifications (forming a total length of several miles), and diminish in size, as the quantity of gas required to be passed through them becomes less. The burners, where the gas is consumed, are connected with the above mains, by short tubes, each of which is furnished with a cock to regulate the admission of the gas to each burner, and to shut it totally off when requisite. This latter operation may likewise be instantaneously performed, through the whole of the burners in each room, by turning a cock, with which each main is provided, near its entrance into the room.

The burners are of two kinds: the one is upon the principle of the Argand lamp, and resembles it in appearance; the other is a small curved tube with a conical end, having three circular apertures or perforations, of about a thirtieth of an inch in diameter, one at the point of the cone, and two lateral ones, through which the gas issues, forming three divergent jets of flame, somewhat like a fleur-de-lis. The shape and general appearance of this tube, has procured it among the workmen, the name of the cockspur burner.

The number of burners employed in all the buildings, amounts to 271 Argands, and 633 cockspurs; each of the former giving a light equal to that of four candles of the description abovementioned; and each of the latter, a light equal to two and a quarter of the same candles; making therefore the total of the gas light a little more than equal to that of 2500 candles. When thus regulated, the whole of the above burners require an *hourly* supply of 1250 cubic feet of the gas produced from cannel coal; the superior quality and quantity of the gas produced from that material having given it a decided preference in this situation, over every other coal, notwithstanding its higher price.

...[Economics of the use of the gas in contrast to candle light examined and calculated]...

The peculiar softness and clearness of this light, with its almost unvarying intensity, have brought it into great favour with the work people. And its being free from the inconvenience and danger, resulting from the sparks and frequent snuffing of candles, is a circumstance of material importance, as tending to diminish the hazard of fire, to which cotton mills are known to be much exposed.

The above particulars, it is conceived, contain such information, as may tend to illustrate the general advantages attending the use of the gas light; but nevertheless the Royal Society may perhaps not deem it uninteresting to be apprized of the circumstances which originally gave rise in my mind to its application, as an economical substitute for oils and tallows.

It is now nearly sixteen years, since, in a course of experiments I was making at Redruth in Cornwall, upon the quantities and qualities of the gases produced by distillation from different mineral and vegetable substances, I was induced by some observations I had previously made upon the burning of coal, to try the combustible property of the gases produced from it, as well as from peat, wood, and other inflammable substances. And being struck with the great quantities of gas which they afforded, as well as with the brilliancy of the light, and the facility of its production, I instituted several experiments with a view of ascertaining the cost at which it might be obtained, compared with that of equal quantities of light yielded by oils and tallow.

My apparatus consisted of an iron retort, with tinned copper and iron tubes through which the gas was conducted to a considerable distance; and there, as well as at intermediate points, was burned through apertures of varied forms and dimensions. The experiments were made upon coal of different qualities, which I procured from distant parts of the kingdom, for the purpose of ascertaining which would give the most economical results. The gas was also washed with water, and other means were employed to purify it.

In the year 1798, I removed from Cornwall to Messrs. Boulton, Watt, and Co.'s works for the Manufactory of steam engines at the Soho Foundry, and there I constructed an apparatus upon a larger scale, which during many successive nights was applied to the lighting of their principal building, and various new methods were practised, of washing and purifying the gas.

These experiments were continued with some interruptions, until the peace of 1802, when a public display of this light was made by me in the illumination of Mr. Boulton's manufactory at Soho, upon that occasion.

Since that period, I have, under the sanction of Messrs. Boulton, Watt, and Co. extended the apparatus at Soho Foundry, so as to give light to all the principal shops, where it is in regular use, to the exclusion of other artificial light; but I have preferred giving the results from Messrs. Philips' and Lee's apparatus, both on account of its greater extent, and the greater uniformity of the lights, which rendered the comparison with candles less difficult.

At the time I commenced my experiments, I was certainly unacquainted with the circumstance of the gas from coal having been observed by others to be capable of combustion; but I am since informed, that the current of gas escaping from Lord Dundonald's tar ovens had been frequently fired; and I find that Dr. Clayton, in a Paper in Volume XLI. Of the Transactions of the Royal Society, so long ago as the year 1739, gave an account of some observations and experiments made by him, which clearly manifest his knowledge of the inflammable property of the gas, which he denominates "the spirit of coals;" but the idea of applying it as an economical substitute for oils and tallow, does not appear to have occurred to this gentleman, and I believe I may, without presuming too much, claim both the first idea of applying, and the first actual application of this gas to economical purposes.[2]

2   The paper seems indeed to be an attempt at establishing priority of invention, something entirely normal by this time.

26

MALTHUS AND POLITICAL ECONOMY

William Petty's work (above) on so-called political economy can be seen as an attempt to make human life a part of the natural order, so as to use the tools of the natural sciences to understand and, potentially, control human society. The chief beneficiary of such work was of course the state, as Petty knew and as Francis Bacon some decades earlier would have realised. For Bacon, control of nature was a legitimate aim of the state, and any extension of the natural sciences to human society itself would surely have chimed with his purposes very well. The Reverend Thomas Malthus followed in Petty's footsteps in many ways, but rather than simply trying to gain some predictive control over matters of population and its increase as an economic desideratum, Malthus had more portentous goals: he wished to derive rules for good governance from what he saw as the inevitability of population pressure in human societies such that there will generally be more people than can comfortably be supported by existing resources of food. He represented his argument in terms of mathematical necessity: unchecked population tends to increase geometrically, as for example 1, 2, 4, 8, 16, 32, 64... (or 1, 3, 9, 27, 81, 243... in the event of greater fecundity, and so on), whereas food supply, he asserted somewhat arbitrarily, can at best be increased only arithmetically, as 1, 2, 3, 4, 5, 6... Consequently, however small the initial rate of reproduction, as long as it was positive it would sooner or later outstrip the potential increase in the food supply, and so the poorest end of society would always be with us. No amount of charitable relief could, ultimately, alleviate this situation; the only recourse was to restrain reproduction as far as possible among the poor. Perfectibility of human society of the sort predicted by such eighteenth-century visionaries as William Godwin was, Malthus argued, impossible. Malthus's book *Essay on the Principle of Population* (1798) went through many revised editions, and made a big popular impact on early nineteenth-century British society; the edition of 1825 was read by Charles Darwin, who took its lessons as an essential part of his own theory of natural selection. Human beings had become, in effect, a part of natural science insofar as they conformed to the same reasoning and premises; it was only a short step to the conclusion that nothing qualitatively special attached to the status of humanity.

Source: Thomas Malthus, *An Essay on the Principle of Population* (London, 1798), extracts from chap. 1.

From Chapter 1

...

It is an acknowledged truth in philosophy that a just theory will always be confirmed by experiment. Yet so much friction, and so many minute circumstances occur in practice, which it is next to impossible for the most enlarged and penetrating mind to foresee, that on few subjects can any theory be pronounced just, till all the arguments against it have been maturely weighed and clearly and consistently refuted.

I have read some of the speculations on the perfectibility of man and of society with great pleasure. I have been warmed and delighted with the enchanting picture which they hold forth. I ardently wish for such happy improvements. But I see great, and, to my understanding, unconquerable difficulties in the way to them. These difficulties it is my present purpose to state, declaring, at the same time, that so far from exulting in them, as a cause of triumph over the friends of innovation, nothing would give me greater pleasure than to see them completely removed.

The most important argument that I shall adduce is certainly not new. The principles on which it depends have been explained in part by Hume, and more at large by Dr Adam Smith. It has been advanced and applied to the present subject, though not with its proper weight, or in the most forcible point of view, by Mr Wallace, and it may probably have been stated by many writers that I have never met with. I should certainly therefore not think of advancing it again, though I mean to place it in a point of view in some degree different from any that I have hitherto seen, if it had ever been fairly and satisfactorily answered.

The cause of this neglect on the part of the advocates for the perfectibility of mankind is not easily accounted for. I cannot doubt the talents of such men as Godwin[1] and Condorcet. I am unwilling to doubt their candour. To my understanding, and probably to that of most others, the difficulty appears insurmountable. Yet these men of acknowledged ability and penetration scarcely deign to notice it, and hold on their course in such speculations with unabated ardour and undiminished confidence. I have certainly no right to say

1 William Godwin, the late-eighteenth-century political radical, husband of Mary Wollstonecraft, and father of Mary Wollstonecraft Shelley.

that they purposely shut their eyes to such arguments. I ought rather to doubt the validity of them, when neglected by such men, however forcibly their truth may strike my own mind. Yet in this respect it must be acknowledged that we are all of us too prone to err. If I saw a glass of wine repeatedly presented to a man, and he took no notice of it, I should be apt to think that he was blind or uncivil. A juster philosophy might teach me rather to think that my eyes deceived me and that the offer was not really what I conceived it to be.

In entering upon the argument I must premise that I put out of the question, at present, all mere conjectures, that is, all suppositions, the probable realization of which cannot be inferred upon any just philosophical grounds. A writer may tell me that he thinks man will ultimately become an ostrich. I cannot properly contradict him. But before he can expect to bring any reasonable person over to his opinion, he ought to shew that the necks of mankind have been gradually elongating, that the lips have grown harder and more prominent, that the legs and feet are daily altering their shape, and that the hair is beginning to change into stubs of feathers. And till the probability of so wonderful a conversion can be shewn, it is surely lost time and lost eloquence to expatiate on the happiness of man in such a state; to describe his powers, both of running and flying, to paint him in a condition where all narrow luxuries would be contemned, where he would be employed only in collecting the necessaries of life, and where, consequently, each man's share of labour would be light, and his portion of leisure ample.

I think I may fairly make two postulata.[2]

First, That food is necessary to the existence of man.

Secondly, That the passion between the sexes is necessary and will remain nearly in its present state.

These two laws, ever since we have had any knowledge of mankind, appear to have been fixed laws of our nature, and, as we have not hitherto seen any alteration in them, we have no right to conclude that they will ever cease to be what they now are, without an immediate act of power in that Being who first arranged the system of the universe, and for the advantage of his creatures, still executes, according to fixed laws, all its various operations.

I do not know that any writer has supposed that on this earth man will ultimately be able to live without food. But Mr Godwin has conjectured that the passion between the sexes may in time be extinguished. As, however, he calls this part of his work a deviation into the land of conjecture, I will not dwell longer upon it at present than to say that the best arguments for the perfectibility of man are drawn from a contemplation of the great progress that he has already made from the savage state and the difficulty of saying where he is to stop. But towards the extinction of the passion between the

2 Postulates had the virtue of association with the foundations of deductive geometry, with its reputation for the certainty of its conclusions.

sexes, no progress whatever has hitherto been made. It appears to exist in as much force at present as it did two thousand or four thousand years ago. There are individual exceptions now as there always have been. But, as these exceptions do not appear to increase in number, it would surely be a very unphilosophical mode of arguing to infer, merely from the existence of an exception, that the exception would, in time, become the rule, and the rule the exception.

Assuming then my postulata as granted, I say, that the power of population is indefinitely greater than the power in the earth to produce subsistence for man.

Population, when unchecked, increases in a geometrical ratio. Subsistence increases only in an arithmetical ratio.[3] A slight acquaintance with numbers will shew the immensity of the first power in comparison of the second.

By that law of our nature which makes food necessary to the life of man, the effects of these two unequal powers must be kept equal.

This implies a strong and constantly operating check on population from the difficulty of subsistence. This difficulty must fall somewhere and must necessarily be severely felt by a large portion of mankind.

Through the animal and vegetable kingdoms, nature has scattered the seeds of life abroad with the most profuse and liberal hand. She has been comparatively sparing in the room and the nourishment necessary to rear them. The germs of existence contained in this spot of earth, with ample food, and ample room to expand in, would fill millions of worlds in the course of a few thousand years. Necessity, that imperious all pervading law of nature, restrains them within the prescribed bounds. The race of plants and the race of animals shrink under this great restrictive law. And the race of man cannot, by any efforts of reason, escape from it. Among plants and animals its effects are waste of seed, sickness, and premature death. Among mankind, misery and vice. The former, misery, is an absolutely necessary consequence of it. Vice is a highly probable consequence, and we therefore see it abundantly prevail, but it ought not, perhaps, to be called an absolutely necessary consequence. The ordeal of virtue is to resist all temptation to evil.

This natural inequality of the two powers of population and of production in the earth, and that great law of our nature which must constantly keep their effects equal, form the great difficulty that to me appears insurmountable in the way to the perfectibility of society. All other arguments are of slight and subordinate consideration in comparison of this. I see no way by which man can escape from the weight of this law which pervades all animated nature. No fancied equality, no agrarian regulations in their utmost extent, could remove the pressure of it even for a single century. And it appears, therefore,

---

3   The geometrical ratio of increase of population seems unproblematic, but the arithmetical ratio supposedly governing the increase in subsistence seems rather arbitrary.

to be decisive against the possible existence of a society, all the members of which should live in ease, happiness, and comparative leisure; and feel no anxiety about providing the means of subsistence for themselves and families.

Consequently, if the premises are just, the argument is conclusive against the perfectibility of the mass of mankind.

I have thus sketched the general outline of the argument, but I will examine it more particularly, and I think it will be found that experience, the true source and foundation of all knowledge, invariably confirms its truth.

Chapter 2

I said that population, when unchecked, increased in a geometrical ratio, and subsistence for man in an arithmetical ratio.

Let us examine whether this position be just. I think it will be allowed, that no state has hitherto existed (at least that we have any account of) where the manners were so pure and simple, and the means of subsistence so abundant, that no check whatever has existed to early marriages, among the lower classes, from a fear of not providing well for their families, or among the higher classes, from a fear of lowering their condition in life. Consequently in no state that we have yet known has the power of population been left to exert itself with perfect freedom.

Whether the law of marriage be instituted or not, the dictate of nature and virtue seems to be an early attachment to one woman. Supposing a liberty of changing in the case of an unfortunate choice, this liberty would not affect population till it arose to a height greatly vicious; and we are now supposing the existence of a society where vice is scarcely known.

In a state therefore of great equality and virtue, where pure and simple manners prevailed, and where the means of subsistence were so abundant that no part of the society could have any fears about providing amply for a family, the power of population being left to exert itself unchecked, the increase of the human species would evidently be much greater than any increase that has been hitherto known.

In the United States of America, where the means of subsistence have been more ample, the manners of the people more pure, and consequently the checks to early marriages fewer, than in any of the modern states of Europe, the population has been found to double itself in twenty-five years.

This ratio of increase, though short of the utmost power of population, yet as the result of actual experience, we will take as our rule, and say, that population, when unchecked, goes on doubling itself every twenty-five years or increases in a geometrical ratio.

Let us now take any spot of earth, this Island for instance, and see in what ratio the subsistence it affords can be supposed to increase. We will begin with it under its present state of cultivation.

If I allow that by the best possible policy, by breaking up more land and by great encouragements to agriculture, the produce of this Island may be doubled in the first twenty-five years, I think it will be allowing as much as any person can well demand.

In the next twenty-five years, it is impossible to suppose that the produce could be quadrupled. It would be contrary to all our knowledge of the qualities of land. The very utmost that we can conceive, is, that the increase in the second twenty-five years might equal the present produce. Let us then take this for our rule, though certainly far beyond the truth, and allow that, by great exertion, the whole produce of the Island might be increased every twenty-five years, by a quantity of subsistence equal to what it at present produces. The most enthusiastic speculator cannot suppose a greater increase than this.[4] In a few centuries it would make every acre of land in the Island like a garden.

Yet this ratio of increase is evidently arithmetical.

It may be fairly said, therefore, that the means of subsistence increase in an arithmetical ratio. Let us now bring the effects of these two ratios together.

The population of the Island is computed to be about seven millions, and we will suppose the present produce equal to the support of such a number. In the first twenty-five years the population would be fourteen millions, and the food being also doubled, the means of subsistence would be equal to this increase. In the next twenty-five years the population would be twenty-eight millions, and the means of subsistence only equal to the support of twenty-one millions. In the next period, the population would be fifty-six millions, and the means of subsistence just sufficient for half that number. And at the conclusion of the first century the population would be one hundred and twelve millions and the means of subsistence only equal to the support of thirty-five millions, which would leave a population of seventy-seven millions totally unprovided for.

A great emigration necessarily implies unhappiness of some kind or other in the country that is deserted. For few persons will leave their families, connections, friends, and native land, to seek a settlement in untried foreign climes, without some strong subsisting causes of uneasiness where they are, or the hope of some great advantages in the place to which they are going.

But to make the argument more general and less interrupted by the partial views of emigration, let us take the whole earth, instead of one spot, and suppose that the restraints to population were universally removed. If the subsistence for man that the earth affords was to be increased every twenty-five years by a quantity equal to what the whole world at present produces, this would allow the power of production in the earth to be absolutely

4 Again, this claim seems unfounded.

unlimited, and its ratio of increase much greater than we can conceive that any possible exertions of mankind could make it.

Taking the population of the world at any number, a thousand millions, for instance, the human species would increase in the ratio of—1, 2, 4, 8, 16, 32, 64, 128, 256, 512, etc. and subsistence as—1, 2, 3, 4, 5, 6, 7, 8, 9, 10, etc. In two centuries and a quarter, the population would be to the means of subsistence as 512 to 10: in three centuries as 4096 to 13, and in two thousand years the difference would be almost incalculable, though the produce in that time would have increased to an immense extent.[5]

No limits whatever are placed to the productions of the earth; they may increase for ever and be greater than any assignable quantity, yet still the power of population being a power of a superior order, the increase of the human species can only be kept commensurate to the increase of the means of subsistence by the constant operation of the strong law of necessity acting as a check upon the greater power.

The effects of this check remain now to be considered.

Among plants and animals the view of the subject is simple. They are all impelled by a powerful instinct to the increase of their species, and this instinct is interrupted by no reasoning or doubts about providing for their offspring. Wherever therefore there is liberty, the power of increase is exerted, and the superabundant effects are repressed afterwards by want of room and nourishment, which is common to animals and plants, and among animals by becoming the prey of others.

The effects of this check on man are more complicated. Impelled to the increase of his species by an equally powerful instinct, reason interrupts his career and asks him whether he may not bring beings into the world for whom he cannot provide the means of subsistence. In a state of equality, this would be the simple question. In the present state of society, other considerations occur. Will he not lower his rank in life? Will he not subject himself to greater difficulties than he at present feels? Will he not be obliged to labour harder? and if he has a large family, will his utmost exertions enable him to support them? May he not see his offspring in rags and misery, and clamouring for bread that he cannot give them? And may he not be reduced to the grating necessity of forfeiting his independence, and of being obliged to the sparing hand of charity for support?

These considerations are calculated to prevent, and certainly do prevent, a very great number in all civilized nations from pursuing the dictate of nature in an early attachment to one woman. And this restraint almost necessarily, though not absolutely so, produces vice. Yet in all societies, even those that are most vicious, the tendency to a virtuous attachment is so strong that there is a constant effort towards an increase of population. This constant effort as

---

5   Such arguments are again reminiscent of Petty (above).

constantly tends to subject the lower classes of the society to distress and to prevent any great permanent amelioration of their condition.

The way in which, these effects are produced seems to be this. We will suppose the means of subsistence in any country just equal to the easy support of its inhabitants. The constant effort towards population, which is found to act even in the most vicious societies, increases the number of people before the means of subsistence are increased. The food therefore which before supported seven millions must now be divided among seven millions and a half or eight millions. The poor consequently must live much worse, and many of them be reduced to severe distress. The number of labourers also being above the proportion of the work in the market, the price of labour must tend toward a decrease, while the price of provisions would at the same time tend to rise. The labourer therefore must work harder to earn the same as he did before. During this season of distress, the discouragements to marriage, and the difficulty of rearing a family are so great that population is at a stand. In the mean time the cheapness of labour, the plenty of labourers, and the necessity of an increased industry amongst them, encourage cultivators to employ more labour upon their land, to turn up fresh soil, and to manure and improve more completely what is already in tillage, till ultimately the means of subsistence become in the same proportion to the population as at the period from which we set out. The situation of the labourer being then again tolerably comfortable, the restraints to population are in some degree loosened, and the same retrograde and progressive movements with respect to happiness are repeated.

This sort of oscillation will not be remarked by superficial observers, and it may be difficult even for the most penetrating mind to calculate its periods. Yet that in all old states some such vibration does exist, though from various transverse causes, in a much less marked, and in a much more irregular manner than I have described it, no reflecting man who considers the subject deeply can well doubt.

Many reasons occur why this oscillation has been less obvious, and less decidedly confirmed by experience, than might naturally be expected.

One principal reason is that the histories of mankind that we possess are histories only of the higher classes. We have but few accounts that can be depended upon of the manners and customs of that part of mankind where these retrograde and progressive movements chiefly take place. A satisfactory history of this kind, on one people, and of one period, would require the constant and minute attention of an observing mind during a long life.[6] Some of the objects of inquiry would be, in what proportion to the number of adults was the number of marriages, to what extent vicious customs prevailed in consequence of the restraints upon matrimony, what was the comparative mortality among the children of the most distressed part of the community

6   A striking early call for social history by Malthus!

and those who lived rather more at their ease, what were the variations in the real price of labour, and what were the observable differences in the state of the lower classes of society with respect to ease and happiness, at different times during a certain period.

Such a history would tend greatly to elucidate the manner in which the constant check upon population acts and would probably prove the existence of the retrograde and progressive movements that have been mentioned, though the times of their vibrations must necessarily be rendered irregular from the operation of many interrupting causes, such as the introduction or failure of certain manufactures, a greater or less prevalent spirit of agricultural enterprise, years of plenty, or years of scarcity, wars and pestilence, poor laws, the invention of processes for shortening labour without the proportional extension of the market for the commodity, and, particularly, the difference between the nominal and real price of labour, a circumstance which has perhaps more than any other contributed to conceal this oscillation from common view.

It very rarely happens that the nominal price of labour universally falls, but we well know that it frequently remains the same, while the nominal price of provisions has been gradually increasing. This is, in effect, a real fall in the price of labour, and during this period the condition of the lower orders of the community must gradually grow worse and worse. But the farmers and capitalists are growing rich from the real cheapness of labour. Their increased capitals enable them to employ a greater number of men. Work therefore may be plentiful, and the price of labour would consequently rise. But the want of freedom in the market of labour, which occurs more or less in all communities, either from parish laws, or the more general cause of the facility of combination among the rich, and its difficulty among the poor, operates to prevent the price of labour from rising at the natural period, and keeps it down some time longer; perhaps till a year of scarcity, when the clamour is too loud and the necessity too apparent to be resisted.

The true cause of the advance in the price of labour is thus concealed, and the rich affect to grant it as an act of compassion and favour to the poor, in consideration of a year of scarcity, and, when plenty returns, indulge themselves in the most unreasonable of all complaints, that the price does not again fall, when a little rejection would shew them that it must have risen long before but from an unjust conspiracy of their own.

But though the rich by unfair combinations contribute frequently to prolong a season of distress among the poor, yet no possible form of society could prevent the almost constant action of misery upon a great part of mankind, if in a state of inequality, and upon all, if all were equal.

The theory on which the truth of this position depends appears to me so extremely clear that I feel at a loss to conjecture what part of it can be denied.

That population cannot increase without the means of subsistence is a proposition so evident that it needs no illustration.

That population does invariably increase where there are the means of subsistence, the history of every people that have ever existed will abundantly prove.

And that the superior power of population cannot be checked without producing misery or vice, the ample portion of these too bitter ingredients in the cup of human life and the continuance of the physical causes that seem to have produced them bear too convincing a testimony.

INDEX

weather 36–7, 91, 108; and navigation
40–2, 44; *see also* winds
weather predictions 62–3, 85
weatherglass 86
Wilkins, John 90
William of Ockham 155n3

winds 85, 104–7; and discovery of new
lands 36–7; hurricanes 108, 158; trade
winds 104–7, 110; and value to trade
104–6; *see also* weather
wounds, curing of 63
Wright, Edward 39–45